*Just at this juncture I received a letter from
Mr Murray — It informed me that delicate
attention to my honour, and feelings, had kept
him silent, but driven, by the malice of his enemies,
from the Continent, he could not depart without
disclosing to me the treasured secret of his soul,
since he might thus risque the happiness of his life
— he could not but indulge a hope, that domestic
felicity might yet be his — he acknowledged he had
long loved me, even from the commencement of
our acquaintance, with ardour loved me, but that
he would have sacrificed his life, rather than have
admitted a thought in this regard to me, which my
own guardian angel would blush to own, but that,
as I had now for many months been released from
my early vows, he presumed to calculate upon a
favourable hearing, and to supplicate, at least for
a continuation of my esteem. I was now, you will
allow, furnished with a fresh motive for admiration
of him, who had at length avowed himself
my Lover....*

Judith Sargent Murray

15 April 1788

Also by Bonnie Hurd Smith

The Letters I Left Behind: Judith Sargent Murray Papers,
   Letter Book 10
From Gloucester to Philadelphia in 1790: Observations, Anecdotes,
   and Thoughts from the Letters of Judith Sargent Murray
Forming a New Era in Female History: Three Essays by Judith Sargent Murray
   ("Desultory Thoughts upon the Utility of Encouraging a Degree of
   Self-Complacency, Especially in Female Bosoms," "On the Equality
   of the Sexes," "On the Domestic Education of Children"
The Repository: A Series of Essays by Judith Sargent Murray
The Reaper: A Series of Essays by Judith Sargent Murray
A Universalist Cathechism by Judith Sargent Stevens

To order these titles, visit www.hurdsmith.com/judith.

Ms. Smith has also contributed chapters on Judith Sargent Murray to
Standing Before Us: Unitarian Universalist Women and Social Reform,
1776–1936 and *The Journal of the Unitarian Universalist Historical Society,*
and biographical sketches for the online *Dictionary of Unitarian Universalist
Biography,* the *Boston Women's Heritage Trail* and the *Salem Women's
Heritage Trail.*

   Bonnie Hurd Smith served as president of the Sargent-Murray-Gilman-
Hough House/Sargent House Museum in Gloucester, Massachusetts, from
1992–6. As the founder of the Judith Sargent Murray Society, Smith lectures,
publishes her research, and maintains a website: www.hurdsmith.com/judith.
She has devoted her professional career to promoting history and culture in
Boston and on the North Shore of Massachusetts.

Copyright © 2007 by Bonnie Hurd Smith
ISBN-10: 0-9791214-0-X
ISBN-13: 978-0-9791214-0-1
Designed by Bonnie Hurd Smith
Produced by ABCO Printing, Penobscot, Maine

Published by the Judith Sargent Murray Society, a division
of Hurd Smith Communications, Salem, Massachusetts.

Published with permission from the Mississippi Department of Archives
and History, Archives and Library Division, Jackson, Mississippi.

"Mingling Souls Upon Paper"

&

An Eighteenth-Century Love Story

BONNIE HURD SMITH

For my mother, Lydia Averell Hurd Smith,
whose scholarly achievements, "female abilities,"
and proud New England heritage produced
a daughter who is irrevocably tied to the
investigation and promotion history.
My mother's enthusiasm for this project in
particular, and for my never-ending work on
our common ancestor, Judith Sargent Murray,
in general, is deeply appreciated.

Acknowledgments
My heartfelt thanks to Paul Brawley for his steadfast loyalty, generosity, and ready ear; to my editor, Cathy Armer, who raises my work to a higher level; to local historian John Hardy Wright and Britta Karlberg of the Phillips Library, Peabody Essex Museum, for their assistance with the manuscript; to Biff Michaud of the Salem Witch Museum and Dan Johnston of Cornerstone Books in Salem for their marketing advice; to Ed Miller of ABCO Printing and Len Bolonsky, book distributor extraordinaire, for help with production and sales.

I am especailly grateful for the wisdom and knowledge of the Reverend Peter Hughes, the Reverend Richard Trudeau and, most importantly, the Reverend Gordon J. Gibson, who not only found Judith Sargent Murray's letter books in Natchez, Mississippi, but told me years ago that the relationship between Judith and John Murray was one of the greatest love stories in American history.

Contents

℘

List of Illustrations   2

Introduction   3
(with brief biographies of
Judith Sargent Murray
and John Murray)

Recipients of the Letters   33

The Letters   41

Resources   199

Index   202

*Yes, best of Men, I am yours in every sense
of the word, and may I cease to breathe, e'er
I cease to acknowledge your unvarying,
and faithful regards....*

—Judith Sargent Stevens to
John Murray, 9 January 1788

List of Illustrations

Cover

Portrait of Mrs. John Stevens (Judith Sargent, later Mrs. John Murray) by John Singleton Copley, 1770–1772, detail. Terra Foundation for American Art, Daniel J. Terra Art Acquisition Endowment Fund, 2000.6. Photograph courtesy of the Terra Foundation for American Art, Chicago.

Portrait of John Murray. Photograph courtesy of the Cape Ann Historical Association, Gloucester, Mass.

Insert

1   *Letter Book 1,* Judith Sargent Murray Papers. Scan from microfilm.
2   *Portrait of Mrs. John Murray* (Judith Sargent Murray) by Gilbert Stuart, ca. 1806. Private collection. Photograph courtesy of the Peabody Essex Museum, Salem, Mass.
3   *Portrait of John Murray* by Henry Sargent. Courtesy of the Sargent House Museum, Gloucester, Mass.
4   *Portrait of Epes Sargent* by John Singleton Copley. Private collection.
5   *Portrait of Julia Maria Sargent* by Gilbert Stuart, ca. 1806. Photograph courtesy of the Peabody Essex Museum, Salem, Mass.
6   *Portrait of Mrs. Daniel Sargent* (Mary Turner Sargent) by John Singleton Copley. Courtesy of the Fine Arts Museums of San Francisco. Gift of Mr. and Mrs. John D. Rockefeller 3rd to The Fine Arts Museums of San Francisco, 1979.7.31.
7   *Saint Lawrence Church*, Alton, England. Photograph from the Francis Frith Collection, Vancouver, Canada.
8   *Gloucester Harbor in 1817.* Courtesy of the Cape Ann Historical Association, Gloucester, Mass.
9   *Home of Judith Sargent Murray.* Photograph by Bonnie Hurd Smith.
10 *Gloucester Universalist Meetinghouse.* Courtesy of the Cape Ann Historical Association, Gloucester, Mass.
11 *Franklin Place/The Tontine Crescent.* From *Return Quick Step* (cover of book of music published by Keith's Music Publishing House, Boston) A TS 1844. Ret. Courtesy of the Boston Athenæum.
12 *Franklin Place/The Tontine Crescent.* Courtesy of the Boston Athenæum.
13 *Franklin Place interior. The Tea Party,* about 1824, by Henry Sargent. Courtesy of the Museum of Fine Arts, Boston. Gift of Mrs. Horatio A. Lamb in memory of Mr. and Mrs. Winthrop Sargent, 1912.
14 *The First Universalist Meeting-House,* attributed to Samuel Smith Kilburn. Courtesy of the Andover-Harvard Theological Library, Harvard University, Cambridge, Mass.
15 *Judith Sargent Murray's grave site.* Courtesy of the Mississippi Department of Archives and History, Archives and Library Division, Jackson, Mississippi.
16 *John Murray's grave site.* Photograph by Bonnie Hurd Smith.

Introduction

John Murray rode into Gloucester for the first time on November 3, 1774. It was probably late afternoon teatime. Not being familiar with the roads, he would have ridden his horse hard from Boston in order to arrive before nightfall. Making his way through Salem, Beverly, and Manchester, John would have come upon a panoramic view of his destination—a hilly hodgepodge of modest dwellings, stately homes, wharves, ships, warehouses, and outbuildings surrounded by massive rocks, sandy beaches, and the ferocious Atlantic Ocean. It must have been quite a sight: this remote island town at once a fishing village, a major trading port, and a natural marvel, all appearing to coexist harmoniously. John was intrigued. He was happy he had agreed to come.

As John rode on, crossing the Annisquam River, smoke from a hundred hearths greeted him. A ripe, "waterfront" wind blew in from the harbor. A day like this in New England was a day of change, he knew, ushering in winter. John was chilled, but invigorated.

Finally facing the venerable Sargent mansion, proudly clapboarded and shuttered in high Georgian style, John dismounted and tethered his horse to the hitching post. A servant approached to relieve John of his tired animal, while another servant politely escorted him through the Sargents' grand entrance hall and into the best parlor.

There, by the fireside, stood Winthrop Sargent just as John remembered him from their recent meeting. Wealthy, influential, and self-confident, Mr. Sargent had ridden almost forty miles to Boston to extend a personal invitation to the famous Universalist preacher to visit Gloucester as soon as he could. John was not in the habit of refusing anyone who believed in his mentor, James Relly, and Relly's theory of universal salvation, but Winthrop Sargent's request was particularly earnest. For several years, Mr. Sargent had hosted meetings in this very home to discuss Universalist theology. John looked forward to a conversation with this distinguished gentleman, hoping it would reveal whether Universalism could take hold permanently in Gloucester.

Next to John's host, rising immediately from the sofa to greet their celebrated guest, was the lady of the house, Judith Saunders Sargent— elegant, gracious, and comfortably conversant on any subject. John immediately felt welcome. He accepted a cup of strong Hyson tea, moved toward a chair by the fire, and settled in for lively discussion and hearty refreshment.

Just then, the parlor door opened and in walked the loveliest woman John had ever seen. But beyond that beauty, she radiated an intelligence and worldliness beyond her youthful years that caught his attention. She curtsied, and extended her hand in welcome. John was not accustomed to ladies behaving in so forward a manner, but he was becoming used to the colonists' informal ways. He took her hand and thanked the stranger for her kindness, looking intently into her dark eyes. She was momentarily at a loss for words, but John had the strongest sense, from her inquisitive regard, that she knew exactly who he was and why his religious mission was important.

John quickly learned that he was locked in a gaze with the Sargents' daughter, Judith Sargent Stevens, who was married to the son of one of Gloucester's most prominent families. She was also a devout adherent of universal salvation and a regular participant in Winthrop Sargent's parlor meetings. How delightful and unexpected.

After what was surely too long a period of time, Judith and John separated hands and regained their composure. Taking Winthrop Sargent's lead, the foursome in the parlor now plunged into animated conversation as the Sargents questioned John about his upbringing in England, his calling to preach Universalism, and his journey to the American colonies. How would he describe the character of James Relly, Universalism's founder? How was Universalism received in England? How had John been treated in other parts of the colonies? The Sargents had read news stories about John, but they wanted to hear from him directly. They were curious, concerned, and engaged.

John answered every question thoroughly and with enthusiasm, basking in the Sargents' hospitality and sincere interest in his work. Before they retired for the evening, Winthrop Sargent asked John Murray whether he would consider making Gloucester his home and serving as the pastor of Gloucester's developing Universalist community. Wasn't John weary of his endless travels as an itinerant preacher? As a matter of fact, he was, and the idea of committing to these good people appealed to John. He liked the Sargents, and he was drawn to their remarkable daughter. She was clearly more capable than the confines of polite society allowed. As her pastor, he thought, he could nurture Judith's spiritual and intellectual development. He also sensed that she could become a sympathetic friend to him.

Emerging from his sumptuous bedchamber the following morning, John set off early for Boston with the promise that he would return soon. His mind was filled with thoughts of Gloucester and the opportunity to reside there as an established clergyman. If he accepted, and if Winthrop Sargent were capable of maneuvering through the legal and political hurdles that would surely result from opposing the established church, John would be the first ordained Universalist preacher in America.

Meanwhile, from her home a short distance away, Judith was thinking about John Murray that morning—in fact, she had been thinking about him all night. No one would call him traditionally handsome, but he had a charisma, a physical presence, and a warm personality that had dominated her father's parlor. It was as if he personified the loving, hopeful message he promulgated. Judith had dozens of questions about Universalist theology, but no one with expertise to whom she could turn. What if John Murray agreed to her father's proposal and made Gloucester his home? She could learn so much from this man. But even if he declined Winthrop Sargent's offer, she thought, perhaps Mr. Murray would be willing to exchange letters.

As a married woman, Judith wrestled with the propriety of such a request for days. Finally, she sat down at her writing desk, quill pen in hand, and took a bold and fateful step by writing:

"My Dear Sir, I am not much accustomed to writing letters, especially to your sex, but if there be neither male nor female in the Emmanuel you promulgate, we may surely, and with the strictest propriety, mingle souls upon paper...I have to request — if your leisure will allow, that you would honour me by a line and I pray you to believe me with all sentiments of esteem your most obedient &c &c."

* * * * *

Introduction

Is this scenario what actually took place? We have no idea. But we do know that from the very first meeting between Judith Sargent and John Murray, sparks flew.

The words Judith penned on November 14, 1774, initiated a fourteen-year friendship with John Murray followed by a twenty-seven-year marriage. They were friends, lovers, equal partners, parents, and grandparents. They supported each other's work, yearned for each other during their long separations, and promoted the optimistic promise of universal salvation. Judith asked if they could correspond and John accepted, setting in motion a poignant story of love, faith, and unwavering loyalty.

*Blessings on the Man who first invented
letter writing — Say I ... although separated,
perhaps thousands of miles, from the object
whom I address, I can utter my sentiments
as freely as if we were sitting face to face
— nay, there are subjects, which an epistolary
correspondence may discuss, perhaps with still
greater freedom than when engaged
in conversation....*

—Judith Sargent Murray
to Esther Sargent Ellery
20 October 1797

JUDITH SARGENT MURRAY
(1751–1820)

Brief Chronology

1751	Born in Gloucester, Mass., on May 5
1750s–60s	Writes early letters and poetry
1765	Begins to use family library to further education
1769	Marries John Stevens; father, Winthrop Sargent, learns about universal salvation and hosts meetings in his home that Judith attends
1770s	Begins to create letter books
1774	Meets John Murray
1775	Threatened with expulsion from First Parish Church for nonattendance
1776	Has herself inoculated against smallpox
1778	Expelled from First Parish with other Universalists
1779	Signs Universalists' Articles of Association
1780	Nurses father through smallpox while Gloucester Universalists dedicate their new meetinghouse, calling John Murray as their pastor; adopts Anna and Mary Plummer; later, takes in Polly Odell
1782	Publishes Universalist catechism
1783–6	Universalists challenge right to independence from First Parish
1784	As "Constantia," publishes first essay, "Desultory Thoughts…," in *Gentleman and Lady's Town and Country Magazine*
1785–6	Spends winter barricaded in house with John Stevens
1786	John Stevens leaves Gloucester for the West Indies
1787	Notified of John Stevens's death
1788	Marries John Murray; meets John and Abigail Adams
1789	Son, Fitz Winthrop, stillborn; publishes poetry in the *Massachusetts Magazine*
1790	As "Constantia," publishes "On the Equality of the Sexes" and "On the Domestic Education of Children" in the *Massachusetts Magazine*; meets George and Martha Washington

1791	Daughter, Julia Maria, born; *Massachusetts Magazine* declares "Constantia" one of its ablest poets
1792	For the *Massachusetts Magazine*, assumes male persona to publish "The Gleaner" column; as "Constantia" publishes "The Repository" series
1793	John Murray ordained as minister of First Universalist Church in Boston
1794	Moves to Franklin Place, Boston
1795	First play, *The Medium, or Happy Tea-Party* (later renamed *The Medium, or Virtue Triumphant*) performed at Boston's Federal Street Theatre
1796	Second play, *The Traveller Returned*, performed at the Theatre; tries to adopt brother Winthrop's illegitimate daughter, Caroline Augusta
1797	Publishes three-volume book, *The Gleaner*
1800	American novelists Henry Sherburne and Sally Wood praise *The Gleaner*
1801	Niece, Anna Williams, moves to Franklin Place; nephews arrive from Natchez, Miss., and Gloucester for schooling in Boston
1802-03	Helps Judith Saunders and Clementine Beach open female academy in Dorchester; publishes poetry in the *Boston Weekly Magazine* as "Honora Martesia"
1805	Writes third play, *The African*
1809	John Murray suffers paralytic stroke
1812	Helps John Murray edit and publish *Letters and Sketches of Sermons*; Julia Maria marries Adam Lewis Bingaman of Natchez.
1813	Granddaughter, Charlotte Bingaman, born
1815	John Murray dies
1816	Publishes John Murray's autobiography, *Records of the Life of the Rev. John Murray*
1818	Moves to Natchez with Julia Maria and Charlotte
1820	Dies in Natchez on June 9

Judith Sargent Murray
Essayist, educator, and promoter of female abilities

Gloucester and Universalism

The Gloucester, Massachusetts, of Judith Sargent Murray's childhood was a thriving colonial seaport in "His Britannik Majesty's" empire populated by hardy, independent-minded, townspeople. Many families, like the Sargents and Saunderses, had immigrated from England in the seventeenth century to pursue economic opportunities. By 1751, the year Judith was born, they had achieved considerable wealth from exporting fish, lumber, and other commodities to England and the West Indies and importing valuable goods. They were distinguished, engaged citizens whose trade activities exposed them to people and ideas from other parts of the world. Judith Sargent was born on May 5 into these two families, the oldest child of Winthrop Sargent and Judith Saunders Sargent, only four of whose children survived to adulthood.

Judith's parents provided a typical education for a merchant-class daughter—reading, writing, and training in the domestic skills of sewing and household management. At the same time, though, the Sargents had hired a tutor for their son Winthrop to prepare him for Harvard College. Judith was keenly aware of the differences between their educations. She wanted to learn more, and under her own initiative read books of history, geography, literature, philosophy, and theology found in the Sargent family library. Judith became an avid reader and a "scribbler" from an early age, writing poetry, historical essays, and letters to family members and close friends.

Like most children in Gloucester, Judith was raised in First Parish Church whose Congregational ministers ruled religious and civic life. She was taught to be virtuous, benevolent, and well-behaved to avoid God's anger. Judith learned that only a few people were predestined for heaven, while most would spend eternity in hell. It was not a particularly optimistic outlook, but Judith's religious life was balanced by her family's self-confident business and political pursuits.

Judith fulfilled the one role expected of her when she married John Stevens at the age of eighteen. She had chosen well and appropriately, selecting the son of a prominent Gloucester family. The young couple resided with John's parents until they could build a house of their own, allowing Judith to live within a short distance of the Sargent and Saunders homes. Their new home would be built in the adjacent lot.

At about the same time, Judith's father read James Relly's book on universal salvation, *Union, or, A Treatise of the Consanguinity and Affinity between Christ and His Church*. Winthrop Sargent was intrigued with the scriptural interpretation Relly articulated, and he began to host gatherings in his home to discuss the new theology. It was a radical departure from traditional doctrine, and Judith was among those who embraced Relly's hopeful, egalitarian view of the worlds here and beyond.

In 1774, when Winthrop Sargent learned that the English Universalist preacher John Murray was lecturing in Boston, he invited him to visit Gloucester. On November 3, John Murray presented himself at the Sargent family home where Judith met him for the first time. Judith asked John if he would agree to engage in a correspondence, and he accepted. While John moved to Gloucester shortly thereafter, he traveled frequently to other parts of New England and depended on Judith's accounts of life in his adopted town while he was away.

At first, Judith's letters were filled with theological inquiry, but soon she was reporting fearful goings-on in Gloucester such as when British warships appeared off the coast in 1775 and Judith and her family retreated for their safety to Chebacco Parish, Ipswich, that winter. Her Loyalist uncle, Epes Sargent, later one of John Murray's most influential supporters, was forced by angry separatists to leave town for Boston.

These were tense times in Gloucester, and not simply because of the war. John Murray's Universalist supporters, including Judith, faced a different kind of battle in 1775 when they were threatened with expulsion from First Parish Church for not attending. John Murray was accused of being a British spy, and he quickly accepted a post as Army chaplain to prove his loyalty to the American cause. During his absence, Judith kept him apprised of Gloucester's desperate poverty while the port was closed. When John returned in 1776, he successfully raised funds to alleviate Gloucester's distress.

By 1778, war activities had moved south, and now the leadership of First Parish took action against the Universalists of Gloucester by suspending Judith Sargent Stevens, Winthrop Sargent, Epes Sargent (who had returned to Gloucester), and others from the church. Instead of backing down, the Universalists, including Judith, signed Articles of Association the following year to create a new religious society: the Independent Church of Christ. Soon after, the Gloucester Universalists built their own meetinghouse and dedicated the building on Christmas Day 1780, calling John Murray as their pastor. Even though Judith was in Boston at the time nursing her father through smallpox, she delighted in the Universalists' significant achievement.

Judith quickly found herself in the role of religious educator for Gloucester's growing number of Universalist children. She had recently adopted two of her husband's orphaned nieces, Anna and Mary Plummer, and temporarily took in a third little cousin, Polly Odell, as well. Before long, Universalist parents urged Judith to write down the lessons she was teaching. She complied, and in 1782 Judith published a Universalist catechism that is today considered the earliest writing by an American Universalist woman. The pamphlet included Judith's first public assertion of male and female equality, a hallmark of Universalism.

In the same year, the Universalists' defiance of First Parish led the ruling ministers to seize valuable goods from Winthrop Sargent, Epes Sargent, and others to sell at public auction. Even though the Universalists had formed their own organization, they were still expected to support the established church—which they refused to do. The Universalists persuaded John Murray, as their leader, to bring their case before the Massachusetts Supreme Judicial Court and argue for the right to separate from First Parish and support their own church. Eventually, in 1785 and 1786, the court ruled in favor of the Universalists and freedom of religion.

A Second Marriage and a Literary Career

Judith's life took a dramatic turn in 1786 when John Stevens revealed just how much his debts had accumulated since wartime trade embargoes and a series of storms had destroyed his cargo and ships. He was embroiled in discussions with his creditors to obtain leniency and avoid debtor's prison. Even John Murray stepped in to negotiate on his behalf. Judith, her husband, and Anna Plummer spent the winter of 1785–6 literally locked inside their home to keep John Stevens safe from the sheriff. That spring, as a desperate last resort, John Stevens secretly left Gloucester for

Introduction

St. Eustacius in the West Indies where he hoped to restore his financial standing by participating in international trade.

Her husband's departure left Judith ill and depressed. Following her physicians' advice, she agreed to a journey in the countryside with Anna Plummer, escorted by John Murray. For the first time, Judith saw John preach to crowds of hundreds of people at a time. Until then, she had not fully appreciated his stature and the effect he could have on so many "hearers" from all walks of life.

Judith learned of her husband's death the following year and resigned herself to life as a widow. But John Murray had other ideas: at the close of 1787 he asked Judith to marry him. At the time, John had made plans to sail for England in January on the advice of his Universalist supporters. His ministry had been challenged again by First Parish, and Winthrop Sargent suggested he leave Gloucester while the Universalists secured a legal ruling from the Massachusetts legislature.

Judith waited many long and apprehensive weeks for a positive decision from the legislature and for her future husband's safe return. When the Universalists received word in their favor upholding the legality of John's ministry a few months later, Judith immediately wrote to John with the good news and he sailed for Gloucester that fall. They married in Salem, Massachusetts, on October 6, 1788. Despite her brother Winthrop's inexplicable disapproval of her marriage, Judith explained to her parents that John Murray was the "choice of my heart."

Before long, Judith was pregnant with their first baby. After a childless marriage with John Stevens, she was elated. She was thirty-nine years old and had just about given up hope. But in August 1789, the little boy they had planned to name Fitz Winthrop was stillborn. Judith nearly died as well, and faced a lengthy, painful recovery.

While she was bedridden, Judith wrote poetry to submit to the *Massachusetts Magazine* using the pen name "Constantia." Her 1784 essay, "Desultory Thoughts upon the Utility of Encouraging a Degree of Self-Complacency, Especially in Female Bosoms," had been well received in *Gentleman and Lady's Town and Country Magazine*, and she hoped to develop an even wider audience for her political and creative ideas. Along with poetry, the following year, 1790, she submitted what would become her landmark essay. "On the Equality of the Sexes," appeared in the March and April issues of the *Massachusetts Magazine*, closely followed by "On the Domestic Education of Children" in May.

Later that year, when Judith embarked on a six-month journey to Philadelphia with John, she experienced a dizzying array of people, places, events, and ideas through the eyes of an acclaimed essayist. Her meetings with President George Washington, Martha Washington, Vice President John Adams, Abigail Adams, and other dignitaries must have heightened her desire to participate in national conversations about citizenship, virtue, philanthropy, female education, and the role of women in the New Republic. Judith knew that as a woman, writing was the only way to have a voice.

When Judith returned home, she was pregnant again at the age of forty-one. This time, though, her maternal hopes were realized when she gave birth on August 22, 1791, to a healthy baby girl they named Julia Maria. Judith's contentment overflowed that year when the *Massachusetts Magazine* declared "Constantia" one of its ablest poets. Despite John's many absences when he was invited to preach outside of Gloucester, Judith now enjoyed a happy family life and a promising literary career, which she was about to advance significantly.

Her decision to create a new column in 1792 for the *Massachusetts Magazine* stemmed from the knowledge that her friends and family knew "Constantia's" real identity. This time, in choosing a pen name, she settled on a masculine identity as "Mr. Gleaner" to engage more male readers in her ideas and avoid being dismissed as a female writer. "The Gleaner" addressed many of the political and social issues that were close to Judith's heart, and "he" developed quite a following. A few months later, as "Constantia," Judith created a second column for the *Massachusetts Magazine* called "The Repository," which included shorter, more reflective, and even Universalist pieces.

Literature, Comedy, and Education in Boston

In 1794, after John had been ordained the minister of Boston's Universalist congregation, the family moved to Franklin Place, Boston, where Judith would be in the center of New England cultural and political activity. News of Judith's arrival prompted Thomas Paine, the editor of one of Boston's newspapers, *The Federal Orrery*, to prevail upon her to create a new column. Judith agreed, and submitted five installments of "The Reaper." In this series, Judith investigated lessons regarding character and virtue that she had "reaped" from real life. To her dismay, Paine not only edited her work but changed words and sentences altogether. Judith refused to submit more columns, not knowing that Thomas Paine would later cause trouble for the Murrays.

Thomas Paine's mean-spiritedness surfaced in 1795 and 1796, when Judith's plays were performed at the Boston Theatre on Federal Street making her the first American—male or female—to be so honored. *The Medium, or Happy Tea-Party* (1795) and *The Traveller Returned* (1796) were comedies about class structure, patriotism, and virtue, and they featured strong female characters. Thomas Paine, himself a hopeful playwright, perhaps resented Judith's success. He not only denounced *Traveller*, he accused John Murray of writing it and serving as the male pen behind Judith's literary efforts. The public spectacle dismayed John's conservative congregation, but John defended his wife's abilities by publishing letters in Boston's weekly newspapers.

In 1796, Julia Maria was a talkative, precocious five-year-old whose early education Judith oversaw herself. Julia Maria used to scold her mother for not providing a brother or sister. Suddenly, out of the blue, Judith's brother Winthrop wrote to her from the Ohio Territory where he held a high-ranking government position. He told Judith about his infant illegitimate daughter, Caroline Augusta, whom he wanted Judith to raise in Boston. Judith agreed unhesitatingly, pleased with the chance to provide a sister for Julia Maria, but Winthrop was never able to persuade Caroline Augusta's mother to relinquish her daughter.

Along with her role as a mother, Judith's domestic duties included managing the family finances. She often had to plead with the Boston Universalist congregation for John's salary. Her decision in 1796 to produce a book was as much to generate income as it was to achieve real literary fame. A shrewd businesswoman, she secured early support from President George Washington and Vice President John Adams (she also dedicated the book to Adams) for her "indigenous," meaning American, production. When the two men agreed to her request, she used their names to attract subscribers from the highest ranks of civic, military, business, and academic circles. When *The Gleaner* appeared in 1798, Judith became the first woman in America to self-publish a book. Two years later, American novelists Henry Sherburne and Sally Wood, among others, praised Judith for *The Gleaner's* timeless importance to social and political thought, and they thanked her for the doors she had opened for emerging American writers.

Young people were very much Judith's focus at home along with those she hoped would read *The Gleaner*. In the early 1800s, her brother Winthrop sent his stepdaughter, Anna Williams, to live at Franklin Place. He sent his sons and stepsons to academies in Billerica, Massachusetts, and Exeter, New Hampshire, as well. Later, "the boys" attended Harvard. Throughout her nephews' years away from home, Judith visited and wrote to them, and hosted them during school vacations. Judith's reputation as an educator expanded still further in 1802, when Judith Saunders, a cousin, and Clementine Beach asked Judith to support their new female academy in Dorchester, Massachusetts, where they hoped to provide the kind of education Judith had always championed for girls.

During these years, Judith published poetry in the *Boston Weekly Magazine* under a new pen name, "Honora Martesia." In 1805 she wrote a third play, *The African*, which was inexplicably rejected by a critic during rehearsal and whose manuscript has never been found.

Judith's Final Days with John, and Without Him

Judith's life changed abruptly in 1809 when John Murray's tireless traveling and recurring illnesses caught up with him. A massive stroke left the right side of his body numb, incapacitating John for the rest of his life. Although his mind was alert and he could still speak, he could no longer travel, preach, or take care of his family. The Murrays were already struggling to make ends meet; Judith was shaken. The Universalist congregation hired a private nurse and sent male members of the congregation each day to move John within his apartment or out to a waiting carriage. Even so, Judith was John's constant bedside companion and she marveled at his patience and good nature.

Having lost the services of their pastor, the Boston Universalists installed the Reverend Edward Mitchell in John's place, much to Judith's delight. He was a Rellyan Universalist from New York who could, hopefully, return the church to more traditional Universalist theology. Ten years earlier, John had inadvertently allowed the Reverend Hosea Ballou to preach in his pulpit. The Unitarian views Ballou espoused at that time were not at all in keeping with the teachings of James Relly, and the Boston congregation had been in theological disarray ever since. Now, perhaps, Edward Mitchell could help. Unfortunately, though, he left after only a short time and Judith found herself refusing to attend church and "sanction by her presence" the Universalists' theological shift.

The same year of Edward Mitchell's departure, 1812, Judith helped John edit and publish a collection of his writings titled *Letters and Sketches of Sermons*. They hoped the book would solidify John's historic role in Universalism and bring them income. While the work was in process, Julia Maria married Adam Lewis Bingaman, a Harvard graduate from Natchez, Mississippi, who had boarded with the Murrays for a short time. In 1813, Julia Maria gave birth to her parents' first grandchild, Charlotte, and both Judith and John were enchanted by the baby's playful presence.

But war with Great Britain disrupted the Murrays' family life as investments failed and American troops arrived in Boston to protect the port. Judith and John feared for their safety, frustrated by the difficulty with physically removing John from Boston if the British set fire to their city as they had done to Washington. Although they survived the hostilities and looked forward to resuming a peaceful life together, John Murray died in 1815 after almost six years of painful confinement. Judith was bereft, having spent forty-one years as his devoted friend and wife. But John had longed to escape the "prison" of his incapacitated body, and she knew they would see each other again in the next world. She was probably relieved on his behalf.

The Universalists held two services for John, one in Gloucester and the other in Boston, where a long procession through the city ended with John's interment in the Sargent family tomb at Granary Burying Ground. Within a month, Universalist friends approached Judith to complete the autobiography John had abandoned in 1774, and she turned to Edward Mitchell for assistance. Judith published *Records of the Life of the Rev. John Murray* in 1816, hoping again to preserve her husband's legacy.

Judith would have preferred to end her days at Franklin Place in the same bed she had shared with her husband. But Adam Lewis Bingaman, who had long since returned to Natchez, had legal control over his wife and daughter and Judith could not bear a separation from her offspring. In 1818, Adam sent word to Boston that he was on his way to escort his family to Natchez. Among the items Judith packed were some of John's papers and the twenty volumes of letter books she had produced throughout her adult life—blank volumes into which she had deliberately copied her correspondence to family members, friends, and business acquaintances.

Very little is known about Judith's time in Natchez, where she lived for the last years of her life in the Bingaman family mansion, Oak Point. By then, her eyesight had deteriorated and it is possible she stopped writing letters because none have been found and her letter books end with a message penned from Boston. In Natchez, Judith was reunited with her beloved brother Winthrop, his children, and stepchildren who no doubt enjoyed spending time with the same "Aunt Murray" who had so lovingly guided them through their education. Judith Sargent Murray died on June 9, 1820, at the age of sixty-nine, and lies buried in the Bingaman family cemetery at Fatherland Plantation. On her mother's gravestone, Julia Maria inscribed, "Dear Spirit, the monumental stone can never speak thy worth."

Judith Sargent Murray's Legacy

Unfortunately, there are no living direct descendants of John Murray and Judith Sargent Murray. The same year that Judith died, her granddaughter, Charlotte, passed away at the age of seven and was buried next to her grandmother. Julia Maria gave birth to Adam Lewis Bingaman Jr. in 1821, but she died within several months, in 1822. Adam Jr. married many years later and raised a daughter who remained single.

It is unclear how many of the young people Judith helped raise continued to advocate for female abilities and a virtuous society. We do know that Caroline Plummer of Salem, Massachusetts, endowed a school for troubled boys in that town and funded a Professorship of Christian Morals at Harvard.

In 1917, Gloucester Universalists and members of the Sargent family opened the former home of John Murray and Judith Sargent Murray to the public as the Sargent-Murray-Gilman House. Today, the Sargent House Museum continues to tell their story.

As for biographies, scholars have long believed the "fact" first reported in 1881 by Rev. Richard Eddy in *The Universalist Quarterly* that Judith's personal papers were destroyed in Mississippi. As a result of this misinformation and without such documents, no biographies were written. A 1923 Sargent family genealogy contains a biographical sketch written by one of Judith's cousins, Lucius Manlius Sargent, who dismissed her published writing as best forgotten. It wasn't until 1931 that a more complimentary story emerged when Vena Bernadette Field published a master's thesis at the University of Maine, but even she had very few resources to draw upon other than Judith's essays.

Introduction

In 1974, Alice Rossi initiated a steady restoration of Judith's role in women's history by including "On the Equality of the Sexes" in *The Feminist Papers*. More recent scholars of women's and early American history have followed Rossi's lead by publishing Judith's own words (see "Resources"). For instance, the Union College Press reissued *The Gleaner* in 1992 and the Judith Sargent Murray Society reissued Judith's Universalist catechism, early essays, poetry, and "Gleaner," "Repository," and "Reaper" columns in the late 1990s. John Murray's autobiography has been reissued or excerpted numerous times.

But the single most important act of restoration was the Reverend Gordon Gibson's 1984 discovery of Judith's letter books in Natchez, Mississippi, at the antebellum mansion Arlington. In 1989, the Mississippi Department of Archives and History preserved and published the letter books on microfilm, thus making them available to researchers. Since 1996, Bonnie Hurd Smith has been transcribing the microfilmed letter books for publication. This volume is part of her multiyear effort.

When Judith Sargent Murray thought about her own legacy, she longed for "affectionate posterity" as an author who had helped to improve society for future generations. As John Murray's wife, she hoped to "rescue his name from oblivion" in whatever way she could. Through the publication of her words, she has finally achieved both—and, as this book shows, also recorded a beautiful love story for posterity.

Judith Sargent Murray was a force, who acted despite the obstacles for women of eighteenth-century society. Perhaps her spirit is best illustrated by her own words in "The Repository" column of May 1793, published in the *Massachusetts Magazine*:

> What a censorious world says of me, cannot offend or permanently hurt me. Was it to commend me, it would do me no real service. I had rather have an unspotted conscience (I may be allowed the expression as far as it is relative to my fellow creatures) I had rather I say be possessed of an unspotted conscience, the acquitting plaudit of my own breast, and the rational award of a serene mind, than to have worlds for my admirers: Without the honied influence of this complacency, I could not but be miserable, nor with it, for any length of time wholly unhappy; and while I am fully resolved to act rightly, the rectitude of my intention cannot but fill my bosom with the

most solacing reflexions. I despise then the low manners of an injurious multitude — it is poor, poor indeed, and I will shield myself in the fair asylum of conscious innocence.

In *The Gleaner*, in 1798, Judith wrote,

> The idea of the incapability of women is ... totally inadmissible.... To argue against facts, is indeed contending with both wind and tide; and, borne down by accumulating examples, conviction of the utility of the present plans will pervade the public mind, and not a dissenting voice will be heard.

Perhaps Judith Sargent Murray's greatest legacy was having the courage to use her "abilities" despite what a "censorious world" might say, and the foresight to document her life.

John Murray
(1741–1815)

Brief chronology

1741	Born in Alton, England, on December 10
1750–9	Moves to Ireland; is introduced to Methodist preacher John Wesley who puts him in charge of boys' religious class; meets Little family and uses their library; begins to preach at about age 18
1760	Hears evangelical Methodist preacher George Whitefield
1760s	Moves to London; studies with Universalist James Relly; marries Eliza Neale; infant son dies; Eliza dies
1770	Leaves England for America; encounters Thomas Potter
1770–4	Travels throughout colonies as itinerant preacher of universal salvation
1774	Visits Gloucester, Mass.; meets Judith Sargent Stevens; settles in Gloucester
1775	Serves as chaplain in Continental Army
1776	Returns to Gloucester; assists poor
1778	Gloucester Universalists suspended from First Parish Church
1779	Gloucester Universalists sign Articles of Association to create their own religious society with John Murray as their pastor
1780	Independent Church of Christ dedicates new meetinghouse
1782	First Parish seizes Gloucester Universalists' possessions in lieu of taxes they refused to pay to the church;
1783	John Murray initiates a lawsuit against First Parish
1785	Travels to Oxford, Mass., to help organize first Universalist convention
1785-6	Mass. Supreme Judicial Court recognizes Universalists' right to independence from First Parish
1788	First Parish challenges John's legal right to perform the marriage ceremony; he leaves for England in January, but returns in October to marry Judith
1789	Son, Fitz Winthrop, dies in childbirth

1790	Helps organize first national Universalist convention in Philadelphia
1791	Daughter, Julia Maria, born
1793	Divides time between Gloucester and Boston Universalist congregations; eventually severs tie to Gloucester; installed as minister of First Universalist Church in Boston; helps found and moderate New England General Convention of Universalists which becomes the U.S. General Convention (see 1837).
1794	Moves family to Boston
1799	At John Murray's invitation, Rev. Hosea Ballou preaches in John's absence causing irrevocable disruption in the Boston Universalist congregation; John Murray presides over funeral service for George Washington
1803	Travels to Winchester, N.H., for important Universalist convention
1809	Incapacitated by a stroke after years of tireless traveling, preaching, and organizing
1812	With Judith's help, edits and publishes *Letters and Sketches of Sermons*; daughter marries Adam Lewis Bingaman
1813	Granddaughter, Charlotte Bingaman, born
1815	Dies in Boston on September 3, buried at Granary Burying Ground, Boston
1816	Judith publishes *Records of the Life of the Rev. John Murray*
1837	U.S. General Convention of Universalists moves casket to Mount Auburn Cemetery, Cambridge, Mass.

JOHN MURRAY
Preacher, organizer, and promulgator of hope

Early Religious Awakenings

Alton, England, where John Murray was born in 1741 to an upper-class family, was a rural market town some fifty miles southwest of London.* Alton was dominated by the Anglican church most people attended, just as John's childhood was dominated by his strict Calvinist father whose fears for John's soul led him to beat and isolate his son. As a consequence, while a child, John perceived religion as a gloomy means to control people's behavior. He later wrote in his autobiography, "I believed that I had nothing to hope, but every thing to fear, both from my Creator, and my father; and these soul-appalling considerations, by forcing a conclusion, that I was but making provision for alternate torture, threw a cloud over innocent enjoyment." Throughout his life, John suffered from depression.

John was a bright but often inattentive student at Alton's Free School, where he made friends easily and exhibited what his father considered a disturbingly outgoing nature. John continued his schooling in Cork, Ireland, where his father moved his wife and their family of nine children when John was eleven. In Cork, John encountered Methodists, at that time a sect of Anglicans whose more social, musical gatherings were a welcome departure from what John had known of organized religion. The Methodists were evangelicals, held religious revivals, and reached out to people from all walks of life in a radical departure from the more solemn worship style and social hierarchy of the religious traditions of John's earlier years. John Wesley, the Methodists' inspiring leader, was despised by the standing Anglican clergy for seducing parishioners away from the established church. He was threatened, sometimes physically attacked, and singularly effective as a preacher of change. He was also an important early role model for John.

After John Wesley came to know the teenaged John Murray he entrusted him with a religious education class of forty boys, encouraging his protégé to lead them in song, prayer, and introspective discussions about their spiritual development. Wesley started John on a path to the ministry, and many Methodists predicted that he would become a "burning and a shining light." At about the same time, an Anglican clergyman also observed John's leanings toward religion and asked John's father to allow John to live with the clergyman's family while he tutored John for college. Unfortunately, John later felt, his father's refusal to relinquish control of his son denied him a college education.

Meanwhile, a Methodist family in Cork, the Littles, had befriended John and encouraged him to read the books in their extensive library, an exciting prospect because John's father had forbidden him to read anything but the Bible or approved religious texts. But now, as a young man, John was free to embark on a self-directed literary education—something he would have in common with his future wife Judith Sargent.

When John was eighteen, he started preaching to large audiences in Cork. He soon attracted enemies and experienced the kind of animosity John Wesley had endured. He also suffered personal losses when an early love interest broke his heart and his closest male friend, one of the Littles' sons, died. John's father died when John was nineteen, after a lengthy illness, and John, as the oldest son, was now expected to manage the Murray family. John felt unable to discipline his siblings as his father had done, nor was he comfortable with the role of provider. He accepted the Littles' invitation to live with them as one of their own children. Before long, the Littles encouraged John to marry their daughter, a prospect that did not interest him. As it was, the Littles' heirs objected to John's presence, fearing he would inherit what was rightfully theirs.

These factors, combined with John's growing doubts about John Wesley's theology, propelled him into a state of despair. He was almost suicidal, he recounted in his autobiography, yet, believing there was a higher purpose in life for him, he decided to leave Ireland. As John wrote in recalling the sad departure from his family, his grandmother told him, "You are, my dear child, under the guidance of an Omnipotent Power; God has designed you for himself; you are a chosen instrument to give light to your fellow men."

On his way to England, John spent a few weeks in Limerick where he heard a sermon by the itinerant evangelical Methodist preacher George Whitefield. John admired the preacher's nondenominational, welcoming style, which seemed more agreeable than Wesley's more rigid ministry. John conversed with him afterward, and, intrigued by Whitefield's independent spirit, he resolved to renew their acquaintance at Whitefield's Tabernacle in London. Meanwhile, when Whitefield was called out of town, John filled the pulpits where Whitefield had been invited to preach—a high honor for such a young man, but John was already a talented evangelical.

John was on the verge of his twentieth birthday when he arrived in England's southwest port of Pill, making his way on foot to Bristol. There, he encountered a group of Methodists who befriended him and urged him to stay—a recurring pattern throughout John's life when he visited new communities. But on to London he went, where he quickly made friends and enjoyed that city's social life of parties, concerts, and the theater while he contemplated what sort of work to pursue. Before long, John ran out of the money he had received from the Littles and he was consumed by an overwhelming sense of failure. He had to pay off his debts, however, and he secured a position in a textile factory.

John despised the drudgery that filled his days, but in the evenings his love for religion drove him to George Whitefield's Tabernacle. John also found himself attending services elsewhere in London, wherever he knew a popular preacher was speaking. After a short time, Whitefield asked John to preach at the Tabernacle and his talent quickly became the subject of conversations in London. John fell in love with a young woman who came to hear him preach, Eliza Neale, and they eventually married despite her family's strong objections to their daughter marrying a Methodist.

Like most of their Methodist friends, John and Eliza were well aware that James Relly, a Welsh preacher, was in London lecturing on universal salvation. As a good Methodist, John despised Relly and refused to hear him. He was even asked to "save" a young Methodist woman whom Relly had been able to tempt away from the Tabernacle. John was surprisingly ineffective; her arguments were persuasive. Finally, John decided to read Relly's book for himself and he borrowed a copy of *Union, or, A Treatise of the Consanguinity and Affinity between Christ and His Church*. Relly's interpretation of the scriptures made sense to him.

Soon after, John and Eliza heard James Relly preach and they were both profoundly affected. "The veil was taken from my heart," John wrote in his autobiography, explaining,

> It was clear, as any testimony in divine revelation, that Christ Jesus, died for all, for the sins of the whole world, for every man, &c.; ... and that every one, for whom Christ died must finally be saved ... We now attended public worship, not only as a duty

... but it became our pleasure, our consolation, and our highest enjoyment. We began to feed upon the truth as it is in Jesus, and every discovery we made filled us with unutterable transport.... I conceived, if I had an opportunity of conversing with the whole world, the whole world would be convinced. It might truly have been said, that we had a taste of heaven below.

The Methodists expelled John from the Tabernacle.

A New Life in America

John's contentment with life ended abruptly when his infant son died and Eliza's health deteriorated. John moved her to the country, hiring nurses and renting a comfortable cottage. But his desperate efforts were not enough. Eliza died, leaving John heartbroken and debt-ridden. Once again, John was overcome by a sense of personal failure. James Relly was the only friend who could comfort him, and he encouraged John to join him as a preacher of universal salvation. Instead, John decided to "close his life in solitude" in America after hearing stories about the New World's independent spirit and plentiful resources. With no connections or plans, John boarded the brig *Hand-in-Hand* bound for New York and served as its supercargo, or business manager.

Before reaching its destination, however, the *Hand-in-Hand* ran aground on a sandbar off the New Jersey coast. Because the crew required additional provisions, John went ashore in search of food. By chance he encountered an elderly farmer named Thomas Potter who had recently built a meetinghouse on his property for itinerant preachers. Potter was waiting for one to come who embraced universal salvation, as he did, and thus there was no doubt in Potter's mind that God had sent John Murray for this purpose. He urged John to preach, but John refused, preferring to leave his past behind and sail for New York as planned.

"The wind will never change, sir, until you have delivered to us, in that meeting-house, a message from God," Potter warned John as John told the story in his autobiography. The wind remained calm for days. John was enough of a believer in God's intervening hand to relent, and he delivered a sermon on Sunday, September 30, 1770, to the friends Potter had gathered. He felt his sense of calling and purpose return.

While Thomas Potter implored John to remain in New Jersey, John was invited to speak in cities and towns in New York, Pennsylvania, Maryland, Rhode Island, New Hampshire, Connecticut, and Massachusetts. He had to go. While he was attracting opposition from established clergy wherever he went, the public was resonating to John's powerful preaching style; his oratory was as effective as any they had heard. In 1774, while John was lecturing in Boston, a gentleman from Gloucester, Massachusetts, named Winthrop Sargent paid him a visit and asked him to preach in that distant fishing and trading port. John agreed, writing in his autobiography:

> November 3d, I repaired to Gloucester, and was received by a very few warm-hearted Christians. The mansion-house—the heart, of the then head of the Sargent family, with his highly accomplished, and most exemplary lady, were open to receive me. I had travelled from Maryland to New Hampshire, without meeting a single individual, who appeared to have the smallest idea of what I esteemed the truth, as it is in Jesus; but to my great astonishment, there were a few persons, dwellers in that remote place, upon whom the light of the gospel had more than dawned. The writings of Mr. Relly were not only in their hands but in their hearts.

John met Winthrop Sargent's daughter Judith Sargent Stevens that day, an encounter whose significance he could not have known.

John decided to make Gloucester his home, but protests to his ministry arose. In 1774, the Reverend Samuel Chandler of First Parish Church preached and published a sermon against John in the *Essex Gazette*. In 1775, Gloucesterians read Boston's Reverend Andrew Croswell's pamphlet titled *Mr. Murray unmask'd: in which among other things, is shewn, that his doctrine of universal salvation, is inimical to virtue, and productive of all manner of wickedness; and that Christians of all denominations ought to be on their guard against it.* Eventually, in 1775, First Parish's new minister, the Reverend Eli Forbes, addressed letters threatening excommunication to seventeen of John's followers including Winthrop Sargent, his brother Epes Sargent, and Judith Sargent Stevens. The town even attempted to have John removed as a vagrant, until Winthrop Sargent deeded him a piece of his own land, thus making John a legal freeholder.

These were tense, volatile days in Gloucester, as patriotic fervor swept through the community. Merchants like Epes Sargent were accused of disloyalty and forced to leave Gloucester. John Murray was named an English spy by some, but friends from Rhode Island asked him to serve as a chaplain in the Continental Army. He accepted, hoping his military service would squash further charges of treason. John encountered clerical opposition in the Army as well, but General George Washington chose to expand his service rather than release him.

After less than a year of service as an Army chaplain, John caught a potentially deadly fever in camp and was forced to return home to Gloucester. Once there, he was instrumental in raising funds to help Gloucester's citizens who were suffering from the closure of their port, though these benevolent activities did little to mollify the First Parish clergy. Instead, the church leadership's campaign against the small group of Universalists in Gloucester escalated in 1778 when Reverend Forbes followed through on his threat to expel them from church membership—an act of potentially enormous legal and social consequence for the outcasts. But instead of renouncing their chosen faith, the Gloucester Universalists signed Articles of Association in 1779 to create their own religious society: the Independent Church of Christ. They built their own meetinghouse on land owned by Winthrop Sargent and dedicated the small building on Christmas Day 1780, calling John as their pastor.

The next several years saw John Murray and the Gloucester Universalists involved in a series of legal disputes with local authorities. Because the Universalists had defied the law and refused to pay taxes to First Parish Church after forming their Association, in 1782 the town seized articles of value from Universalist believers to sell at public auction. In 1783, John brought the Universalists' case before the Massachusetts Supreme Judicial Court by arguing for the legal right to create a religious organization independent from the established church. Eventually, in 1785 and 1786, the court ruled in favor of the Universalists, thereby allowing them to realize a monumental victory for all American citizens.

The Universalists' victory was short-lived, however. In 1787, First Parish challenged John's authority to perform the marriage ceremony and the Universalists advised John to leave Gloucester for his safety. He decided to return to England to visit his mother whom he had not seen for eighteen years. But before he left, he wrote from Boston Harbor to the recently widowed Judith Sargent Stevens and asked her to marry him.

Sailing for England in January 1788, John had no idea if he would be reunited with Gloucester or Judith again. His apprehension gave way to a triumphant return to the country of his birth, however, where he was frequently asked to preach and dubbed "the most popular preacher in the United States." After a few months, John received word that the Universalists had successfully petitioned the Massachusetts legislature to declare his ministry legal and he boarded a ship to Boston, sharing his passage with John and Abigail Adams who were returning from an ambassadorial mission. The Adamses heard John preach on the ship and struck up a friendship that would last for many years.

When John arrived in Boston, Governor John Hancock hosted a reception in his honor. While his departure from Gloucester had been a necessary but painful decision, John's absence, and the Universalists' petitions, had finally, after many years of opposition, solidified John's stature as a beloved preacher of the Gospel. His hard-won success was crowned that fall when he married Judith Sargent Stevens in Salem, Massachusetts, and participated in a second, more traditional ordination service in the Gloucester meetinghouse on Christmas Day. The Universalists published notices of their pastor's calling in newspapers throughout New England to thwart further challenges to John's ministry. Truly, 1789 was a new beginning for John Murray.

The Move to Boston

John and Judith began married life together in Judith's Middle Street home in Gloucester where John had been lodging for many years. He continued to travel, as his health allowed, to help Universalists in other communities organize their own societies. Before long, Judith was pregnant and John prayed for a safe delivery. Perhaps he would have a second chance to realize a fulfilling family life. But, tragically, their son, Fitz Winthrop, was stillborn. John feared for Judith's life, as she lay ill for many weeks. But she recovered, and the two of them journeyed to Philadelphia in 1790 where John helped organize the first national Universalist convention and represented the New England states during the convention's deliberations. On John and Judith's return trip to Gloucester, John presented the convention's resolutions to President George Washington in New York (the seat of the new American government) to explain, as a courtesy, the growing Universalist movement in America.

Back home, in 1791, Judith gave birth to a healthy daughter they called Julia Maria. Both parents were ecstatic. Simultaneously, the Boston Universalists were urging John to accept a position as their minister. With a new family, he needed to increase his income and likely was intrigued by the idea of living in the New England "Metropolis" with its intellectual, literary, religious, and political activity. John's congregations agreed to allow him to divide his time between Gloucester and Boston, but, eventually, the thirty-seven-mile distance became impractical. John established his friend the Reverend Thomas Jones of Wales in the Gloucester pulpit in 1793, and on October 23, the First Universalist Church in Boston installed John as their pastor. In 1794, John moved his family to an elegant townhouse at Franklin Place in Boston.

John's years in Boston were filled with service to his congregation, travels to advise emerging Universalist congregations around New England, and days of recovery from exhaustion when he returned home. The Boston Universalists were slow to pay his salary, unfortunately, and John was often embarrassed by the state of his finances. Judith's literary career, meanwhile, was blossoming after almost ten years of publishing poems, essays, and plays. Her 1798 book, *The Gleaner*, sold well and bolstered the family coffers temporarily. But money was scarce, and John found himself accepting an increasing number of invitations from far-off congregations in order to supplement his income.

In 1798, before departing for one such engagement in Philadelphia, John had arranged for the young minister Hosea Ballou to preach in his Boston pulpit. John had no idea that Ballou would promulgate a theology blasphemous to Universalists in his church. In other Universalist pulpits, Ballou was in the forefront of a shift toward Unitarianism that would ultimately succeed—a new interpretation of the meaning of Christ's death and his relationship to mankind. John, however, was immovably Trinitarian, and would never have allowed such ideas to be preached in his church. In fact, Ballou's theological views caused serious distress and division within the Boston Universalist congregation when he spoke in 1799. When John finally returned home, he was so ill from a tumor in his side he could only minimally calm his parishioners. Division remained, and Universalism continued to change throughout Boston and far beyond.

In 1809, his relentless efforts on behalf of Universalism ended unexpectedly when he suffered a stroke that resulted in paralysis to the right side of his body. Although his mind was alert and he could speak,

John was bedridden for the rest of his life—no longer able to preach, debate, travel, or provide for his family. John's congregation hired a nurse and sent daily "watchers" to help move and attend to him. Yet as ill as he was, John insisted on shaking the hand of Boston's new Universalist minister, his friend the Reverend Edward Mitchell of New York, during his installation ceremony. Perhaps, he hoped, under Edward Mitchell, the Boston church would return to Rellyan Universalism and halt the intrusion of Unitarianism. When Mitchell departed for his native New York in 1812, the Universalists installed the Reverend Paul Dean, a conservative minister whose leadership, they hoped, would appeal to John.

The Preacher's Legacy

John confessed to Judith that he felt "imprisoned" in his "helpless" body. Judith's letters describing his state of mind report that he longed for an "escape" to the next world. But first, to reinforce the original ideas of Universalism that had strayed so far from James Relly's 1759 book *Union*, John asked Judith to help him edit and publish his writings. He would at least leave behind a written testament of the truth as he saw it. John published *Letters and Sketches of Sermons* in 1812, hoping to generate income along with renewed interest in Rellyan Universalism.

As his investments failed during the early days of another war with Great Britain, John feared for the safety of his family. His frustration reached new heights as American troops arrived in Boston to defend its port. The British had already set fire to the capital city, Washington. What if Boston suffered a similar fate? How could John care for his loved ones—and, equally important, how would his lack of mobility endanger their lives?

Eventually, tensions with Great Britain subsided and Judith and John hoped to resume their peaceful lives together. But on September 3, 1815, John Murray died at the age of seventy-five after almost six years of painful incapacitation. A lifetime of useful service to God and to the public had ended. The leaders of his former congregations organized two services for him—one in Gloucester and the other in Boston where, after a long procession through the city, John was interred in the Sargent family tomb at Granary Burying Ground.

Following John's death, Universalist friends asked Judith to complete and publish his autobiography. John had abandoned the project in

1774 when he settled in Gloucester. Hoping to preserve her husband's legacy, Judith published *Records of the Life of the Rev. John Murray* in 1816. Reflecting the posthumous creation of John's autobiography, the earlier parts, from John's original manuscript, are highly detailed and self-reflective, while the later sections, Judith's additions, are a brief summary of the events of John's life from 1775–1815. Only three sentences describe their lives together as husband and wife:

> Mr. Murray's last marriage was the result of a strong and holy friendship, founded upon the rock of ages; and, originating in devout admiration of redeeming love, it is fervently hoped, and unwaveringly believed, that this union will be perfected in another and a better world. One son, and one daughter, were the offspring of this marriage. The son surrendered his innocent life in the birth; the daughter still survives, the prop, and consolation of her widowed mother.

Since John Murray's death, others have sought to honor him as well, including the United States General Convention of Universalists, which, in 1837, moved John's body to the new and prestigious Mount Auburn Cemetery in Cambridge, Massachusetts, and erected a handsome monument to him. (At Granary Burying Ground, no marker or inscription had identified his final resting place.)

In addition, seventy-one years after John's death, in 1886, the newly formed Murray Grove Association purchased the property in New Jersey where John first arrived and erected memorials to the story of John Murray and Thomas Potter. Today, the Murray Grove Conference Center hosts the John Murray Distinguished Lecture Series and publishes its proceedings.

John's autobiography has been reissued many times over the years, with each edition adding new insights and additional material. In 1920, on the 150th anniversary of John's arrival in America, Frederick A. Bisbee published *From Good Luck to Gloucester*, the first biography of John Murray. In succeeding years, scholars have included John in histories of Universalism, Gloucester, and progressive religion in America (see "Resources" section).

Although John and Judith Sargent Murray have no living direct descendants, John Murray's Universalist descendants abound. The Universalist church in Gloucester, the Independent Christian Church, preserves his legacy through programs and exhibits. The Sargent House Museum, John's former home on Middle Street, is open to the public as a historic house museum. Although Universalists and Unitarians joined together in 1961 to form the Unitarian Universalist Association, the history of Universalism and its early leaders has received renewed interest. The New Massachusetts Universalist Convention was founded in 1998 to host conferences, publish, and generally "fan the flame of Universalism in New England and Beyond." Most recently, Universalist enthusiasts established a Universalist Heritage Center in Winchester, New Hampshire, in 2006.

For almost two hundred years, scholars, ministers, and Universalists have variously referred to John Murray as the singular Father or Founder of American Universalism. But to do so is, in fact, a disservice to the dozens of disparate communities where the message of universal salvation had independently taken hold even before John Murray's arrival in 1770. Perhaps the most fitting title is, simply, as the historian of Universalism, Russell Miller, suggests, Founder of Organized Universalism in America. It is also accurate to state that because of John Murray's steadfast, inspiring, strategic work, he changed American religious life for the better—as he used to say, from "hell" to "hope." He would charge his congregations to join him in spreading the "good news of Universalism" by preaching,

> Go out into the highways and by-ways of America, your new country. Give the people, blanketed with a decaying and crumbling Calvinism, something of your new vision. You may possess only a small light but uncover it, let it shine, use it in order to bring more light and understanding to the hearts and minds of men and women. Give them, not Hell, but hope and courage. Do not push them deeper into their theological despair, but preach the kindness and everlasting love of God.

* An interesting story about John Murray's ancestry is described in Letters 615 and 632. While his maternal ancestors were from English minor nobility, John's paternal family was comprised of Scots who were killed in the 1745 uprising, and French Catholic aristocrats who converted to Protestantism. If John's father and grandmother had been willing to renounce their faith, they stood to inherit a small fortune. They refused, but, many years later, John appears to have had the opportunity to collect what his family had been denied.

The Recipients of the Letters

(other than John Murray, and
listed alphabetically by last name; in some
cases, names and birth/death dates were not available)

"Mr B of Philadelphia"

An unidentifiable Universalist friend.

Adam Lewis Bingaman (1795–1869)

Adam Lewis Bingaman, a native of Natchez, Mississippi, and the son of wealthy planters, boarded with the Murrays in Boston while he attended Harvard College. After he graduated, he married Julia Maria Murray, the daughter of John and Judith Sargent Murray.

Julia Maria Murray Bingaman (1791–1822)

The only surviving child of John and Judith Sargent Murray, very little is known about Julia Maria. Judith educated her at home during her early years, and sent her to nearby female academies in Boston later on. Julia Maria also studied music, dance, painting, and elocution. She was, reportedly, a talented performer of dramatic pieces. To date, no journals, letters, or other writings of hers have been found. She married Adam Lewis Bingaman and, later, died in childbirth at the age of thirty-one.

"Mr J. G—"

This is an unidentifiable member of the Boston Universalist congregation.

Esther Sargent Ellery (1755–1811)

"My Sister" or "My Sister E" is Judith Sargent Murray's sister, Esther, who married John Stevens Ellery (1748–97), a Gloucester merchant. Esther moved to Franklin Place, Boston, after her husband died. Judith was always close to Esther's children, John ("Jack") and Sarah ("Sally").

The Recipients

Catherine Gardiner (see Catherine Goldthwaite Gardiner Powell).

Rev. John Sylvester John Gardiner (1765–1830)
Addressed by Judith as "Rev. and Respected Sir," Rev. Gardiner was the rector of the Episcopalian Trinity Church in Boston and the grandson of Judith's cousin Catherine Goldthwaite Gardiner Powell.

Catherine Goldthwaite (see Catherine Goldthwaite Gardiner Powell).

Eleanor ("Nellie") Parke Custis Lewis (1779–1852)
"Mrs Lewis," as Judith called her, was the granddaughter of George and Martha Washington. Judith met her in 1790 when Nellie was eleven years old, and maintained a correspondence with her for many years.

Rev. Edward Mitchell (1768–1834)
Mitchell was a Rellyan Universalist minister from New York City. He spent a brief time serving the Boston Universalists after John Murray's stroke, but returned to his native city after less than two years. At the end of Judith's life, Mitchell was the only Universalist minister she supported—the only one who had not strayed from John Murray's Rellyan theology.

"The Mother of Mr Murray"
Judith never met John Murray's mother, who lived in London. Mrs. Murray was a widow, whose sole support was derived from her two surviving sons (including John). At this time, we do not know her first name.

"Miss N. P."
An unidentifiable Universalist friend.

Mary Parker (1759–?)
One of the daughters of Noah Parker (see below).

Noah Parker (1734–87)
A Universalist mechanic, blacksmith, and poet in Portsmouth, New Hampshire, Noah Parker became the first Universalist preacher in Portsmouth, thanks to John Murray's encouragement.

"Mr Parkman"
One of the Murrays' financial advisers.

Mary Pilgrim
The Pilgrims were Universalist friends of John Murray's in Hampstead, England.

Anna Plummer (1767–1826)
Judith and her first husband, John Stevens, adopted Anna Plummer when she was thirteen years old along with her sister, Mary, who eventually went to live elsewhere. Anna and Mary were two of John Stevens's orphaned nieces. As a young woman, Anna went to live with her sister Mary in York, Maine, when Mary married Jonathan Sayward Barrell. Anna married Jonathan after Mary died.

"Doctor Potter of Wallingsford"
This is probably the son of Thomas Potter, John Murray's first American supporter (see "Introduction").

Catherine Goldthwaite Gardiner Powell (1747–1830)
A cousin on the Saunders side of Judith's family, Catherine was a close friend and confidante of Judith's throughout her life. Catherine married first Doctor Sylvester Gardiner of Newport, Rhode Island, a Loyalist. After he died, she married William Powell, a Boston merchant. At the end of her life, Catherine lived in a grand Boston mansion and was known as "Madame Powell."

Rev. Robert Redding
Judith corresponded with this Universalist minister from Truro, England, a colleague of John Murray's, about publishing her letters and reissuing her book, *The Gleaner*, in his country.

Joseph Russell (1735–95)
Joseph Russell was a Boston merchant, philanthropist, and Universalist who was a strong supporter of John Murray's especially during the Gloucester Universalists' legal battles. He also tried to help Judith's first husband, John Stevens, negotiate with his creditors.

The Recipients

Anna Parsons Sargent (1769–1860)

Anna Parsons was the daughter of Captain Thomas and Sarah Sawyer Parsons of Newburyport, Massachusetts. She married Fitz William Sargent, Judith's youngest brother, and became one of Judith's closest female friends. Judith visited Anna and Fitz William's large family each summer in Gloucester.

Catherine Osborne Sargent (1722–88)

Judith's "Aunt E— S—" was married to her uncle Epes Sargent, a wealthy Gloucester merchant who was one of John Murray's key supporters during the Universalists' early legal battles. Catherine and Epes were Loyalists who were forced to leave Gloucester for Boston. However, they later chose to return and take their chances. Catherine's son, who was also named Epes, was Judith's closest male friend.

Epes Sargent (1748–1822)

Judith's cousin Epes Sargent (see above) served as Gloucester's first collector of the port before he moved to Hampstead, New Hampshire, to pursue his agricultural interests. He was married to Dorcas Babson Sargent. As Judith's close friend and adviser, he often reviewed her manuscripts before publication. Judith was a regular visitor to his home in Hampstead (which still stands on East Road), and Epes's children were frequent guests in the Murrays' home in Boston. Judith wrote often to "the children at Hampstead."

Esther Sargent (1776–1865)

One of Epes Sargent's daughters (see above), "Miss E. S. of Hampstead" grew up to marry Dr. John Dixwell of Boston.

Fitz William Sargent (1768–1822)

Judith was seventeen years old when her brother Fitz William was born. She helped raise him, and remained close to his family when he married Anna Parsons. Like many Sargent men, Fitz William pursued a life at sea as a merchant, becoming quite successful. He eventually retired from Gloucester to a rural retreat in Newton, Massachusetts. His descendants include the artist John Singer Sargent, and the botanist Charles Sprague Sargent who also founded Harvard's Arnold Arboretum.

John James Sargent (1781–1801)

This son of Epes Sargent of Hampstead, New Hampshire, was a favorite guest at the Murrays' home in Boston. Sadly, during one visit, he contracted an unknown illness that caused his death at the age of twenty.

Judith Saunders Sargent (1731–93)

Judith's mother was the daughter of Captain Thomas Saunders and Judith Robinson, both of Gloucester. The Saunderses were wealthy merchant-class citizens. Captain Andrew Robinson, this Judith's grandfather and Judith Sargent Murray's great-grandfather, is credited with building and naming the first schooner for which Gloucester became famous.

Lucy Saunders Sargent (1752–1840)

"Mrs L Sargent of Sullivan" was Judith Sargent Murray's relative in two ways, first, as one of her mother's nieces, and, later, as the wife of Judith's uncle Paul Dudley Sargent. The Sargents lived in Sullivan, Maine. One year younger than Judith, Lucy was one of her closest female friends.

Mary McIntosh Williams Sargent (1764–1844)

Mary was Judith's sister-in-law, her brother Winthrop's second wife. The daughter of James McIntosh and Eunice Hawley, Mary's first husband was David Williams. All of these individuals were born elsewhere but found their way to Natchez, Mississippi, with the opening of the Mississippi Territory. Winthrop Sargent served as the Territory's first governor, retiring after the election of Thomas Jefferson. While she was married to David Williams, Mary had four children: David, James, Anna, and Mary. Anna lived with Judith in Boston for several years while she pursued her education; David and James were sent north to Exeter Academy and Harvard College. "Aunt Murray" kept a watchful eye on all three of these children who were so far away from their parents.

Mary Turner Sargent (1743–1813)

Alternately known as "Mrs Sargent" and "Maria," Mary was one of Judith's dearest friends and the wife of Judith's uncle Daniel Sargent, a leading Boston merchant. Judith was a regular guest in their home, delighting in their many children. One of Mary's sons, Henry Sargent, was an accomplished artist who painted the last portrait of John Murray (see images section).

Winthrop Sargent (1727–93)

Judith's father first went to sea at the age of thirteen, becoming one of Gloucester's most successful merchants. Although largely uneducated, he insisted on a different life for his children. Mr. Sargent was politically prominent on the patriotic side of the American Revolution, serving on Gloucester's Committee of Safety and as a government agent throughout the war. With David Pearce, he owned a privateering vessel. After the war, Mr. Sargent was appointed as a member of the state delegation that ratified the Massachusetts Constitution. Someone, reportedly a Mr. Gregory of England, gave Winthrop Sargent a copy of James Relly's manifesto of Universalist theology, *Union, or, A Treatise of the Consanguinity and Affinity between Christ and His Church*, and Mr. Sargent invited family and friends into his home to discuss the concept of universal salvation put forth by Relly's book. In 1774, Winthrop Sargent invited John Murray to Gloucester, initiating the first legal ruling for freedom of religion in America, the founding of the nation's first Universalist society, and the building of the first Universalist meetinghouse. He was also responsible for introducing his daughter Judith to John Murray.

Winthrop Sargent (1753–1820)

Judith's brother, younger than she by two years, played a leading role throughout her life. As his childhood playmate, Judith observed the intellectually challenging early education he received that stood in stark contrast to her own. This discrepancy propelled Judith into a lifetime of advocacy for female education. Winthrop served as an officer in the Continental Army under General George Washington, and Judith was enormously proud of her soldier brother. Winthrop's service in the Northwest Territory as secretary of the Ohio Company and, later, as the first governor of the Mississippi Territory, also added to Judith's affection for her brother. Winthrop sent his two sons, two stepsons, and one stepdaughter to Boston for Judith to oversee their education. He also asked Judith to adopt his illegitimate daughter, which he was never able to arrange. At the end of Judith's life, when she moved to Natchez, she was reunited with this beloved brother and his children. However, Winthrop also caused Judith a great deal of pain when he opposed her marriage to John Murray and broke off communication for over a year. Eventually, he relented. Winthrop's first wife was Rebecca Tupper who died along with her child. His second wife was Mary McIntosh Williams, a wealthy widow from Natchez (see her description) who owned a sizable slave plantation.

William Sullivan Esquire
The corresponding secretary of the Washington Monument Association, a group formed in 1811 to commission an equestrian statue of the late president for Boston, Mr. Sullivan visited John Murray in 1812 to request a donation. Today, the statue may be seen at the Massachusetts Statehouse, in Doric Hall.

"Mrs Terrell" or "Mrs Terrill"
This is an unidentifiable Universalist woman.

Anna Williams Thompson
The stepdaughter of Judith's brother Winthrop, Anna Williams lived at Franklin Place for several years while she attended school. When she returned to her home in Natchez, she married a Mr. Thompson.

Elizabeth Stevens Elwell Walker (1736–1819)
Elizabeth Stevens of Gloucester was Judith's sister-in-law, the sister of her first husband, John Stevens. She married first Jacob Elwell; for her second husband, she married Robert Walker. "Madame Walker" was a regular fixture in Judith's life.

Sarah Wheat
The daughter of Universalist friends of John Murray's in New London, Connecticut, Sarah Wheat was one of the many young people with whom Judith maintained a correspondence.

"Mrs Woodrow"
Mrs. Woodrow was the matriarch of a prominent Philadelphia family who John Murray came to know during his many visits to Philadelphia. Mrs. Woodrow's daughter, Mary, married first Dr. Barnabas Binney (who is famous for discovering Deborah Sampson's female identity while she was disguised as a male soldier in the Continental Army) and, secondly, Judith's friend Dr. Marshall Spring of Watertown, Massachusetts.

The Letters

Judith Sargent Murray's endearing words on John Murray

"best of Men"

"Dearest friend"

"Respected Friend"

"Dear to my heart"

"my too partial friend"

"The Man of my heart"

"all I wish him to be"

"The Choice of my heart"

"kind, and most indulgent"

"an instrument of great good"

"Tender, delicate, and manly"

"My dear, my protecting friend"

"the World is not worthy of you"

"the enchantment of your pen pervades every faculty of my bosom"

"to be loved, and admired, it is only necessary he should be known"

"A Man of sense, of cultivated understanding, a strictly moral Man"

"blending the characters of friend, and Lover, of husband, and Protector"

"I am too well acquainted with the many virtues which adorn your mind, to regard you as an ordinary person."

"For myself, it is out of my power, to be other than your friend, and I could willingly submit to you the investigations of my most secret thoughts."

"Yes, Murray, I esteem you for your worth, my whole soul is compelled to admiration of your uncommon Virtues — I have never ceased to esteem you, nor do I know an action of your life incompatible with the elevated point of view, in which I have ever beheld you."

The Letters

Excerpts from the letters of Judith Sargent Stevens Murray are used with permission from the Mississippi Department of Archives and History. Spelling and punctuation are unchanged. The headings of the letters vary; some are numbered, some are not; some include the recipient's name, others do not. Words or punctuation enclosed with brackets ([ ]) indicate additions to the letters by BHS.

The italicized paragraphs prior to each letter are an attempt to set the stage for what Judith Sargent Murray wrote.

$\mathscr{L}$

With this letter, Judith Sargent Stevens initiated a lively, freewheeling correspondence with John Murray that enabled the two friends to "mingle souls upon paper" long before they were able to marry. The "Mr Relly" Judith mentions here is James Relly, the founder of Universalism in England. His "writings" refer to Relly's book, Union, or, A Treatise of the Consanguinity and Affinity between Christ and His Church, *which is considered the defining document of Universalism.*

Letter 14 to Mr Murray
Gloucester November 14 1774

My Dear Sir

If I am not mistaken in the character of the person I have the pleasure to address, it will be most agreeable to him, that I should lay aside all that awe, and reverence, which his unquestionable superiority demands, and approach him with the freedom of a sister, conversing with a brother whom she entirely esteems — I am not much accustomed to writing letters, especially to your sex, but if there be neither male nor female in the Emmanuel you promulgate, we may surely, and with the strictest propriety, mingle souls upon paper — I acknowledge a high sense of obligation to you, Sir, I have been instructed by your scriptural investigations, and I have a grateful heart — Your revered friend, Mr Relly, had taught me by his writings, the rudiments of the redeeming plan; but you have enlarged my views, expanded my ideas, dissipated my doubts, and led me to anticipate, and with sublime, and solemn pleasure, the coming of the resurrection [—] Those whom you have honoured by your social visits, will of course be solicitous for a repetition of the favour — The Gloucesterians wish they possessed a magnetic influence, which would irresistibly attract you to their circle — Nay, I believe, so extravagant is their self Love, that they would not hesitate, were it in their power, to establish you among them during the remainder of your life. For my own part, I cannot entirely condemn them, for when I reflect upon the benign influence of your message, upon its salutary, and universal efficacy, and the mild benevolence, with which you condescend to elucidate its nature, my own wishes are perfectly in unison with theirs. I have to request — if your leisure will allow, that you would honour me by a line and I pray you to believe me with all sentiments of esteem your most obedient &c &c

John clearly agreed to Judith's proposition, because her next letter is addressed to him as well. John has asked Judith to "reveal" what her religion means to her, and she obliges. This is the first time she expresses her "astonishment" at the way John has been treated by those who oppose Universalist doctrine.

Letter 15 To the same
Gloucester December 6th 1774

If the character of the Usurer be ever tolerated, it should when the Commerce is wholly intellectual, when the interest of the mind is abundantly promoted, when we would accumulate a fund for eternity. Give me leave, my honoured friend, to ask when you reflect upon the consolatory views with which you have been indulged, upon the splendid displays of redeeming love which have been made to you, are you not constrained to acknowledge, that it is yours to disseminate, that to you it belongs to communicate, both in speaking, and writing? — Yet you bid me show you what the God Man hath revealed to my soul — Alas! my dear Sir, I can much better meditate on the blissful vision than express my sense of its immensity — here the gift of utterance is denied, and I can only admire in silence. When I contrast my days of ignorance, with those on which the Sun of Righteousness hath dawned, I am wrapt in pleasing wonder, at the amazing height of my elevation. Formerly I saw, but sought to <u>veil</u> the inconsistencies which obstructed the path of reason — I could not investigate, my religious Code, and I forbear to analyze — At every step absurd contradictions started up — I struggled to suspend reflection and I imposed upon my self implicit faith. But the morning broke, and reason exults in her emancipation, the lucid flowers of perception spring up — beneath her feet — and the rays of conviction dart, with elucidating influence, athwart the visual ray [and] enraptured I exclaim — truly our God all gracious "had not created but to bless" and although his erring children may [question], the correction of his paternal hand, yet they shall ultimately be rendered up immaculate, and happy in redeeming love — I confess I earnestly wish for the meridian of the day of grace — I pity those who still wander forlorn and benighted, but I anticipate the fullness of their bliss when Emmanuel shall reveal himself, radically one with them

Suffer me to say, I am astonished at your reception in this our World; at the low malice of your persecutors — your message is benign, and surely we ought at least to acknowledge the benevolence of the system — Will you allow me to ask a question, the answer to which, will not take you out of the walk you so steadily pursue? Who was Melchisidec — Moses, we know, describes him as one of the kings that met Abraham upon his returning victorious from the pursuit of his Adversaries — but the Apostle in his epistle to the Hebrews introduces him in a mysterious point of view — "Without Father, without Mother, without descent, having neither beginning of days, nor end of life." This description would lead us to hail Melchisidec as the Ancient of days, were it not immediately added "made like unto the son of God, abiding a Priest continually."

My husband, and my family, wish to be respectfully remembered to you — May the peace you so abundantly communicate, revert back into your own bosom — May you experience the divine influence of that serenity, which results from goodness, and may you never want the consolation you are so wonderfully calculated to bestow.

From letters like the following one, it is obvious that John has inquired about Judith's thoughts and activities. Whenever she traveled, if John did not escort her, Judith wrote lengthy, descriptive letters to oblige him. Often, as in this case, she engaged him in philosophical discussions. What did it really mean to be a Whig? A Tory? Specifically, did being a Tory condemn her uncle Epes Sargent (Mr S—) to harsh treatment because he did not support separation from England?

The Letters

Letter 18 to Mr Murray
Gloucester June 17th 1775

you demand an account of our last week's peregrinations and solicitous to evince my readiness to fulfill the duties of a punctual Correspondent, I hesitate not to meet your wishes — We commenced our little tour on thursday, the morning was beautifully serene, and the earth was cloathed in its richest verdure — At a short distance from Gloucester, we were accosted by a person of a decent appearance. You will conjecture his character, from the ensuing conversation — as our party consisted only of my sister, and myself, I suppose he felt authorized to address us very familiarly "Ladies your most obedient — You has it very pleasant" — Rather warm we think Sir — "Pray where are you from Ladies?" — From Gloucester Sir — "Pray are you driven from thence?" No Sir, we drive — "Ah — Pray are not most of the people driven from that Town?" The females I believe have pretty generally left that place — "Pray is Mr S— gone, or doth he remain there?" — He remains there Sir — "Does he intend to remain there?" — I believe he does — "Perhaps he thinks himself safer than any other person" — I fancy not. — Why should he Sir? — "His principles you know." What are they Sir? — "Why he is a Tory." I believe it would be difficult to prove Mr S— a Tory, Sir. True, he is a friend to peace and he is a Lover of Order — But, if an invariable attachment to the interests of America constitute a Man a Whig, then I believe that title belongs to Mr S— as much as to any of the Congressional Members: "Pray do you not suspect your self of being a Tory." I am a Woman Sir and therefore do not pretend to constitute myself a judge of the contest so unhappily subsisting — but I may be allowed to assert a fact, I sincerely rejoice when I hear of the prosperity, freedom, and welfare of my country — With regard to the terms Whig and Tory I am free to own I do not understand them — I have heard they are of various signification — but I am not soli[ci]tous to define them — "If you were to talk so favourably of Mr S— among Whigs, you would be called a Tory" Possibly — but having the honour to be nearly allied to Mr S— I have listened to him in the most confidential moments, and I admire his integrity, the universal benevolence of his character — Sir, Mr S— is a Citizen of the World, and it is only necessary to know him, and you will assuredly love, and honour him — Fortunately, the parting of the road, separated us from this disagreeable associate — We reached Byfield about the hour of dining, and were received by our relatives, who are sheltered there, with every possible mark of the most cordial affection — My Aunts are situated in the midst of a woody Vale, surrounded by tall oaks, and hills almost perpendicular — Early on friday morning we pursued our way to Salisbury, over a beautifully level road, and, if I held the pen of description, I would assay to sketch the fascinating views, which, as we passed along on either hand seized, and commanded our admiration....

While their friendship blossomed, Judith and John were both affected by the colonies' approaching separation from England. During John's service as an Army chaplain, Judith wrote to him describing the terrifying presence of the British warship Hope *off the coast of Gloucester.*

Letter 20 To Mr Murray
Gloucester July 28th 1775

You wish for some particulars relative to our publick affairs, and indeed they have [hardly] varied since you left us — upon the day of your departure, the arrival of a schooner belonging to his Britannick Majesty, threw our people into great alarm — Immediately the drums beat to arms, the [bells] sounded portentously, and the streets were filled with the goods of the terrified inhabitants — [Females] running up and down, throwing abroad their hands, the most heart affecting distress visible in their almost frantic gestures, when to heighten the misery of the scene, the Captain of the schooner dispatched a special messenger to the family of the Sargents, soliciting permission to visit them, and begging that some fresh provision may be sent on board, for which he will make ample payment, and disavowing at the same time all intention of hostility — "No, no, no" was the purport of the answer, worded in as strong terms as language could embody. We continued in a state of distressing suspense, through the whole of friday, saturday and sunday — all our men bearing arms even to their place of worship, but Monday confirmed our direful apprehensions — [viewing] maneuvres on board the schooner, it was believed the war was coming up to the landing, Words are inadequate to describe the panic which took possession of the bosoms of the more timid sex, while our Men bravely prepared for opposition — Captain Dawson, however, again dropt Anchor; this in some measure quieted the minds of the people, but toward the close of the day, an event took place which hath alarmed the most judicious among us, Some of our ill advised Townsmen have very indiscreetly fired on the schooner, as she lay in the road, and we have great reason to fear that the Town will fall a sacrifice to their imprudence, indeed it is not improbable, that we may be devoted to destruction — the innocent may too possibly be involved in one common ruin with the Guilty!!

Judith lets John know how much Gloucester is suffering during the early days of the war. Meanwhile, her husband, John Stevens, has secured an inland retreat for the safety of their family and Universalist friends in nearby Chebacco Parish, Ipswich (today's town of Essex). Judith asks John to join them when he returns from the Army, which he does in 1776. Today, the house where John Murray resided still stands on County Road in Essex.

Letter 22d To the same
Gloucester October 1st 1775

... The present unnatural contest hath augmented the miseries of our little Town, to an almost incredible degree — Persons formerly in easy circumstances, are now greatly depressed, while the poor are involved in every species of suffering, to which the sons and daughters of indigence can possibly be subjected — My Dear Sir, you who are at the fountain head of intelligence, is there no hope of an accommodation, will not the rich blessings of peace again illumine our Land? Or is the peerless Goddess fled forever from our borders?

... Upon a supposition that we shall be compelled to abandon our Sea Ports Mr Stevens has provided a little asylum — It is I confess a dreary spot, yet it will answer for a temporary retreat ... I trust we shall not be forced to fly, but if we should, and your inclination should ever lead you to traverse the wilds of Chebacca, you will be received with every demonstration, of that regard which you so well merit.

In one of many letters written to her cousin Catherine Goldthwaite, Judith discusses her admiration for John Murray and her desire for her friends to meet John and learn about universal salvation.

Letter 31 To the same
Gloucester March 3 1776

… The paragraph in your letter respecting Mr Murray, is truly just, his merit is indeed great — Your sentiments of this gentleman would have been highly grateful to your angelic sister — You should not have laid such restrictions, upon me relative to your letters — If you could divest yourself of that diffidence, which, however amiable, in this instance counteracts my wishes, you would be convinced that no one can read your performances, without being charmed with the fair Authoress — I am, however, religiously bound by your injunctions — I did not show your letter, but, as I received it in the presence of Mr Murray, I could not deny myself the pleasure of reading for him, some passages — you may believe he is truly grateful — you are both very dear to me, I am solicitous you should be better known to each other — I am sure you would mutually give and receive pleasure....

Judith tells John that she has had herself inoculated with smallpox, a life threatening procedure. She had seen firsthand how pox victims were treated— carted off to a pest house and left to die, usually alone. She feared for her father's health, given how often he traveled for political or business reasons. If Judith survived the inoculation, she would be able to care for him. She underwent the procedure in secret, not wanting to cause her parents or John Murray concern. She survived, and in fact did nurse her father through the pox. Luckily, John Murray never contracted the disease. Judith is being a bit flirtatious in this letter, denying that she probably was quite beautiful and graceful.

Letter 49 To Mr Murray
Gloucester July 15— 1776

Once more, dear Sir, I resume my domestic employments — My circumstantial journal may possibly reach you — but lest it should not, it may be well to give you a brief account of particulars — I had the small pox rather severely — Inoculation hath not enabled me, as an individual, to speak lightly of this malady — My kind friends left nothing, in their power, unessayed, which they conceived might mitigate my sufferings.... I have had the small pox very full, the disfiguring marks of which still remain [—] I do not wonder that persons possessing beauty, are shocked at the approach of this Despoiler.... I am free to own, that were beautiful features, and a graceful person mine, I should have regarded their loss, as a truly melancholy deprivation.... Thus have I condensed particulars, in which your benevolence induces you to claim an interest, and, I have only to add, my best wishes for the success of your truly divine Mission —

It is unclear which "little Essays" Judith has sent John. Perhaps they were some of the essays she published in the 1790s; perhaps not. What's interesting, though, is that she has shown John her work in progress for his comments.

Letter 51 To Mr Murray
Gloucester November 23d 1776

I have just one moment to embrace an unexpected opportunity — It is true I have scribbled some pages since your departure — these I might send forward, but having proposed a certain plan in the progress of my work, influenced by — What shall I call it — Perhaps caprice, I do not choose to forward my production until it [is] finished. Possibly my little Essays may meet you in Providence for I intend forwarding them by post.... you ask if I am happy — cheerful, composed, &c &c? Why, my dear Sir, I am occasionally tolerably serene — Perfect happiness is, you know, "a bold word for mortals" — I do not believe it is attainable — certainly not desirable, in the present State — Probably I have as great a share of contentment as [I have a] right to have — Nay of this I am positive, for consummate Wisdom, He who hath allotted me my portion, cannot err. When a forward, and ill disposed child, is fretting at a tender and judicious Parent, a sensible person will not be disturbed at its repinings — View me, dear Sir, as this ungrateful child, and let not the calm surface of your bosom be ruffled, at my querulous statements — But I must hasten to close — My Uncle and Aunt E. S. by whom you will receive this letter are on the wing

Judith has written a circumstantial and intimate travelogue for John while he is away in Rhode Island and she is visiting Newburyport, Massachusetts, and Derry, New Hampshire. These brief excerpts show Judith's daily communication with him.

Letter 55 To Mr Murray
Newbury Port Summer of 1777

Will you, my friend, accept a letter, written journal wise, and intended merely for the amusement of the moment — I apprized you in my last, that I had a little tour in contemplation. I left Gloucester thursday evening, accompanied by Miss — I smile at the metamorphose your perceptive faculties have undergone, yet I cannot forbear acknowledging, that your rude barren scenes, steep rocks, and wide waters, partake much of the sublime, but I must still avow my fondness for rural prospects, and spreading oaks, ever verdant pines, and all the gay variety the woods produce....

The Letters

Thursday Night

I am retired to my apartment, have wound up my watch, and am preparing to resign myself into the arms of the image of death ... I have had a wearisome day — searching the shops, in the vain hope of furnishing myself, with some little necessaries, of which I stand in great need....

Wednesday Morning — Sun just rising

While the horse is putting to the Carriage, I will take leave to greet my revered friend with the salutations of amity — May this day prove to be most happy — I am charmed with this Mansion and its environs ... you have been often here, to you, therefore, they are familiar — The views are really paradisical — But the Carriage is ready and I am gone....

Haverhill — Eleven O' clock

We arrived here about an hour since....

Thursday Evening

Well such a day! But you shall hear all — and methodically too — Let me consider — I parted from you expressing my regrets, fears &c &c at the idea of abiding in the Inn — We soon after walked out to the shops, for the purpose of procuring some articles of which we were in want — The weather was intensely warm, and we much fatigued.... We were entirely unacquainted with the roads we were to pursue.... We reached this place sufficiently fatigued with our day's jaunt

Friday Evening Newbury Port

Late this evening we are thus far on our way homeward.... Overtaken by a violent thunder storm, and hasting to a sheltering roof, we have been thus delayed — In this Mansion, however, I am at home — my youthful Host is, as I said, obliging and the domestics attend me with the most flattering observance — a pleasing proof this, of the regard with which I am distinguished by their superiors — Early in the morning, we commence our return to Gloucester — Being weary, I seek the balm of sleep —

Gloucester Saturday evening

It was late before we reached Home.... The demonstrations of pleasure given by my friends at my return from every little absence, are truly grateful to the best feelings of which I am possessed.... Respected Friend, Farewell

The Letters

Here, Judith unburdens herself to John about a disloyal friend, concern for her brother Winthrop who was serving in the Army, and for her country. John was her confidant on many subjects.

Letter 69 — To Mr Murray
Boston March 31st 1778

... My spirit last evening was greatly agitated, my feelings have been wounded, I have been most cruelly treated by a female from whom I had every reason to expect the utmost exertions of tenderness — What a void doth the defection of a friend create in the soul, a prime source of consolation unexpectedly cut off, the mind agonized, and forlorn, seeks in vain for relief, every pleasing sensation seems to have fled, and, for a time, we refuse to be comforted.... This morning my Father received a letter from my eldest brother, he is not pleased with the adventitious life of a soldier — He ardently wishes for something decisive, as he expects to continue in the service of his country, until the close of the war, which judging from appearances, he supposes will find him despoiled of health, destitute of occupation, and penniless — Oh! America! America! is it thus you encourage your bravest sons —

Judith is in Boston nursing her father, Winthrop Sargent, through smallpox as well as attending to her aunt Mary Turner Sargent. This is the first of many letters in which Judith expresses her constant concern for John's health, and her belief in the singular value of his life.

Letter 73 to Mr Murray
Boston April 2d 1778

Dear Sir, I am now to demand your felicitations, The small pox begins to make its appearance, and the symptoms are abating — yesterday Mr Noble put your obliging favour into my hands — The sentiments you express of me, are highly flattering, and I am truly grateful.... I have, I confess, devoted but a small share of time to you, but you will readily accept my apology — My Father hath very naturally demanded my closest attention, both he, and my brother, have been, and still are, very ill — In truth this same small pox, even in its mitigated state is still poisonous to our Nature.... Mrs Sargent too has many claims upon me.... We expect you with pleasure but my Father unites with me in conjuring you not to commence your journey hither, until the weather proves propitious —

The state of your health is very low, and you ought always to remember, how very many are interested in a life so valuable — Mean time allow me to commend you to the care of Heaven —

John Murray faced opposition and even danger for preaching the concept of universal salvation and attracting a growing number of followers. His message threatened the established, Calvinist order of Gloucester's First Parish Church that upheld the traditional doctrine of predestination. Universalism "dispersed" Calvinism's "dark clouds" and many people responded favorably. John was frequently denounced in sermons and pamphlets, "assaults" to which John felt he must respond. Judith was always his stalwart supporter, as she shows here.

Letter 102 To the same
Gloucester September 17th 1778

... Thou Murray, art engaged in dispersing those dense clouds, which presumptuously o'er shadow our intellectual sun, and it is hence I pronounce thee happy — Go on, dear Sir, and may the God whom thou delightest to serve, grant thee success. You wish to know if I have proceeded in the work which I had commenced — Alas! No — for although I have frequently made the attempt, I cannot please even my own partial self — How well digested is your plan, or rather how strong is truth — I do assure you, when you were so unceremoniously, and so publicly assaulted by the bold question[ers] universal palpitation seized me. When you sat down, and again when you arose, my cheeks were alternately flushed, and pale, and, during the torrent of interrogations, I could scarcely breathe — nor wonder, for if I have not yet found the path of truth, where alas! shall I turn? But, when I listened to the judicious, the calm responses of our Apostle, my soul became calm, assured, and perfectly confiding — May God forever bless you, indeed He hath blessed you, by thus [causing] you to encounter the various difficulties and to surmount them too by [whom] you are surrounded — May the presence of the Almighty still continue your never failing support.

Judith is able to dismiss her headache by chatting with the "friend of her soul." In the next letter, she credits John with guiding her spiritual journey— a recurring theme throughout her letters to him.

Letter 134 To the same
Portsmouth August 29 1779

Well, at length I have a tranquil moment, [tho] my head is pained, and my heart is heavy, but what then, I will seek to [dismiss] every unpleasant sensation, in chatting with a friend — With the friend of my soul — he who hath led my steps into the paths of truth....

Judith despised war throughout her life, having witnessed its devastating effects on families, businesses, and communities. Here, "prizes" (foreign ships) captured by privateers are sailing into Gloucester Harbor. She shares her thoughts at this moment with John.

Letter 135 To Mr Murray
Gloucester September 16 1779

... I sigh for the superiour heroism of ... ancient times, and I regret that I was not born in the days of other years — Now, deceit is deemed a virtue, and he who can most successfully dissemble, is the most renowned Chief — hark! what explosions are those — I have inquired, the other prizes have passed the Fort and the roar of arms proclaim the joy of our people. I too would rejoice, but the Ghosts of the departed arise, and the grief of the aged, the widow, and the Orphan, is great — Waft me some friendly spirit, far from the din of War, from the inauspicious greetings of those instruments of death.

John often asked Judith her opinion of him.

Letter 140 To Mr Murray
Gloucester October 18— 1779

You are solicitous for my opinion of you — Is it possible, dear Sir, you can entertain a doubt in this respect? I have often said, and thus called upon I now repeat, that I can never view you in a disadvantageous light — I am too well acquainted with the many virtues which adorn your mind, to regard you as an ordinary person....

Judith poses more theological questions following one of John's sermons, feeling quite "free" to speak plainly to her pastor.

Letter 141 To the same
Gloucester October 21st 1779

The weather is gloomy — but my spirit is calm — It is stayed upon the rock of ages — The clock from the neighbouring steeple hath just struck eleven, it warms me not to pass the hour unheeded by — I come then, revered friend of my soul — and that my coming may not be unprofitable, I will give you the result of my meditations upon the four first verses of the seventy second Psalm, which this morning fixed my attention — I pray you would have the goodness to turn to the verses....

Days later, their theological discussion continues. Meanwhile, John is having another episode of self-doubt. Judith tells him to carry on even in the face of growing opposition—he is one of very "few" who have been called upon to deliver his Universalist message.

Letter 146 To the same
Gloucester November 17th 1779

"Yet I feel pleasure in the consciousness that I last night faithfully delivered the truth, as it is in Jesus, to a large and attentive audience — while I continue so to do, I shall at least possess the approbation of my own Mind, be the [consequence] what it may" — Such is the exordium of your last letter — and here then, my friend, I would rest — This sentiment is worthy of a Christian, and of a Philosopher — will you not persevere in drawing consolation from a source so rational. Why should you allow the multitude of events, which take place among your various connexions, thus to oppress you — Hath not your great Master assured you, that narrow is the way, and few there are who walk therein — Must you then repine at the economy of Omnipotence — Is not God the supreme Governor — doth He not possess unerring wisdom, and is He not the great omni Parent of the Universal family, and are not [all terrestrial] concerns, subjected to his controul — Deny this, you who acknowledge the divinity of Revelation, if you can be so egregiously, so absurdly inconsistent — For me, my friend, did you ever expect all who heard, and professed to admire, would become physically [affected], why are you so astounded at the truth of revelation, of a Revelation which you [hope] to gild your hopes of future happiness — start not, Murray at the plainness, nor the ... freedom of this question —Friendship sanctions....

Judith has received John's recent letters with great delight during this pivotal time for the Gloucester Universalists. They have decided to sign Articles of Association and create their own religious society separate from First Parish Church, thus accelerating their "rapid progress" toward establishing Universalism's "tidings of peace." This act was in direct defiance of the church, which had earlier expelled the Universalists for not attending. According to this letter, John asked Judith to burn his letters. Naturally, Judith is horrified by the idea. It is not clear if she obeyed him, but most of John Murray's personal letters are missing.

Letter 149 To Mr Murray
Gloucester November 28 1779

... yesterday the clock had struck twelve, my pen was thrown aside — I sat pensive, and alone, gloomy was the theme in which I had been engaged — your packet was brought from my Mother's — Open went the seals, first one, than another, my eye ran greedily over the multiplied sheets — reading here, skiping there, vainly wishing to swallow the whole with a single glance — At length I sought, and found the dates, and turning to the last page, I eagerly drank in every line — tears, joyful tears bedewed my face, smiles lighted up gladness in my countenance, and sacred pleasure suffused my soul — The rapid progress of the heart elevating tidings of peace, and imperishable salvation — Great God — I exclaimed Great God it is enough — I prostrate myself before thee, in thankful, in silent [praise] — and now, arising from the peaceful and salutary slumbers of the night, I proceed to express my pleasures, and my regrets, as I behold you improving the early dawn, to bless me by the page, dictated by affectionate esteem.... Are you my friend serious, with respect to the requested bonfire to be light up at your death? and must I resign those scared honoured pledges of as pure a friendship as ever glowed in a mortal bosom — Must I give up those sacred repositories of esteem, dictated by wisdom, written with the pen of elegance, and crowned by the rich diadem of sincerity — I have collected with care, have smiled over multiplied pages, numbered their beauties, and cherished them with maternal fondness — Can I then devote them to the devouring flames — No, surely no — such a sacrifice would resemble the funeral piles which were said to be collected in days of yore — It will be forbidden by every feeling of amity — What a meeting with your friends — How tenderly pathetic are your descriptions — My sensations, during the recital, are indeed ineffable — I could not delineate — every pulsation

beats to joy, and the enchantment of your pen pervades every faculty of my bosom — Farewell the equal flow of serenity is no more

Judith is never shy about her high regard for John, placing him far and above the unidentifiable "Mr P—" in her estimation.

Letter 161 To Mr Murray
Gloucester September 21— 1780

No, positively No, I will never consent to rank P— above Murray — P— is by no means destitute of foibles, here hath he been protracting, till the week is wasted even until thursday, and yet he is not gone! ... Viewing you as a mere Man, we do not exact from you the gift of prescience — "He," saith a celebrated Writer, "who hath once prevailed upon himself to break his connexions, and commence a wandering life, very easily continueth it" — We do not calculate, trust me we do not, upon fixing our reverend Wanderer, we only wish to determine upon what footing we stand. Will you forgive the freedom of these animadversions, Trusting that you will, I lay down my pen in hope —

When Judith adopted thirteen-year-old Anna Plummer, her husband's orphaned niece, she wrote the first letter describing the event to John Murray.

Letter 168 To the same
Gloucester December 2d 1780

Well, dear Sir, my little Girl is at length come and an idea of the importance of the charge disposed upon me, absorbs every faculty of my soul, I wish my cares could have commenced earlier, it is difficult building upon the foundation of another. I should be glad the mind which I have to form, might be unbiased by prejudice. I wish — in short I hardly know what I wish — Heigh! Ho! — ah! me — would I were in any other character — But peace my soul, and give me, O! thou God of consolation to pursue unrepining the path pointed out by providence....

The next letter illustrates the expanding role John Murray played in the Sargent family as their pastor and friend, in this case, as the messenger of bad news. Judith is in Boston nursing her father through smallpox, as she long ago suspected she would have to do. They will miss the Christmas Day dedication of the Gloucester Universalists' new meetinghouse—the first one in America. At this time, among Protestant sects in coastal Massachusetts, only Universalists and Episcopalians celebrated Christmas.

Letter 171 To Mr Murray
Boston December 24— 1780

I have, I do assure you, my Dear Sir, been most religiously bound by my promise. I really flattered my self I should at Salem have obtained a mitigated account of the situation of my suffering brother, but alas! my intelligence was but too true.... I conjure you, Sir, by that sacred friendship which so uninterruptedly subsists between us, by every tie I entreat you to take of your precious health, every necessary care. I trust I shall soon be with you — God grant this expedition does not prove illusive — To you I assign the task of breaking to my Mother, the illness of my brother — Dear, blessed Woman, her infirmities are many — Winthrop is her darling, her health is low, and her tenderness of the most anxious description — you will pity, you will sympathize with her — I know it is a painful task which I impose — But what taxes have you not already paid for a friendship of little or no intrinsic value — With respect to performing divine worship in the new Temple to morrow, it appears to me, while the Family of its Founder is involved in a situation so truly melancholy, there would be an indelicacy, if not an impropriety in opening it — you however can best decide — In all events, you are in possession of my best wishes — What a Christmas!!!

Clearly, as much as Judith is writing to John, he is writing to her as well, in this case, while she is in Boston.

Letter 179 To the same
Boston January 2d 1781
Evening of January 2d

Just at one O clock arrived Mr Stevens. What letters! how many sheets? God forever bless you, Sir, I almost regret that I have not now time to respond, but it is past twelve O clock, I have called on many of your friends this evening, Colonel G— and family, Mrs Perkins — Mrs G— &c &c they were severally solicitous respecting your health — again, and again I repeat my thanks for your indefatigable attention — Not one of my friends are either able, or willing, thus to oblige me — they are conscious of this and hence their consent I should address my circumstantial details to you

— But early on the morrow I am coming — yes I will, in person, express my gratitude, and study, by my every action, to merit your esteem —

Judith has been writing a Universalist catechism for children with which she is not quite happy.

Letter 190 To Mr Murray
Gloucester June 2d 1781

Yes Sir, I confess I have discontinued my usual method. Imposing duties have engrossed my time, and the cares either real or imaginary of the present insipid state of Being, employing my fingers have not left me a moment to arrange my ideas upon paper. Sacred periods have been devoted to the page of inspiration — I have proceeded with the prophet, and with my friend, yet I am not pleased with myself — Recollection fails me, and I come short, very far short, of the Excellence at which I aimed....

How "sad" Judith is and how "dreary" her home is without John's presence whenever he had to travel on one of his endless "tours of benevolence." John is a boarder in her house at this stage of their friendship.

Letter 201 To Mr Murray
Gloucester September 20— 1781

And art thou then gone, to be here no more! forbid it ye guardian spirits, whom we devoutly implore to shield our revered friend, and to protect him in this his tour of benevolence — Slow, sad, and solemn, did yesterday descend, among the periods now no more — In vain we strayed in pursuit of peace, among all the apartments of this solitary, and now frightfully spacious abode! alas! the heavenly descendant, sweet peace, had made one in the train of departed friendship — The room allotted to you appeared a dreary desert: Deep glooms brooded there, and your empty chair, stared upon us, wildly vacant.... Through respect, as if by general consent, your seat was left empty[,] by mistake a cover was placed for you — fortunate accident — I will improve upon it — My table shall continue its accustomed order, nor shall any one occupy the vacant chair — Thus I will indulge my feelings, untill you again fill the appropriated spot — should you no more return — I cannot help it — It is in vain I enlist reason [and] fortitude.... Friendship, bereaved Friendship demands its dues —

The Letters

Judith reveals how John's letters and attention make her feel.

Letter 208 to Mr Murray
Gloucester November 6th— 1781

That I have received your letters, that I have read them with attention, and that I am truly grateful, will not, I presume, be for a moment doubted — But, my too partial friend — your soothing compliments can never by me be merited — why then should they elate — and yet, strange as it may seem, it is never the less true, that the sweet sensations which now play about my heart, proclaim that praise, even although undeserved, doth however exhilarate....

In this letter to Noah Parker of Portsmouth, New Hampshire, a Universalist preacher recruited by John, Judith discusses her fears for John's health and the "progress" of her catechism. Thanks to Noah Parker, Daniel Fowle, the publisher of the New Hampshire Gazette, *printed Judith's catechism in Portsmouth in 1782. It was the first locally published Universalist catechism and the earliest work by an American Universalist woman. It would immediately help John Murray and other congregations teach Rellyan Universalism to the growing number of Universalist children. Months later, the catechism was reissued in Norwich, Connecticut, where John Murray was a frequent visiting preacher. It is reasonable to assume that he caused this to happen. (To download a copy of the cathechism, visit www.hurdsmith.com/judith.)*

Letter 219 To Mr Parker
Gloucester January 31 1782

... your Son ... will give you an account of the indisposition of Mr Murray, and he will tell you, it is of a nature to require every moment which can be spared from unavoidable domestic cares — Indeed we have been greatly alarmed about our friend — To us his life is very necessary, nor are we yet without apprehensions, that his useful course is nearly run — He is confined to his bed by a fever ... loss of appetite, and constant complaints of lasitude — I rejoice to learn that the Doctrines of the Redeemer flourish in Portsmouth.... With respect to the writings to which you advert, I have to say, first of the Catechism, Anna cannot copy for the press, she is too young in the writing way and I have already urged my own apology. I confess I have almost come to a resolution to destroy not only the catechism, but every other production of my aspiring pen — Mr Sewall, while at Gloucester, very undesignably, no doubt, greatly discouraged me, by pointing out errors, which, a deficiency in my education prevents me from distinguishing — In short — in short — I am unequal to the efforts I have presumed to make, and it was better I consigned to oblivion the arrogance of a mind, which ought to be sensible of its own inability — But considerations of this description, may not always sway, I shall probably, when leisure will allow prepare for you a copy of the Catechism, which you will be at liberty to suppress, or to publish, concealing however the name of the adventurous Author —

Here, Judith presumes to tell John how he should allocate his time, and that he should put more effort into writing for publication. Become a "quill driver" she tells him, write to her more often, and "omit nothing!"

Letter 237 To Mr Murray
Boston June 17— 1782

Fitz William has at length handed me a packet from my friend — The air of sincerity which it breathes is as refreshing to my spirit as the evening zephyr, after the intense heat of the summer's sun, and that I am most grateful, my future words, my future actions shall evince. The Ode which you have transmitted is beautiful — The soul of the Preacher, thus enlarged, could the evening be other than divine — To listen to the proclamation of redeeming Love, to unite in celebrating the descending, the incarnate God, is surely a taste of heaven — May your expectations, so often frustrated, no more deceive you, may you be blessed with content, with that content which will ensure felicity — Permit me, however, once more to repeat — If you do not possess self approbation, it will be in vain to calculate upon serenity — God is my witness I had rather be assured that my actions were conformable to rectitude, than to have the assembled World for my admirers — Self approbation ensures peace, while discord at home is pregnant with most corroding sorrows. I know you have often condemned your self for abiding with a circle so comparatively small, while you have many opportunities abroad of publishing truth more extensively — But perhaps were you to recollect, that Triflers generally compose the multitude, and that reason, deliberation, and sentiment, are usually found among the select few, you would be better able to reconcile with your duty, your abode in Gloucester. No, Sir, I cannot fain what I do not feel, my power only extends to the occasionally placing the lights, and shades in an advantageous point of view. I confess, to express myself in the Andrean style, I have always had the most irrepressible desire, to see you a quill Driver — I know you have materials, and I think your usefulness would be more extensive, certainly more permanent, than in the method you at present pursue. But it would not be so conducive to your health — I am of a different opinion — I never could believe that extremes were salutary, either to the mental, or corporal system — Uniformity is productive of advantage, as well as beauty, and certainly consequences the most pleasing result therefrom — Exercise ought undoubtedly to occupy a part of every day, but surely it should not be steadily pursued for one, or more, and then wholly neglected — Some such plan as the following might, I presume to dictate, I would suggest — In the first place you should rise in the morning as early as might consist with your feelings, when you should, if the weather were propitious, make a constant practice of walking to that part of Town, where you were [first lodged —] you might amuse yourself for a couple of hours in those agricultural pursuits of which you are so fond, the hours from breakfast until eleven o- clock, should be appropriated to writing, and the remainder until dinner to reading, and conversation — The ceremony of dining gone past, your horse should be got up, and after a ride of considerable extent the evening should be concluded by giving, and receiving visits — Events decidedly extraordinary should alone have power to supersede, or even controul this method — Regularity is essential to every solid attainment, and you will, dear Sir, observe, that exercise [is] a part of my plan — Order describes the Prince of Peace, and confusion marks the progress of the Prince of darkness — Method is a prime source of good — Harmony is its first born, and the business proper to the several periods of the day, performed in due season, prevents distraction, and redeemeth time.... Do not, however, let my pen embarrass you — Recollect that to enforce obedience is beyond my power, for although friendship may suggest, it should not presume to command — I wish you happy in whatever situation you may be, and I do most earnestly entreat you, to pursue undeviatingly the path which your judgment shall point out, as most likely to procure felicity — If you are sure of your measures, contentment will gild your hours, if not, you must be unhappy. But lest this sheet should fall into other hands, I take leave to observe, for the purpose of obviating a suspicion, which might arise in some minds — I have no [rights] to enjoyments in another, and a better world, of these we are beyond a doubt. I purposely avoid touching upon the subject of your reiterated sufferings — Gracious God! but let me still preserve my resolution — How was it possible you could pursue your journey — how, with such apparent equanimity, address the people — how hold your pen — but I have done — Redeemer of Men preserve the friend, and once more restore him to health, and to his admiring, and numerous connexions — I pray you, when next you write, be very particular relative to your situation — for heaven's sake omit nothing — you have kept the present account back so long, that I am extremely apprehensive — alas! alas! — but you will, you must, again return — May all good Angels waft you on your way, I must hasten to a close — I shall else be too late for the post — May the peace of God be with you, May his irradiating countenance be, at all times, your support, and abiding consolation —

This will not be the first time someone accuses John of writing Judith's work.

Letter 243 To Mr Murray
Boston June 28— 17[82]

... I have not an objection to your being supposed the Author of the Catechism although it appears to be holding you up rather in a capricious point of view and we should be at a loss to conceive of a motive for your assuming the former....

In the same letter, Judith expresses her gratitude that he has finally written.

... The packet by Mountford I have received, and heretofore acknowledged, and I have now only to admire your indefatigable endeavours to entertain, and inform my mind.....

Here, the two friends discuss what they are reading, a favorite pastime, and Judith explains her life-long preference for letter writing and quiet conversation. She signs her letter in a particularly affectionate way.

Letter 251 To the same
Gloucester July 17 1782

Your last favour remains unanswered, but want of opportunity, and not deficiency in attention, hath prevented me from paying it that respect, with which the letter before me opens, as a sacred truth, and it is fraught with consolatory ideas.... The opera of Voltair is pleasing — I think it does him honour as a Writer, it is descriptive of a fine imagination, and it exhibits all that burst of thought, which is an indispensable requisite in a poetical career.... I thank you for your explanation of the origin of the Knights of Malta — how frequently have you enlightened the uninformed mind — This communication is a badge of your calling.... Are you not astonished that being this day to entertain a large company, who are to dine, drink tea, and spend the evening, I should thus scribble on without mercy either upon myself or you — Recollection however impels me to resign the pen, first assuring you that I am, with accustomed Amity, unalterably yours &c &c

This is the first letter in which Judith acknowledges her husband's accumulating debt. Written to John Stevens's sister, Elizabeth Stevens Elwell Walker, Judith begins to document a tragic personal drama that won't end well.

Letter 312 To Madam Walker
Gloucester October 8— 1783

The period since I received the last favour of my honoured Correspondent hath been repleat with glooms — often have I essayed to write, to assume a language foreign to my soul, to display upon paper expressions of a mind at ease.... Mr Stevens, when fate made our destinies one, was master of a sum, which in almost any business, supposing but moderate success, would have secured competency — This sum was, however, so absorbed in the Vortex of unsuccessful Navigation.... The commencement of the War between Great Britain, and her Colonies, together with the paper currency which it originated, relieved us from the demands of Creditors ... [but] our Creditors are again Clamorous, and although they are not as numerous as formerly, yet they demand their dues, nor have we means of satisfying them....

John is traveling again, and he has once more confided his feelings of self-doubt to Judith. This time, though, he has revealed his ongoing struggle with depression. Such intimate exchanges occur throughout their letters to each other as John and Judith buoyed each other up in moments of despair.

The Letters

Letter 341 To Mr Murray
Gloucester May 17th 1784

Thus time moves on — and the last day will come,
When sighs will cease, and joys eternal bloom:
When hopes and fears no more shall agitate,
When we shall be beyond the power of fate;
When passing to the realms of perfect day,
The torch of faith shall point the brightening way.

Thirteen days since your departure are now gone past, they are with the years of other times, their sorrows shall no more perplex, nor their illusive joys arise, like a meteor shooting athwart the sky — I have not marked them, I do not wish them to be registered, I consent they be consigned to oblivion, that they be enveloped in the impenetrable shades of forgetfulness — yet some white moments have marked their progress, they were gilded by the receipt of letters from dear, absent friends, among which, your epistles were not the least esteemed — Never was I more unpropitiously situated for writing, almost every moment of my time is demanded, and so much are my domestic calls encreased, that my hours are, of necessity, surrendered — and, indeed, why should I write, not a subject worthy of a suspension of my avocation presents — one continued round, producing the same objects, gives me to conceive I am actually treading the very identical path which I have so often and so painfully pursued. At this period of our friendship, professions are not necessary, of my esteem, and consequent respect, you may always assure your self, and should any thing material take place, I will be careful to apprize you.... Meantime I will as concisely as I may, note the particulars your favours contain. If you do not possess tranquility, we shall certainly regret — you have many connexions, all warmly attached to your person, and office — you are passing from one circle of friends to another — perhaps a love of variety is not peculiar to you — it unquestionably governs more, or less, every son, and daughter of Adam — Nature in the exuberance of her diversifications, prepares to regale, to the utmost of their wishes, her favourite children — she is adorned for you, with every blooming sweet, you will be secured wherever you may sojourn, with the most sincere friendship, the important, and peaceful nature, of your embassy, will ensure your welcome. your investigations will light up the smile of reason, in the countenance of the intelligent, and your message will diffuse through the enraptured spirit, the most holy, and sacred pleasures — while a sense of having well performed your duty, will give a zest to every high raised enjoyment — O! Murray why are you not happy — borrow but the lucid ray, beaming from the sun of gratitude, and mounting to the Author of your existence, and you will then drink as deeply, at the fountain of felicity, as your present mode of being will admit — For my own part, I know of no situation which more necessarily ensures happiness to a benevolent mind, than the power of communicating knowledge, and consequent happiness — knowledge of the highest kind, that sacred knowledge, which can only be perfected in the mansions of blessedness — yes, I am free to confess, I can conceive no higher felicity, this side the regions of immortality, than that of raising the depressed spirit, irradiating the benighted mind, dispersing the clouds of darkness, and giving the child of sorrow, to behold the light of life —

Judith reports to John on her health, diet, and her birthday. She often referred to the human body as a "clay built tenament."

Letter 347 To Mr Murray
Gloucester June 12— 1784

You say, my respected friend, I cannot oblige you more than by a regular, and scrupulous attention to my own health, and by calling in a physician as an auxiliary — Surely this clay built tenement is not so very important a concern — We should smile, were we to see a person set about repairing a shattered building, which, in fact, as intercepting some enchanting prospects was much better levelled with the ground, yet feeling a kind of attachment to the antiquated ruins he is still seeking to prop them — But seriously, I am indeed under a uniform regimen — I eat no butter, nor any thing of which that ingredient makes a part of composition, sauces of all kinds, vegetables excepted, I have wholly relinquished — To supper, you know I have long since bid adieu — I make no use of animal food, except that which is termed white meat, and I take that part very dry — I go not abroad but under the cover of an azure sky, and when the ground is properly prepared, by the intense rays of Dar Phoebus — twice, every day, I have recourse to medicine, for which my stomache hath been properly prepared by an emetic — tomorrow I am to begin a course of the cold Bath, and, to crown all, I have as tender and humane a Physician, as ever blessed a grateful patient. Thus you see, I am as attentive to myself, as you could wish.... My last birth day completed the thirty third year of my age [—] your wishes respecting it — — — But it is past — It is with the days of other years, and I rejoice that its pleasures, or its infelicities will no more return....

Judith tells John how much she enjoys his letters and engages him in a discussion about mankind's natural desire for freedom. Time and again, we see that Judith is comfortable asserting her own views with John, and even disagreeing with him.

Letter 351 To Mr Murray
Gloucester June 18— 1784

... I repeat that I derive much satisfaction from your letters — if you receive as much pleasure, as you communicate, your enjoyments are by no means inconsiderable — That I have known and distinguished you, seems to me to be honourable to my character, and, in my bosom, friendship does not suddenly expire — I admire your descriptions, if they be not as sublime as though you had made the tour of Italy for the purpose of sketching them, they are certainly as beautiful.... I cannot agree with you, I do not believe a propensity to slavery inherent in mankind — Religion, false Religion, may shackle them with fetters forged upon the anvil of superstition, but this is an accidental effect, wholly foreign is our nature, while a love of liberty is a spontaneous sensation, which is the beauteous growth of every bosom — Freedom is the first flower which buds in the soul, and the hand of discretion is necessary, for the purpose of lopping the luxuriance of its growth — Let us, my friend, wait, patiently wait, for the salvation of our God — what, although error exalteth itself, yet shall all things terminate in the general good — Our apprehension, and surprise, at the sudden appearance of what, to the eye of reason, seems calculated to sap the very foundation of our dearest hopes, are unquestionably natural — but firm is the rock on which we stand — Nor Men, nor angels possess the power to undermine its imperishable base — Priests may publish, Clergymen may combine — but Emmanuel will rise triumphant, and his God head shine conspicuous, although the whole artillery of impious wit, may urge its most deadly shafts — Let them stand in opposition to the God Man, let them endeavour to strip the Redeemer of his hard earned laurels, to seize his crown, to dethrone their rightful monarch — God the Sire of their spirits knows their frames, that they are but dust and he will, most certainly, have compassion upon them, upon the ignorant, and those who are out of the way, and, under his beneficent wing, he will ultimately gather them, thus sheltering them from every evil....

In this playful, flirtatious letter, Judith has sent John "silver" hairs she has plucked from her head! I suspect the "papers" and "parcel" that made her so happy were from John.

Letter 353 To Mr Murray
Gloucester July 9th 1784

... Let me see — What more have I to say — O I have news for you, combing my hair this morning, as I beheld its motley appearance, I felt my veneration for this tenement considerably encrease — Antiquity, you know, inspires this passion, and, from henceforth, acknowledging the superiority of my character, I advise you to yield me all proper observance, and, to the end, that you may be duly impressed with adequate ideas of my consequence, I have plucked from amid the dark shades by which they were surrounded, a sufficient quantity of those silver teguments to evince the authenticity of my title, to that respect which I claim, and, carefully wrapping them in a piece of paper, you will find them severally inclosed in this sheet, and I require you, and all my other friends, to consider them as so many proofs of my indubitable right, to that attention which I shall not fail to exact.... With what unusual levity I trifle on! In good truth I possess, this morning, a high degree of serenity — Can you guess the reason? Think you it proceeds from the important discovery I have made, which undoubtedly invest me with a considerable share of dignity? Or rather may not this calm, be in part occasioned, by a whisper I have received, that there is now waiting for me with good Mr Williams a number of papers with a parcel all of which will most assuredly be this very evening presented to me — From which of these sources do you suppose my tranquility proceeds? If you have not sufficient sagacity to determine this question, depend upon it you shall never be called upon to decide in any matter, which involves the peace of, or is of any great importance to me — but I beg pardon, I had forgotten to whom I was writing —

Judith describes a recent outing in Gloucester while raising some interesting philosophical points about the treatment of animals. Judith always preferred a vegetarian diet.

Letter 358 To Mr Murray
Gloucester August 4— 1784

Solicitous to collect for you, every thing which may in any degree
interest, or amuse I take leave to transmit you an account of a party which
we have recently formed for eastern Point — you will not expect a superb
description of our little Circle — Imagination might doubtless supply the
gilded banks, the purple sails, the richly waving streamers, with the most
magnificent Canopy, which the looms of Persia could furnish — Fancy
might listen to exquisitely harmonious sounds — Flute, han[d]boys, harps,
violins, french horns etc etc etc which our oars, glittering amid the azure
stream, were in exact unison [—] Performers might combine their odours,
impregnating with richest fragrance, the surrounding atmosphere — In
the virgin train the Loves and graces might appear, Minerva might lead the
Matrons, and from assembled Gods, and Goddesses we might select every
Deity, which could aid our purpose, and heighten the scene — Venus we
might arbitrarily associate with Diana, While cupids reveled in the smiles
of Vosta [—] But the fact is, nothing of all this happened — Egyptian
magnificence presided not, nor was Cleopatrian luxury combined — yet
cheerful confidence, smiling amity and social pleasures were there —
These crowned our movements, doubling, and enhancing every pleasure
— We were received at my Father's wharf into a boat, which from its size,
necessitated us to divide our company — The distance to my brother
Fitz William's pleasure barge was however small — This barge has been
lately fetted up, in a high style of elegance and stars fancifully displayed,
produced a most agreeable effect — The cabbin is neat, and much more
spacious than I had conceived — The water was smooth, the sky serene,
the Maidens chanted in concert, and at intervals familiarly chatted — by
one circumstance, however — I was really pained [—] I have never before
made one of a party, where fishing was considered as any part of the
amusement, nor had I seen any of the fishing tribe, in the act of struggling
for life — The Cod, the Haddock, and the variously decorated Mackrell
were displayed upon the deck, with shouts of barbarous exultation, and
although expiring, they assayed, as in their nature element, to make their
way over the unyielding boards! by ruthless hands they were seized[,] kind
but in one thing, that they prolonged not the misery of the sufferers — for
the liberty of the little captives it was in vain I supplicated, neither could
I reprieve those, who, in gay meanders, unconscious of impending evil,
pursued their briny course — My intreaties were probably imparted to

affectation, although, rightly considered, they would only have afforded an added proof of the necessity of habit to reconcile such savage customs — but not being seconded by any other female, drawing my Calash, as a veil to the view intercepts of the helpless, struggling, inoffending beings, I remained silent — On our landing, we rambled about, according to our various inclinations, among the rocks[,] hills, and vallies which you must recollect[,] the grounds destined to our amusement abound — The place is indeed highly romantic. The umbrageous grove presented a shelter from the perbendicular rays of Apollo, and the wide Ocean perceptible, through the foliage, elevated and variegated the prospect — The trees are now cloathed in their most beautiful verdure, and the earth hath received her carpet of vivid green — Nature hath fashioned, in the midst, a rocky plain, which answered as a convenient substitute for a tea table; the Lads soon boiled the kettle, and the fragrant stream was unmixed with slander — Innocent mirth presided, and festive glee reigned in every countenance — The luxury of the repast was heightened by the fish, which had been deprived of life! Strange, that from the depredations of the despoiler, even the deep cannot protect — that Man cannot step forth, in pursuit of his own pleasures, without sacrificing upon the altar of a depraved appetite, a number of harmless beings! — We returned in the cool of the evening, the moon cloathed in meridian splendour, lent her aid[,] she seemed to regard us with peculiar approbation, and when her various disposition led her half concealed, amid the verdant trees, her resplendent light, not being with drawn, the mild lustre of her beams, were in a great degree heightened by contrast — all that Homer, or his immortal embellisher, all that Milton, Young etc etc had said upon the Night's fair Empress rushed at once upon my memory, thus combining to enhance, and to render interesting, the enchanting view — We returned home serenely gay — It seemed as if every benevolent Genius hovered round — The tide too, proving propitious, we landed without the aid of the small boat, and dispersed to our several homes, highly satisfied, with the pleasures of the day —

Judging by the next letter, it seems that John provides Judith with his own travel journals while he is away.

Letter 362 To the Same
Gloucester August 7th 1784

... I have not of late written you so copiously as usual, but I am generally surrounded by a Circle of friends, who, if the pen is in my fingers, are calling out, that I am robbing them of their dues — yet, I have repeatedly written — I have received your multiplied favours — and I am impatient for a continuance of your journal....

Judith was especially "apprehensive" regarding John's health when he was on the road and she was not readily available to care for him. At this moment, she has no idea where he is—somewhere in Connecticut, she tells Noah Parker.

Letter 366 To Mr Parker
Gloucester September 5th 1784

I do dearly love the partiality of my friends, and could I persuade all the world to cherish a predilection for me, I should not hesitate to scribble on, to the end of the chapter, while the efforts of my pen, should be dispersed far, and wide ... I will ... at some future period, attempt — at present my mind is occupied by apprehension for Mr Murray — he is ill, and we are ignorant at what place — It is two weeks since any direct tidings have reached us — he was then very low — his letters were descriptive of the paroxysms of a fever, and were only interspersed with rational observations [—] At present, common report says he hath left Norwich, and is again dangerously upon the road — His friends are greatly alarmed, and are sending a nephew of Colonel Foster's in search of him, to make inquiries into his situation, and to return, as soon as possible, while in the interim, we remain, you will not doubt, in painful suspense....

"Every faculty of her soul" is anxious about John's health.

Letter 369 to Mr Murray
Gloucester September 11— 1784

The account of your ill health hath reached us — Mr Foster is setting out to make particular inquiries, and, taking up my pen to address you by him, I reiterate my wishes for your restoration, and your felicity — We endeavour to erase from our bosoms, the alarming apprehensions, which the intelligence we have received but too well authorizes, but they will at times obtrude, and great is the havock which they make — If you have any request to make, you will have the goodness to forward it by Mr Foster, should you solicit the attendance of any of your adherents in Gloucester who ever it may be, will hold him, or herself, in readiness to obey your summons, consider what friendship, christian friendship demands, especially when it hath more than Young's revolving suns, to bring it to perfection — Let us, respected Sir know exactly how you are, and what are your wishes, and believe me you will find a disposition, in every heart, to comply with your desires.... We entreat you to take care of the small remains of your health, and we commend you to the protection of heaven — May all good Angels hover round you, suggesting to your sick mind, the most soothing images — and shielding you from every evil — May returning health smile upon you, and may you yet be loaned, a blessing to a world which it is probable may never fully estimate your worth — Farewell, my friend, every faculty of my soul, is expanded in aspirations to the throne of grace in your behalf O! may the united wishes of your venerating friends, be crowned by an assump[tion] of peace —

Judith asks John not to show her letters to anyone.

Letter 370 To the same
Gloucester September 13— 1784

Yours, of the 9th instant, is this moment handed me — We are, dear Sir extremely alarmed on account of your health — the air is cold and bleak, uncommonly so for the season — such chilling blasts how unfriendly to the suffering invalid.... I had rather you would not give a copy, of the lines you mention, until I review them — I repeat, I take no copies of my letters to you, secure that they will be returned, agreeably to promise, to my own more deliberate inspection — I am content to let them go, rude an[d] undigested, warm as they flow from the heart, and penned amid a scene of incumbrance, every line written during the hurry of a circumscribed hour, nor is time afforded me, to correct, yet I am easy in this consideration, that it is always in my power, to recall my letters, and, supposing them to possess any degree of merit, to bestow upon them the finishing of leisure....

Judith has sent her catechism to Mary Pilgrim of London, a Universalist friend of John Murray's. Judith openly confesses her admiration for John, who, in turn, has expressed his admiration for Judith's catechism.

Letter 381 To Mrs Pilgrim City of London Old England —
Gloucester October 31— 1782

Your letter, my dear Madam, furnished me with an added motive, to bless that all pervading cement, a Saviour blood, which thus unites the wide extensive Circle, and although the broad atlantic rolls between its component parts, gives them, by the sweet powers of sympathy, to mingle souls.... If my little Catechism meets your approbation, it will possess a claim to my esteem, of which it hath hitherto been destitute — The story of its birth, and introduction to a censorious world, the preface truly gives — I am not my dear Madam a Parent — My years are not greatly multiplied — yet I have had the presumption to take upon me the charge of two orphan girls — My task is arduous, and perhaps the tenderness of a Mother is requisite, to support the mind, and to render tolerable the difficulties which too often spring up in the path of Education — My memory, standing in need of an assistant, I was induced to write — my friends earnestly requesting, I was induced to publish — Mr Murray was then in Philadelphia — but, upon his return he approved, he could not but approve, the sentiments he had instilled.... Yes, my friend, we are right happy in the teachings of a Murray, we pursue with gladdened hearts the writings of the apostolic Relly, and searching with sacred joy the inspired Volume, we bow with holy rapture at the feet of Him, with whom is the residue of the Spirit — We are fond of communicating with the members of the body of our blessed Lord, however widely they may be scattered, and hence we receive, with becoming gratitude, the information of our friends — Mr Murray is not at present with us, it is probable he will write before an opportunity of forwarding this letter presents....

John has finally returned to Gloucester. Hopefully, Judith writes to Winthrop, she can nurse him back to health.

Letter 398 To My brother
Gloucester March 1st 1785

Since I had last the pleasure of writing to my dearest brother, I have again been, and indeed still am, engaged in a melancholy attendance upon a sick chamber.... Mr Murray hath been brought, by a complication of disorders, to the very gates of the grave — Every hope of his Physician vanished, and we repeatedly believed, his spirit had fled — The windows of his apartment, preparatory to the last solemn office, were at length thrown open — when a salutary breeze recalled the fleeting inhabitant, and it is now feebly fluttering in its decaying tenement — The death warrant seems issued, and I doubt its execution is only delayed....

John's health was so precarious the newspapers reported his demise.

Letter 403 To Miss Mary Parker of Portsmouth
Gloucester April 15— 1785

... The News Papers have doubtless announced to you the death of Mr Murray, but, my dear, even News Papers are not always to be depended upon — The good Man hath indeed been brought to the gates of the grave, but he is now, thanks to a preserving God, gradually recovering....

John is not completely well, but he departs nonetheless on a journey to Providence, Rhode Island. Here we read that he is shopping for Judith.

Letter 409 To Mr Murray
Gloucester June 2d 1785

I should, my dear Sir have written you this morning, by Captain Foster, had I not been informed you intended leaving Boston this day, but being honoured by your letter, just received from the hands of Captain G— I gather from its complexion, that this hasty line may yet be in time for your perusal — It is late in the evening, and I have only this moment heard of an opportunity by sunrise in the morning, yet I am induced to scribble a line, trusting it will be expressive of my gratitude, for your friendly attention [—] We are happy to hear that the paroxysms of your Organs are [much] lighter — Our superfluous fears we give to the wind, trusting they will be wafted beyond our reach, and in their stead encouraging sweet hope, our bosoms have become as calm, as yonder cerulean sky — your friends being anxiously solicitous for your perfect restoration, very naturally hail, with the most grateful sensations, every propitious symptom, and our wishes are, that you should not surrender your physician, so long as it is necessary you should be under his care — We trust you will implicitly follow his directions, and we hope that with returning health, you will entwine tranquility of mind — While, for the rest, we resign to unerring providence. Do not make yourself uneasy about the fur, the kind I wanted was such as Miss P— wore round her hat — I do not doubt my hat is fashionable, I know it is handsome, but it is not becoming, and the last is with me the most material consideration — the white fur would change its effect — I am told there is some in Salem. Possibly Mrs A— might procure it for you — and if not, it is of too small importance, to merit a second thought — Good night my friend, may your repose be calm — May the angel of tranquility watch around your bed, and may tomorrow's dawn, behold you in possession of health, and every attendant blessing —

Judith's love for John is quite evident in this letter.

Letter 411 To Mr Murray
Boston June 17 1785

I dreamed last night you had a very severe return of your ague [—] God grant, this dream may have played me as false, as all my hopes from this debusive World have hitherto done.... Yes, Murray, I esteem you for your worth, my whole soul is compelled to admiration of your uncommon Virtues — I have never ceased to esteem you, nor do I know an action of your life incompatible with the elevated point of view, in which I have ever beheld you — [Ease then] by contrary suspicions the bosom of your friend — that shadows are inseparable from humanity we well know — What then — they do but serve to render Virtue more resplendant.... While I am writing the heavens begin to gather darkness, the East wind to blow and the clouds to pour forth the copious shower — I trust my friend you will make provision for this sudden change wisely considering that a constitution broken like yours must be treated with the most exact observance [—] May providence guard you in your every movement and may you gently descend the vale of life.... I give you leave to understand my fervid wishes for your felicity implied in every sentence, in every word whether they be expressed or not — you will please to present to the worthy Circle in Providence my respectfully affectionate regards — you will expect a line from me by Post and you will believe me to be, with all sincerity your faithful friend —

Judith confesses more love and concern.

Letter 412 To the same
Boston June 20th 1785

The letter of my respected friend is come safe to hand and I am truly grateful for its contents [—] I do assure you I was not displeased with the account of your regrets on my departure [—] Congeniality possesses for me not a few charms — I think, strictly speaking, that I am not ill natured and yet I protest I would not wish any one who I particularly esteemed to remain perfectly tranquil during the first moments of separation.... The saturday after next, barring accidents, I hope to reach home, where, if I may meet you, dear Sir, it will not a little enhance the felicity, always attendant upon rejoining those connexions, to which we are naturally, and almost of necessity attached — I am told you are still indisposed, and I am fearful you are not sufficiently attentive to yourself — What regimen do you observe, and how does it affect you? My friends cannot suffer alone — I have a tear of commiseration ready to mingle with theirs — O! that the Physician of value would restore you to health....

In 1783, John Murray filed a lawsuit on behalf of the Gloucester Universalists. Despite creating their own religious society, the Universalists were still legally obligated to support First Parish Church. When they refused to pay these taxes, the town seized valuable goods from the Universalists to sell at public auction. John's law suit would not only absolve the Universalists from supporting another church, it would ensure the same freedom for other religious organizations. After many hearings, the Massachusetts Supreme Judicial Court responded in the Universalists' favor in 1785 although a final ruling was not handed down until the following year. Judith was involved in all of these legal actions, writing to John with the good news in June.

Letter 416 To Mr Murray
Boston June 25— 1785

Joy, joy, joy to you my honoured Friend — Law is exalted, and Freedom clappeth her hands for joy — Outrage, violence, and unbridled power shall no more stalk unmolested abroad — but the sons of this our commonwealth, rising upon the broad base of civil, and religious equality, shall boast, from their happy Constitution exemption from the Tyrannic sway of despotic arrogance — God I thank thee — agreeably to thy sacred injunctions, I would call no Man Master — I would only prostrate at the shrine of Omnipotence — yet this unexpected prevalence of rectitude is strange!! The authenticity of my intelligence cannot, however, admit a doubt — Auspicious era — investigation unappalled by censure, is now triumphant, nor shall ignorance be again permitted to forge fetters, for the free born mind — Authorized by the Legislator, No individual will henceforward dare to make us afraid — happy — I repeat — most happy arrangement, and, once more, my friend, I pray you to accept my congratulations — The judges, blinded by prejudice, gave their opinion against toleration, and the charge to the jury, after the leadings, was so full in favour of our opponents, that Mr W— positive in regard to that decision, deigned not to wait the event — but forthwith took horse, and departed home, with the pleasing intelligence that the case had gone in favour of the riotous purloiners of our goods! And you will readily conceive the consequent dejection of our friends! The jury continued their deliberations from eight in the evening, until four the ensuing morning, when lo! Contrary to the conclusion both of friends, and foes, they gave in a verdict in favour of the oppressed Complainants — Colonel C— was like a madman — while Doctor Plummer elated, no doubt, to a very extraordinary degree, immediately mounted his horse, and fraught with the Capital, and truly elevating tidings, reached Gloucester with most surprising expedition —

Judith and John enjoyed a mutual admiration.

Letter 421 To Mr Murray
Boston July 7th 1785

... For myself, it is out of my power, to be other than your friend, and I could willingly submit to you the investigations of my most secret thoughts — I am really surprised at your hasty return to Portsmouth — Great must have been the disappointment of the Gloucesterians, and equally been their mortification — Miss Osborne too — but, my dear Sir I do not mean to censure you — you no doubt had your motives, and I dare say you believed them discreet — To bear the burdens of the weak, is a duty suited to the exertions of benevolence, and it is altogether worthy the amiable character of my friend, thus to devote himself — I am happy in your esteem and while I retain your approbation, it will serve as a testimony, that I am not wholly destitute of good, and amiable qualities. There is, however, in friendship, a tender equality which gives birth to the endearing sentiments of affection, and, allow me to say that while I am this side my grand Climacterie I do not wish, or I am not over solicitous, to inspire my friends with reverence veneration and all that — My confidence in you I have never lost, I yield to your word the most extensive credit — To call in question your veracity, would, in my opinion, argue not only a deficiency in candour, but in reason, I have every inducement to believe you are motivated by sincerity, that you are impelled by the feelings of the moment, and that your heart, upon all occasions, dictates to your tongue....

Judith offers more advice to John about his health.

Letter 429 To Mr Murray
Gloucester August 15th 1785

I thank you, my dear Sir, for your last favour, for every instance of your regard I sincerely thank you. The combining want of leisure, and of [opportunity] prevent my enlarging agreeably to the dictates of my gratitude. you will, however, accept a line, by way of acknowledgement, which is the only compensation that my present situation, and feelings, will allow.... I rejoice your day at Cambridge was productive of so much pleasure — May your pleasures ever more encrease, and may your anxieties diminish — I pray you, however, to beware of the varieties of the table, and remember, that poison lurks in every dish — It may indeed be to you, a matter of indifferences, whether you are continued upon this globe, or whether you are called hence — but you do not love pain, and your constitution hath been so repeatedly shocked, as to render it absolutely necessary, if you should enjoy a tolerable share of health, that you should pay the most scrupulous attention to the quality, as well as the quantity of your food. I know you are far from being intemperate either in meals, or in drinks but such is now the situation of your frame, that what ought heretofore be deemed the strident regimen, would now operate as a fatal excess — That I have your happiness at heart I flatter myself you will not doubt, and I consequently take it for granted you will not be offended at the freedom of my remarks....

In 1785, Judith's uncle Epes Sargent published a pamphlet that explained the Universalists' arguments for establishing their own independent organization. In response, the Reverend Eli Forbes of First Parish Church published an "Answer" condemning John Murray and Universalism in a sternly worded pamphlet. John Murray counteracted with a broadside, or flier, for public display. In the following letter, Judith is once again his fiercely protective defender.

Letter 443 — to Mr Murray
Gloucester October 30th 1785

I take it for granted you have seen the elaborate publication of Mr F— and I am presuming enough to collect your sentiments, by my own — Never surely was the attention of the public called to any thing more illiberal — What impudent barefaced assertions, what injurious insinuations! And how replete with malevolence! — Our friends are divided in their opinions, some think it will be best to pass it by with silent contempt, others warmly assert, that truth ought to be defended[,] that some one ought to stand forth, to plead the cause of justice, and that the villany of said piece ought to be detected, and brought forth to the view of an impartial publick — What steps you, Sir, or any one in your behalf may be inclined to take I am yet to learn — My present wish respecting the matter, is, that if Mr F— which I confess is pretty evident — doth not merit a refutation, he may at least be told how unworthy he is to be refuted — Can any thing be more false than the ridiculous sentiment which, in his second page he puts in your mouth, as making a part of your address to the Gloucesterians! — I well remember the materials from which this gross misrepresentation is fabricated … in fact the publication of F— abounds throughout with such unfair representations, such false conclusions, and such undisguised malice, that if I could persuade myself Rectitude, a love of justice, the influence of reason, candor, and benevolence, with a sacred regard to genuine liberty, were, at this period, more prevalent in this our world, than their opposites, I should view the event with all the tranquility in the gift of assurance — but as it too certainly is not the reign of integrity, I wait the consequences, and with trembling apprehension — Yet, let us suppose the worst, they can never chase us from the bosom of a tender Redeemer — how ever they may curtail our temporal liberties, they can never ban our access to the Throne of Grace.…

As John Stevens's financial predicament deteriorated, Judith grew increasingly apprehensive about what would happen to her.

Letter 446 To Madam Walker
Gloucester December 5th 1785

… I have been assailed by many an adverse wound. The embarrassments of my husband, are, to me, a never failing source of unquietude [—] That he can answer every demand, which can be made upon him, I doubt not

— but in such an arrangement, he leaves himself wholly destitute — yet, may he square his conduct by the most rigid rules of [propriety] — Our ill success through the past summer, hath still further involved us, indeed, I am ignorant to what amount — Mr Stevens hath made every possible effort, and declining health is the consequence of his anxieties and his efforts — judge, dear Madam of my prospects — Did I not look beyond the present scene, should I not be justified in questioning the equal distribution of Him, whom connecting our future destination, I now hail as the impartial parent of the Universe?

Here, Judith details her plans to support her household without any income from John Stevens. At the same time John Murray has been meeting with their creditors, hoping to persuade them to sign a Letter of License. Such a document would give John Stevens more time to repay his debts and keep him out of debtor's prison.

Letter 450 To my Mother
January 1st. 1786

… I will tell you, my honoured friend, how I mean to conduct — I shall have no occasion for dress you know, it would not be proper for me — What little I shall want my needle will supply — I shall neither visit, nor be visited, ceremoniously, I [do not] experience the least regret in yielding up these forms — I have cultivated a large acquaintance, not because I took pleasure in the kind intercourse they attach, but because I would not appear singular — because I would appear equal in my regards — I am now furnished with a melancholy excuse for declining any unnecessary attentions, and thus I shall redeem many an hour to devote to my Mother, which I have hitherto idly squandered — No call pursuing company, I have no occasion for keeping a Maid servant, and not keeping a Maid servant, one fire will be sufficient — What an amazing expense will then be spared — With strict economy, we may be able to support our very small family — You know, dear Madam, that ordinary living is conducive to health, and, if I should wish for the luxuries of life, I can say, I will arise and go to my Father — If Mr Murray, who hath ever been to us an angel of peace, can obtain for Mr Stevens a Letter of License every emolument of my husband's business — for until he is extricated from his present embarrassments, I will not derive the smallest advantage from his gains, may, at the expiration of the given terms, be impartially divided among his Creditors — This will induce them to continue his freedom, and thus we may ultimately be emancipated from all our difficulties — This, my beloved Mother is our plan [—] allow its execution, and tranquility may again be mine — I would have visited you this day — accustomed as I am, upon a New Year's day, to rejoice in the benignity of your smiles — but, although it would have been a consolation to have beheld you — to have attended the evangelical teachings of our common friend, and to have joined the Circle and your hospitable board, yet I could not, at present, stand the inquisitive gaze of the indifferent, or the censorious — Farewell — dearest Madam — Grant me your maternal sanction, and I shall be satisfied —

Judith was profoundly grateful to John for his efforts on behalf of her husband. Sadly, though, he was unsuccessful. Their chief creditor, "Mr F— I—" could not be satisfied and he called in the local sheriff. This series of letters to John Murray documents the unfolding events that resulted in John Stevens's departure from Gloucester.

Letter 455 to the Same
Gloucester lat[e] on the Night of January 14— 1786

I received the letters of my indefatigable Friend, just at the close of day, but being for many hours prevented [from] reading them I was subjected to all the tortures of suspense! I have now, however, perused the faithful sheets, and every line hath furnished added testimonies of your disinterested attachment to me and mine — Low leaves this place early in the morning and consequently I have only time for a hasty reply — Accept, best of friends, our united thanks — poor, in every sense, it is not permitted us to yield a recompense more adequate to the services rendered — This business is indeed fraught with too much labour for you, particularly when your precarious health, and the deep interest you take in our affairs, are considered — But to whom else can we look or what mortal is so capable of assisting us? God grant your invaluable health be not the sacrifice — Sire of Angels, and of Men, protect, we beseech Thee, protect our friend…. We cannot, Dear Sir, think of your returning here, with an intent to go again to Boston, during this inclement season — surely it would be abundantly less fatiguing, to tarry there longer, than by repeating your journey, amid the severity of the present Winter, to endanger a life so consequential to a numerous circle of admiring friends — However we ought not to dictate — The part you act, is certainly uncommon, you are heaping your favours upon those who can never recompence, and at the same time soliciting them to make known their every want, that you may be thus enabled to devise the means of gratifying them — O! that your possessions were as ample as your heart, for then the Universe would not contain a son, a daughter of penury, and you are still solicitous to add to the debt of gratitude another and another item — We can only say, may God reward you — To ... every one who hath kind intensions in regard to us, or who commiserate our misfortunes, we are truly obliged — But for you, Dear Sir, Gratitude hath erected a throne in our bosoms, and she will offer, at the shrine of Friendship, the purest, and most refined obligations — We can never discharge the mighty debt which we owe to you, but, we must repeat, this consciousness is not painful — No, by no means, it rather irradiates, and elevates our most pleasing reflections — Farewell —

Letter 458 To the same
Gloucester January 20— 1786
Friday Evening

Alas! my friend how are all the smiling hopes to which the first page in your letter gave birth blasted by its conclusion — "Some will not sign this Letter of Licence" In vain then, my dear Sir, are you thus unwearied in your kind exertions, Vain is the humane indulgence of those, who sacrifice at the shrine of benevolence — for alas! the unyielding and obdurate, will unite to bend fast our chains! and to entail upon us a bondage, to end only with our lives — My poor distracted mind, harrassed and weary, hath not where to repose itself — yet, stop my complaining pen — In Christ Jesus I have peace [—] He hath opened the prison doors — He hath paid that debt, which no Creditor could have remitted, and which no indulgences would have enabled me to discharge — In the divine character of my Redeemer, my emancipation is legibly stamped, it never can be erased, and I shall e'er long enter His presence, where is perfect freedom [—] Come then and let me gird up the loins of my mind — let me be going — I have delayed but too long — Felicity awaits me upon the shores of blessedness — and I will no longer hesitate to join the celestial train.

Saturday Morning

I have seen my Father, who is of [the] opinion that if you apply to my Uncle, he would influence Mr P— to accord to the act for liberating my husband — My Father informs me, when he was last in Boston, my Uncle set his name to a letter of licence, in favour of a friend of Mr P— who stood indebted to him to a very large amount — Neither did he receive, or demand a dividend — The person was Mr Joshua Blanchard, and in a short time from the date of his confinement, he was again permitted to open his shop as usual.....

Saturday afternoon

F— I— is in Town, I am exceedingly alarmed — He hath sent a messenger by Mr E— S— requesting an interview with my husband, he wishes to see him without a witness — Mr E— S— proposed the presence of my Father to whom F— I— particularly objected, and he added, that he must see Mr Stevens alone, something of consequence had taken place, proper only for the ear of Mr Stevens, and he would never communicate it to any one else!! I trembled, my whole frame was agitated in the extreme — What a request! — What can he mean —! Circumstanced as we are? Mr Stevens has written him a line informing him that we can only confer with him by letter. We wait the event with great anxiety —

Saturday Night twelve O'clock

Gloomy hath been the period since I last raised my pen — Mr E— S— returned with a letter from Mr F— I— declaring it was impossible to communicate his business by letter! He had questions to ask that could not be written! he should be exceedingly gratified by a personal interview — he would pledge his sacred word of honour, that he was alone, and that he possessed no powers, that could possibly injure Mr Stevens his sole intention being merely what he had avowed [—] We believed it best to deliberate, upon a question which might be attended with such important consequences, and to consult our friends — Just at that juncture, my Uncle reached Town — To take counsel of him, we judged would be proper — and we dismissed Mr E— S— with an assurance that we would send an answer to Mr F— I— in the course of a few hours — My Father, and Uncle were summoned, they did not coincide in sentiment — My Father considered it too great a risk to admit Mr F— I— My Uncle said the pledges given in this gentleman's address, to Mr Stevens, were too highly important to be forfeited — What could we do — every thing, we were sensible, depended upon our observing the strictest vigilance — yet we had a favour, a very essential favour to ask of Mr F— I— Was it advisable to irritate him by an apparent suspicion of his honour [?] It was in his power, by with holding his name from the Letter of Indulgence, as effectually to imprison Mr Stevens, as if every Creditor were to embody for the purpose of abridging him of his liberty — After much consultation Mr S— addressed the gentleman to the following effect —

Saturday evening

Tomorrow being sunday, I shall, in one view, be upon terms of equality with you, I can then see you with greater ease to myself — I have laid down a mode of conduct, from which I may not depart with out incurring censure — I have refused admitting many of my friends, they would have just reason to be offended, if I should not be uniform in my observance of stated rules — I am, Sir, with respect &c &c

Mark now the sad, sad event — Mr F— I— had a Sheriff waiting, who, engaged in Salem, came on with him as far as the entrance into the Town — there he was directed to stop, and so soon as the intent of our deliberations were known — Mr Wait was brought forward and a writ was served upon my Father (—upon a supposition that he held effects belonging to Mr Stevens in his hands!) ... Thus is my honoured father involved in a series of difficulties upon my account — Oh! that my ... Mother, when she [went] to nourish me at her maternal bosom had conveyed me [to] a peaceful lodging in some narrow house — Doubtless her [tears would have] bedewed the clay cold face of her first born — but time would, long e'er this, have assuaged her grief — I should have lived in her pleased remembrance, and in yonder worlds of light, she would have hailed her white robed Cherub — How sad, alas! is the reverse — I am now made the unhappy cause, that her pillow is nightly wet by the fast flowing tears of commiseration, her bosom is torn by anxiety and she bodes a thousand evils — My father too, how keenly doth he feel, tender, and compassionate, his manly bosom confesses all the Parent, and he is awake to the finer feelings of the soul — Nor is this enough [—] he is now to be involved in all the intricacies of an injust prosecution — his honour, never before suspected is called in question, and he is reduced to the necessity of appearing in a court of justice, to vindicate a reputation hitherto considered without a stain — Where alas! shall I hide me from these rapidly succeeding storms! My weary head would sink, gladly sink to everlasting repose. My Cousin presented me your letter — we thank you for it — That in the midst of such fatigue you still preserve your health, is to us [an] item of consolation, and for this intelligence, we lowly bend at the shrine of Him, who is the giver of every good, and perfect gift — We are surprised at your removal, and also at the place of your present residence, and we cannot say that it affects us agreeably....

Sunday

I no sooner entered the breakfasting parlour this morning, than Mary, almost breathless, came running to me — Here Ma'am, I have found these papers pinned upon our door — The first was a summons in the usual form, declaring our goods and Estate attached at the suit of Mary I— widow — The second a summons at the suit of Mr W— of Salem!!! scarce had I seated myself, when in burst Mr F— I— [—] my mind highly irritated, and deeply wounded I was at a loss how to address him — he still persisted in wishing to see Mr Stevens alone — We replied we had no secrets, the part we had acted would bear examination, and we were not solicitous to shun the light — Our wish was to satisfy our Creditors — This was the principal reason which had induced Mr Stevens so earnestly to solicit for a letter of licence, but it appeared that he, Mr F— I— had been very active against us, for which we could assign no reason — he had already received more than his original debt the asurious interest only remaining unpaid — We were surprised he should inquire if Mr Stevens had brought his furniture from England! When he for many years had been accustomed to the same articles, now displayed, during the periods when he, and his, had been entertained at our dwelling — Sir, we added, we possessed our furniture, such as it is, from the paternal indulgence of our kind Father — Such are the scenes under our present observation, and such must be our subjects, of [which] we continue to write [—] Is it not better that we resign the pen?

Monday Evening

Understanding that Mr E—S— goes to Boston early on the morrow I make up my letter to Night — At dawn of day, a loud rap at the door summoned me to the key hole — Who is there? The usual interrogation — The well known voice of my Uncle, assured me a friend awaited — A Friend — My mind, before much softened, the dear and tender application melted me into tears, and I unbarred, and unlocked the door silently petitioning, that he might indeed prove his right to this sacred character, by such exertions, as were abundantly in his power — In the course of his visit, our affairs being introduced, with trembling hesitation, unaccustomed as I am thus to supplicate I solicited his favour, in behalf of my husband — Listen to his patient reply "Depend upon it, my dear, if Mr Stevens recovers his liberty I will do for him, all in my power: there will be no risk in putting vessels into his hands, and I will spare no exertions to aid his honest endeavours.["] Thus, dear Sir, it would really be for the interest of Mr F— I— and others to allow Mr Stevens to employ himself in this service — Tell them so — Possible his assurance may be attended with salutary effects — Has Mrs H— no interest with Mr B— and, if she has, might she not be induced to influence him to assent to this letter of indulgence? Farewell dear and honoured Friend — May God protect you, and crown you with much felicity, as gratitude, unabounding rectitude, called into action by a thousand acts of kindness, would exalt to bestow — That we wish to see you, let the solitary hours which pass, be our witnesses, but who is there, who doth not, perforce submit to necessity?

Letter 459 To the Same
Gloucester January 24 1786

My Uncle is of the opinion that Mr Stevens will not obtain his liberty! Mr E— S— was here last evening — he pronounces our application too prompt — What an event judging World! — and how easy it is to condemn [—] If the Creditors of Mr Stevens determine, finally to exercise lenity toward him, how little will they consult their own interest to confine him during the summer months, or even through the present season [—] The precise time when he could be collecting crews, and making preparations for a spring Fare, which is decidedly the most lucrative of any in the course of the year and, by consequence would be the most advantageous to the gentlemen, for whom he wishes to labour — But I am weary of conjecture, and of suspense — My Mind, I verily believe, cannot long support the pressure, which with every hour acquires additional strength [—] The dreariness — the solemn stillness of this my prison — the many evils with which I have to contend — the impenetrable glooms which envelop my future prospects — My reason, as I apprehend, will be the ultimate sacrifice — it already totters — it may soon be dethroned — The iron gates of despair, grating horribly as they turn, are thrown wide open to my affrighted view — one step further, and they will close upon me forever!!!! ... Is it not extraordinary, that Lawyers should depend so materially in their opinions, respecting recording the deed? — I am really apprehensive, that this unhappy business, will terminate in the ruin of my Father! — Suspense, cruel suspense, how it corrodes, and drinks up the very principles of life — My heart sickens, and every hope hath well near expired — I cast my eyes around my prison walls — every thing assures the colour of my fate, no cheering image presents, no pleased expectation, hath its residence here — It is in vain I endeavour to rise superior, every nobler principle seems overwhelmed, in one common wreck — With regard to temporary matters I see no refuge but despair, an absolute relinquishment of every brighter prospect, and a gloomy acquiescence in the evils, in which we are so irremediably involved [—] Gratitude, I am aware, is not the growth of every bosom, and it must be uncommonly vigorous, if it be not choaked by the rampant growth of religious prejudices — Surely, my Friend, those Creditors who wish to see, in what manner the property of Mr Stevens has been disposed of have never attended to his letter of address — Doth he not there say, that misfortunes have involved him in debt, that he had been necessitated to dispose of his house, and furniture, and that his vessels had been repeatedly attached? What, my dear Sir, can he add to this account? It is true he might have drawn out a long list of particular losses, he might have demonstrated that the property of which he has been despoiled by the Banks, and which hath been absorbed in the bosom of the Ocean, far exceeded every demand which could possibly be made upon him; he can exhibit upon his book, no less than eleven thousand pounds Lawful Money, out standing debts, of which, the probability is, he will neve[r] be able to retain a single farthing — All this he can make clear — but, my friend, will this answer any valuable purpose, will it satisfy a single Creditor? Is this the state of his affairs which they require, let them but grant him permission, and he will immediately wait upon them, with a regular account of all his proceedings, what further can he offer? — If they suspect our integrity, we can only regret....

Judith and John Stevens literally locked themselves inside their house to prevent the sheriff from taking John to debtor's prison.

Letter 460 To Madame Walker
Gloucester January 31— 1786

You, my dear Lady, have known this house in better days, when comparative happiness was ours — in other words, when liberty was the prime Mover of all our actions — Now, the corroding apprehension, that an enemy is constantly laying in ambush for our destruction, furnishes the ... necessity of bolts, and bars, which alike exclude both friends, and foes. Nor can any one, however tenderly interested, gain admittance here, until gloomy suspicion, in the pale emaciated form of your once unsuspecting friend hath recognized the voices, or examined the appearance of the Candidate for entrance, and then, as though for some dark crime, we remained in durance [—] the bolts and bars are thrown back — The door grates mournfully as it turns, and, with trembling caution, the guest is allowed to approach [—] Such is the present scene, and so complicated [is] the [complaint] which has been produced, that I scarce indulge a hope of its termination [—] Mr Murray to whose generous benevolence we owe the most [tender] obligations, hath been unwearied in his endeavours to procure our enlargement — But alas! his most arduous efforts, have hitherto proved unsuccessful!! yet to what end detain Mr Stevens a prisoner for life? — he hath committed no fault adequate to a punishment so severe — The integrity of his heart acquits him of intentional error, his every step hath been pursued by misfortune and one sad event, hath unavoidably produced another!

Judith is ill, depressed, and shut up in her home.

Letter 466 To Mr Murray
Gloucester February 12 1786
SundayMorning

I write now in bed — I am indeed extremely ill — your removal to your present lodgings, is precisely what I have expected, and wished [—] May they answer your most sanguine wishes — Forgive me for not writing, I am reduced very low — for six successive nights, I have not obtained a moments rest, but by the use of laudanum — Farewell

Judith's health continues to decline.

Letter 468 To Mr Murray
Gloucester February 18— 1786

We are not, revered Friend, we never were, insensible of the very important obligation we are under to you — Very inadequate are the returns it hath been in our power to make — yet our experiences bear as witness, that we have been ready, as far as we might, to evince our gratitude

— you say I have been very ill, and yet have written — but, Sir, do you not know, that my head was never before so violently seized — you left me very ill, yet my then state was perfect health, compared to what I have since suffered — for the space of twenty four hours, I entertained not the smallest idea, of being detained a prisoner in this vale of tears, through the course of an added week — nay, it was for some hours expected, that every moment as it rose, would witness my release — Indeed Sir I have not been, nor am I now, capable of writing — My head swims, my hand trembles, and a painful lasitude seems gradually to absorb my faculties — My distressed husband must answer for himself — It is, you must have observed a work of labour to prevail upon him to take up his pen and, in truth, I have, for a very long time, felt myself unequal to every arduous effort

In plain truth, the displeasure you seem to have conceived against us, has almost broken our hearts — I hope, indeed, that happier times await us for the present are very dark —

While Judith is indisposed, she still worries about John Murray. Meanwhile, John has enlisted the help of Joseph Russell, a wealthy Boston philanthropist, to negotiate a settlement with John Stevens's creditors.

Letter 470 To the Same
Gloucester February 20th— 1786

How are you my dear Sir — O! that health and happiness attend our invaluable friend — We should then, at least by reflection, partake very materially his felicity — your illness greatly alarms us — My Father is very apprehensive in regard to you — Will you consult some able physician — With regard to my health, I have to say, it is not worse — yesterday I was carried out in my Father's Chaise closely wrapped in a bed blanket — so no fear of taking cold you see — In truth, my feelings assure me, that Nature is not yet wearied with efforts, to preserve this frail Being, in its present mode of existence — The unexemplified generosity of Mr Russell, hath penetrated my soul — Would to heaven — but to express myself upon this point I must be indulged with steadier fingers, and a less disordered head, and, in the mean time, I can only say gratitude will ever reign triumphant in my bosom — Will you tolerate your friend if she is solicitous to owe to your exertions yet one more obligation — you have delicacy, you have penetration, and with those accomplishments, you blend address[es]

The Letters

Judith lets John Murray know about her husband's plan to leave Gloucester for Saint Eustacius in the West Indies to reestablish himself and pay off his debts.

Letter 480 To the same
Gloucester April 21st 1786

    … Mr Stevens hath not embark[ed] with Captain Hough — So we have obtained a short reprieve — But in two weeks from this date, the ship Favourite belonging to my Father, sails for St Eustacia, and then, if our Creditors still continue obdurate — Mr Stevens will hasten to that Asylum of the unfortunate — My heart, I confess, consents not to this arrangement, yet it is countenanced by every friend — My opposition has been strong: and although I am now silenced, I am not, however, convinced of its utility — It is supposed we shall be able to make terms with our Claimants, when they shall know my husband is beyond their reach, and the poor Man flatters himself, that in the course of a few months, he shall be able to return blest with liberty, and competency — May He, with whom is the issue of events, crown with success the arduous undertaking….

Ignoring her doctors' advice, Judith continues to write letters. But she does follow their prescription for country air by planning a journey with young Anna Plummer. John Murray has offered to escort them.

Letter 481 To Madam Walker —
Gloucester May 5th— 1786

    I have with great reluctance complied with the instructions of my Physicians, who hath strictly prohibited me the use of pen, ink, and paper, I however steal a moment softened by the intermission of peace, and I hallow it by yielding it an offering upon the altar of amity…. With regard to my health, it is in truth very low, the Physicians in Boston, and else where, who have been consulted concur in prescribing a journey, and Country air. This recipie I have found it difficult to follow [—] My friends are all necessarily engaged — I am, however at length preparing to commence my route — My Anna with me in the Chaise, and Mr Murray, by way of Escort, on horse back….

Writing to John clearly had a healing effect on Judith. Perhaps chastising John about his health did as well!

Letter 485— To the same
Gloucester May 29— 1786

Your letter by Mr Hough, was handed me some moments since, and although it is now the evening of the day, and I have pained head and aching heart, and have, besides, so recently paid my duty to you, yet I cannot deny myself the pleasures of scribbling, by way of acknowledgement, another and another line — There now, if I do not merit applause, I wonder who in the world does! — but, to be serious — and your hint respecting our common Creditors, is surely calculated to render me so — I entreat you will use your utmost endeavours to soothe and to soften matters, as far as they will bear — Heigh Ho! how long will it be, e'er I shall find my way out of a Labyrinth, in which my peace is so cruelly entangled — I am pleased to learn you are in better health, but I am apprehensive, although your abstaining from animal food, may be attended with salutary effects, yet you will be essentially injured by omitting the generous glass of wine, which you have proved so beneficial —

To restore Judith's strength, Judith, Anna, and John Murray traveled through southern Massachusetts, Rhode Island, and Connecticut. Along the way, John was asked to preach and he always obliged. For the first time, Judith witnessed the extent of his popularity. While John had his detractors, his charisma and powerfully optimistic message attracted large crowds and loyal friends.

Letter 492 To my Father
New London June 23 1786

To write to you, my dear Sir, and to my Mother, must ever strictly consist with both my inclination, and my duty. Much have I regretted that the fatigue, consequent upon my journey hath hitherto prevented my addressing you, and I employ with superior pleasure the moments of returning health, to express my high sense of obligation for every act of kindness — your paternal goodness penetrates my soul, and my bosom glows with suitable regards — Mr Murray hath from time, to time, apprized you of the situation of my health, and if you have received all his letters, you are not ignorant of the progress we have made — I owe much to this good Man — all who love me, had they no other reason, would remember him with distinguishing favour — his attentions to me have been unwearied, he hath, in every particular consulted my wishes, and my own dear father, could not have been more solicitous respecting me, than

Mr Murray hath been — I think the state of his health is rather better, than when he left home — He is now gone to pass three days in Stoughton, at which place he has many friends — It is hardly possible to delineate the happiness which attends his stops, wherever he disseminates the word of life [—] The head made white by time, Individuals in the meridian of their days, and those in the bloom of youth, throng around him, every hand is extended, and every heart is open while welcome, welcome a thousand times repeated, is wafted from every tongue! — "God Almighty bless you Sir, we had thought no more to behold your face in the flush, right happy is the hour which hath brought you once again among us — Blessed Man — surely never one instrument, merely human, was ever made productive of so much peace to the children of Men" — Such are the exclamations which hourly vibrate upon my ear — Tears of transport descend upon the furrowed cheek, and tender gratitude, is painted upon the face of beauty — At every stage the idolized preacher hath been discovered — "May I presume, upon your name Sir — Is it not Murray — ?" They are answered in the affirmative and pleasure and admiration, immediately take place in every feature "Thank God for giving us to behold you, long have we wished for such an opportunity " — Then follow a succession of important questions, and the Preacher promulgates, with heart felt energy, the message of his God — Notwithstanding the resolution of Mr Murray, to suspend, on account of his indifferent health, his public labours, he has not been able to resist the pressing solicitations of the people — The first sunday after his departure from Gloucester, he preached in the Court House at Taunton, the second in the Court House at New Port, and the approaching Lord's day, he will meet the people in the same convenient receptacle in this City — Crouds gather round him, and characters the most respectable throng to hear, while every attendant is wrapped in fixed attention — Hundred[s] there are, who cannot obtain seats. yet no signs of lassitude appear, every eye is attentively fixed upon the speaker, until the big tear proclaims a fullness of satisfaction — This animates our friend, and his discourses partake a proportionable degree of energy — To listen to the conversation of the people, must warm the heart of every Lover of the Redeemer — While returning from public worship, with uplifted hands, and eyes, they reiterate — ["]what sublime, what salutary truths — how clear, and how consolatory — Would to God we could be indulged with a repetition of these golden opportunities, When in Gloucester and what fascinating powers doth it possess — We cannot say, but this we know, that

its inhabitants are beyond expression happy" — All this, and much more, I have repeatedly heard, and accompanied by an expression of countenance, which no words can convey

Letter 495 to my Aunt E— S—
New London June 26— 1786

… Mr Murray hath not been able to withstand the solicitations of the people, he hath repeatedly and publicly delivered his message of peace — crouds have gathered round him and every countenance expresses pleased attention — Strange as it may seem — to form an idea how much Mr Murray is believed, we must leave Gloucester. Many persons follow him, wherever he appears, with a kind of devotion, that is rather descriptive of idolatry, than of common admiration [—] even his most trivial expressions are treasured, and detailed with pious rapture — They keep the anniversary of the hour which first brought to their ears his message of peace, with demonstrations of sacred joy, and they think he hath not been equalled, among the children of men, since the days of the Apostles.…

Back home in Gloucester, Judith receives troubling news from John Stevens.

Letter 521 To Mr Murray
Gloucester September 8th. 1786

Fatigued by writing the inclosed letters, I must, my respected friend, pray your acceptance of a few lines, instead of the many pages to which you are undoubtedly entitled — I grieve at the omissions of which you complain — Let it, Sir, be your consolation, that death, assuredly waits you; that, although the stroke be delayed, it will ultimately be made sure; and, as you must learn from experience, that all your supplications, doth not accelerate the progress of the severing angel, I think you should cease to petition a being, so inexorable.… I am pleased to learn your passage proved propitious — A Coalition of our Creditors! Why this looks auspicious [—] Possibly the result may be fortunate — My last accounts from St Eustacia were not favourable — Again I say, I will hope the best — Adieu — exhausted strength renders it necessary for me to lay aside the pen —

In the next letter, Judith responds to John Murray's recurring self-doubt as we would expect.

Letter 522 — to the same —
Gloucester September 11th 1786

... you complain, or rather you reflect upon yourself, as a loiterer — Pray my respected friend when and where have you loitered? Have not your public labours been so unremitted, as to injure your health, until at length, from real indisposition, you have been compelled to deny petitioning multitudes — I regret that your bosom admits so large a share of inquietude, and, I add if you be not at peace with yourself, you would do well to pursue a path that would more certainly lead to mental tranquility — From my soul I wish you every felicity, and, counseling your interest, I cannot but be desirous, you should embrace some plan, that might at least endow you with serenity — Adieu. I am, and ever will be, your faithful, and, revering friend.

Judith places her concern for John's safety over her own needs.

Letter 532 To Mr Murray
Boston November 11— 1786

I assure you, my dear Sir, it gives me pain to hurt the feelings of any one, and especially of a friend so respected, yet I cannot approve, whatever may be my gratitude for your intention, of the journey which you contemplate to this Metropolis — It is unusual for you to repeat your labours in this place, in such quick succession, should you make your visit at this time it will certainly be imputed to me.... Farewell — may God forever bless you

Judith describes a Christmas dinner scene for her brother Winthrop that illustrates John Murray's importance to the Sargent family. "Jack" and "Sally" are Judith's nephew and niece, the children of her sister, Esther. "Miss Saunders" and "Miss Plummer" are two young cousins from Salem, the latter, Caroline Plummer.

Letter 542 To my brother
Gloucester December 7 1786

Setting round a noble Christmas fire at my Father's about five in the evening, but I will give you the group, just one thing formed a semicircle, about the blazing hearth — First my Mother with [marks of] tranquility in her fine face ... seated in her easy chair, she exhibited, as in strict propriety she ought, the principal figure. Next, at her left hand, the chimney was at her right, for being Christmas day, we were assembled in the front parlour sat Mr Murray and by the conscious satisfaction which swelled his features, I imagine he was reflecting upon the consolatory subject, which he had been attempting to investigate, through the preceding day — Close at his elbow appeared our sister, dress is supposed, by some, to bestow upon the female additional charms and the season gave Esther an opportunity of exhibiting sovereign beauty, to the greatest possible advantage — Jack and Sally were seated beside her — Miss Saunders, and Miss Plummer, in the holyday Garments — Fitz William uncommonly agreeable, while your humble servant, had the honour of fronting her Mother, at the opposite side of the Chimney — a general silence succeeded the various chit chat of the hour — It was one of those pauses in conversation, in which each individual seems to acquiesce, and retiring into their own bosoms, as if by common consent, there to indulge the pleasures of retrospection, anticipation, or, in short, precisely as fancy shall lead. I had called up to my view the circumstances of last Christmas day, the many events which have since revolved, a sigh found its way and, a tear was with difficulty arrested in its progress, by being successfully dispersed over the eye, e'er it made its appearances in the too ready drop....

Judith's letter to Doctor Potter is filled with praise for John Murray and their mutual "Cause." This man is probably the son of Thomas Potter, the New Jersey farmer who befriended John when he first arrived in America in 1770 (see "Introduction").

Letter 552 To Doctor Potter of Wallingsford
Gloucester April 8th— 1787

... Yes, my friend, the God of universal nature is, indeed, love, and it is impossible, with a mind rightly turned, to trace his omnific footsteps, without experiencing the animating glow of sacred devotion, enkindling in the bosom — My last summer's pleasing excursion, hath furnished me with abundant matter for reflection, and, as you rightly judge, my conceptions of the plastic power of the self existent first Cause, the great informing soul, which breathes through a speaking Universe, cannot but be enlarged, cannot but prostrate my spirit, with all the rapture of sublime admiration.... The Cause of Mr Murray is good, his language is energetic, and, of course, I cannot wonder, that your serious, sensible Villagers, have been swayed by the combined force of eloquence and truth — Whenever Mr Murray quits his Gloucester friends, they cannot but regret, he is, however, independent of us, and, I suppose, altogether his own Master — Proud Word — especially when the lips of truth inform us, it is not in man that walketh to direct his steps — My respectful Compliments, if you please, to Mrs Potter, and the other individuals who compose your household — I am, with much esteem, dear Sir, your obligingly grateful friend —

Apparently, John Stevens has set sail for Gloucester.

Letter 553 To Madam Walker
Gloucester April 13th— 1787

... I have been for some time past in hourly expectation of seeing my husband — his prospects in the West indies are miserably blasted, his health is still further impaired, and he stands in need of the peaceful retreat of his own home, to recruit his exhausted spirits — I anticipate the hour of his arrival — my soul will not then be subjected to those alarms, which for some weeks past hath drank up my very life, and, no longer a prey to suspense, a measure of tranquility will be mine....

John Stevens's death comes to Judith in a vision.

Letter 554 To My Brother
Gloucester May 5th 1787

... The very night of his departure, I dreamed that I was desolate and forlorn, placed in a dreary situation, I remained unprotected and alone, and gloomy despondence was suffered over my whole soul — when, suddenly, lifting my eyes I beheld my husband, standing before me — Present to myself, I experienced no alarm, I reflected that by the last accounts he was in St Eustacia and I was unapprised of his intention of returning — I know not how he had reached home, or how he had found his way to me, for I believed I had quitted the mansion in which he had left me — His countenance was perfectly serene, and without uttering a word, he regarded me with utmost attention; surprised at his tranquility, and ... amazed that after so long an absence he did not deign to address me by a single sentence, my hasty temper became unduly irritated and I reproachfully interrogated — From whence can proceed your composure, your taciturnity? Do you not see the wretchedness which surrounds me? Surely you are strangely altered! How often have you asserted that you felt for my sufferings abundantly more heavily than for your own, and that to ensure my happiness, you would cheerfully submit to almost any species of misery! yet now, behold, the reverse seems to [be] conspicuously manifested — Contentment is yours, even while you witness the depth of the calamity which involves me! Did I hold the pencil of the painter, I would exactly delineate the expression which took place in every feature while I then remarked — It is not in the power of time to erase it from my memory — It partook a mixture of tenderness and that kind of pity which in the same moment gives an assurance of self-complacency; every feature indicated superiority, and he seemed to say "you are unconscious of my situation, otherwise you would neither wonder at, nor censure the sobering joy, the rational felicity, to which my countenance is an index — and, casting upon me an eye of the most penetrating intelligence, as if he were eager to convey information truly important, which upon his lips was affixed the seal of silence — such was my dream, and strong was the impression which it made upon my soul and quitting my bed I inserted in my memorandum book — <u>Thursday night eleven o-clock — eighth of March — 1787</u> It was the first time I had been thus influenced by a dream — but such was the agitation of my mind, that I regarded it as the passage of some most favourable event — This moment "perhaps," said my labouring mind, the scale begins to turn — Fortune is at length weary of persecuting the honest, the industrious Man, and she will henceforth array herself in smiles. I acquainted my Mother, and my sister, with my dream and the hope it had inspired — But alas! the middle of the month of April, produced Captain Webber from St Eustacia — We inquired, and we learned that <u>on thursday night eleven o'clock eighth of March — 1787th</u> Mr Stevens expired!! and thus is finished, thus forever closed, the melancholy scene....

In the next letter, Judith tells Catherine Goldthwaite (who has married Doctor Sylvester Gardiner of Newport, Rhode Island) that she is reluctantly settling into her new life as a widow. Meanwhile, John Murray has offered to escort Catherine to Gloucester to visit Judith.

Letter 562 To Mrs Gardiner
Gloucester August 15th 178[7]

... Yes, my Cousin, my mind hath been deeply wounded, my health sacrificed, and my spirits proportionally distressed. Nor will the lenient hand of time possess the power to soothe my soul to peace — Habit, it is true can meliorate, and reconcile us to almost any situation, but regrets can vanish, when circumstances daily conspire, to remind us of any sad reverse of fortune, when upon the wing of every passing hour, is borne some melancholy memento — No, my charming friend, Competency however little my frugality might induce me to term such, smiles not upon my widowed state, there is scarce anything which I can call my own, and dependence, with all its pleasure blighting influence involves in clouds the moments of reflection — Yet I would not unbecomingly deplore, time itself is fleeting, and my days will e'er long be numbered — your silence respecting your promised visit gives us pain — Mr Murray would take pleasure in escorting you from Boston, to Gloucester, and he would, with due respect, attend your appointment — Should I have an opportunity of seeing you once more at Newport, you may calculate that I will readily embrace it....

During John's latest illness, Judith is happy to assist him by writing, in this case, to Joseph Russell.

Letter 563 To Mr Russell
Gloucester August 15 1787

... Mr Murray being confined by a serious attack of a bilious colick — Mrs Stevens is deputed his occasional secretary....

While John is en route to Philadelphia, Judith reaches out to him in a moment of loneliness.

Letter 574 To Mr Murray
Gloucester October 4— 1787

Such a length of time hath elapsed, and so many distressing events have succeeded, since last I employed my pen to you, that my depressed mind, retracing the gloomy past, feels itself hardly equal to the exertion, which even the fabrication of a letter requires — yet my gratitude is solemnly engaged, and your solicitations, that I would resume a correspondence, once so pleasing, are too often reiterated, to be passed in silence — Alas! Sir, He for whom your kind cares were employed, now sleeps in the dust — Seven long months [and] four days, have revolved since the period which witnessed his enlargement — In his Elysium, in the paradise of his God, beyond the reach of clamorous Creditors, his enjoyments are unbroken, and they will be perfected, when reuniting with his friends, he shall behold the family of Man complete [—] You, Sir, have frequently witnessed my tears, have marked and obligingly commiserated [with] a lacerated mind struggling with those combining sorrows which a variety of circumstances have conspired to produce — Whence then, you will pertinently question, this recurrence? I can only say, that folding my paper, and preparing myself to write, the whole series of my misfortunes rushed upon my mind, and I had not sufficient self Command to forbear tinging my frontispiece, with the hue of past calamities…. Wherever you are, and whatever may be your engagements — May the rich blessings of our Redeemer abide upon you

Penning Judith a letter from Philadelphia, John has apparently offered her financial assistance.

Letter 575 To the same
Gloucester October 16th — 1787

… How strangely variable are human resolutions — My reasons for not writing to you, during your absence, amounted, in my view, to an absolute prohibition, and I had made up my mind accordingly — and yet, behold, the petitioning sheet is put into my hand, and the supplicating voice of friendship is heard…. My income, you know is at present entirely suspended, for however liberal your offers may be — Having drank at the fountain head of justice, my feelings will not allow me to avail myself of your generosity — You must not expect to hear from me again in Philadelphia — farewell and receive warm from my heart, my very best wishes —

Now, their relationship takes a romantic turn.

Letter 582 To Mr Murray
November 10— 1787

I cannot, my dear Sir, leave Town without expressing my gratitude for your attention to me, in transmitting me so circumstantial an account of your movements — To say I am highly obliged is far short of those

impressions which acts of kindness have ever stamped upon my soul —
When the warmest sentiments of the heart are engaged, it is difficult to
find words adequate to the sensations they produce — Examine then your
own bosom upon similar occasions, and let that delineate the energy of
my feelings — Devoutly do I bend before the preserver of Men, and at
the prospect of your restoration, the voice of thanksgiving is upon my
lips [—] Penetrated by a proper sense of the value of a life so precious, so
extensively useful, I am solicitous Application should be made, of those
means which may conduce to its continuation, or at least to its well being,
while existence may be prolonged.... My kind Father, whose health and
spirits are in a great measure restored, hath made a journey to Boston, for
the purpose of accompanying me to Gloucester — May God forever bless
my friend

*At the close of 1787, Judith's father and other prominent Universalists advised
John to leave Gloucester for his safety. First Parish Church was challenging
the legality of John's ability to perform the marriage ceremony, and it was
unclear how long it would take to secure a ruling from the state legislature.
John decided to sail for England to visit his aging mother after eighteen years
of separation. But before he departed from Boston Harbor, he wrote to Judith
and asked her to marry him if he was able to return. Now, Judith feared an
"eternal separation" from John. Crossing the Atlantic Ocean during the winter
months was a dangerous undertaking. What if he perished? What if he decided
to remain in England with his family?*

Letter 589 To Mr Murray
Gloucester January 15th— 1788

Were I to draw my conclusions from principles, deduced from the
experience, and observation of every age, I should make such an estimate,
as to justify me in believing it of little consequence to you, whether I address
you in this way — Inconsistency is, or ought to be, the mother of your sex,
and a fondness for change is, almost invariably, the motive of your actions
— No sooner doth the conceding fair one, with snidest confidence, avow
her approbation, than her predilection evidently depreciates, and it is well
if her tranquility can obtain, even a second consideration — Deducing, I
say, my ideas from a general train of events, I should make up my mind
accordingly — but influenced, in some measure by the Christian system,
I exclaim "It is not in Man who walketh to direct his steps" and it ought

to be measured in the archives of truth, although found in the page of the Poet, that every individual must perforce fill the Circle marked by heaven — I cannot, in any other view, acknowledge the necessity of your voyage, and although your perseverances in a resolution so precipitously taken, may by the indifferent, be dignified by the character of manly fortitude — yet I, who suffer by its execution, cannot forbear striping it of its false gloss, and bestowing on it, the less pleasing feature of inflexibility — your attachment to me hath been delicate, highly generous, disinterested, virtuous, and honourable — But, I have in some instances experienced, that you have received from Nature, an obdurate heart — yet that heart, is as dear to me, as the vital stream from which flows this continuity of existence — How could you, Sir, if your passion for me be ardent as you delineate, resist petitions so movingly, and so reiteratingly urged? but you are my friend, and it did not become you to concede to womanish complaints — Do you believe me severe, you would perhaps change your opinion could you take a view of my situation — Storms are all around me, and no cheerful voice vibrates upon my ear — Upon sunday, January sixth, you sailed from Boston, and on the following tuesday the elements seemed combining, as if determined to produce the universal wreck of Nature — Judge what were my reflections — Why, my friend, did you depart? — But it is past, and perhaps you have, e'er this, shot the gulph — Tuesday probably signed your passport to the realms of blessedness — Yet my friends solicitous to soothe [my mind] that by the storm on tuesday you were not endangered — Well it may be so — and you may return — I will woo the cherub Hope and, in my agonized bosom, I will endeavour to erect for her a seat — One thing is true, I sigh for the pillow of resignation, upon which to repose my weary head — How often have I trusted — and, alas! how often been deceived [—] But, no matter — My Redeemer hath said, I shall have peace beyond the grave — And O! thou God of all grace, and consolation, grant unto thy supplicant, such acquiescence, as may ensure a uniform submission to thy well — Peace, Warblers — peace — The Birds in yonder enclosure are chanting most melodiously — Yet, to me, their notes are discordant — Surely they should not thus attune their little throats, when the harp of their mistress is, by the rude and unexpected hand of misfortune, most gloomily unstrung [—] But if there be in nature a universal sympathy, these binds would not thus sweetly course, if ill had betided our benevolent friend — if indeed the little songsters may be supposed in any sort influenced by gratitude — this thought is as rich as it is whimsical, and I will cherish it

— Well then, sing on my innocent companions — ye shall cheer my hours, and your enchanting lays, shall be to me, as the most benign presagements — It is not the absence of a friend for a few months that could possess the power thus to distress — but I am tortured by apprehensions, the months evince an eternal separation [which fills] me with frightful aspect, in the face, and it hath, indeed it hath, murdered the tranquility which was again reestablishing in my bosom — your friends in this Town are warmly affectionate, and the late unjust award originates in their bosoms, feelings properly indignant — but, alas! there is no one to lead them, and they are a scattered people [—] I have received all your letters, and I entertain a proper sense of every testimony of your esteem — they are indeed as dear to my heart, as my future hopes of happiness…. December 27th you departed — what a gloomy period hath since revolved — My feet hath not once passed the threshold of my door — My friends murmur — I do not yet wish to offend them — but I have not spirits even for the smallest effort — Besides, where can I go, what place can I enter, in which your image will not present itself — I cannot open a book, I cannot see a face — I cannot hear or recollect a sentiment, which are not pregnant with mementos of what I once possessed — of what I have now lost — too probably forever lost — your apartment — but to me its doors are effectually barred — No more I approach its hallowed retirement — Some of your friends have called upon me, fixed melancholy and heart felt chagrin printed upon their countenances for they are at length deeply sensible of your worth — Blessings do most truly brighten, as they take their flight — After shocks so repeated, after evils so accumulated, that they exist is to me matter of astonishment — Why hath not the rude hand of adversity crushed this being of an hour — For this last stroke I was all unprepared — Fool that I was — unconscious of the bursting storm, I had fondly began to anticipate moments of tranquility, but dark clouds gather round, and I am continued a Mourner in the Universal Family — yet I know that paternal Deity is unerring in his allotments, and my most earnest petitions to the throne of grace is for acquiescence in his divine arrangement — The present season is indeed truly distressing — How, how on the wings of sacred of virtuous friendship, I would have flown to have soothed the smallest [affliction] of Body or of mind which could have assailed you — Was it not barbarous — Bitter in the cup — yet, impelled by necessity you must have acted precisely as you have done — My heart is continually urging this apology, and affectionate amity is soothed by its defence — The most efficacious means were, as I believed attempted — I offered to accede to your wishes — but to oppose its incontrovertible negative, fate triumphantly arose, and our Teacher became obdurate — your hearers in this place, will make every possible exertion — Our little meeting — Gracious Father — I do not believe that I could support a view of this consecrated Fame — Did we imagine upon last Christmas Day — that the sweet voice of truth would so soon have ceased — I am alone in the midst of my tears — But again, I say, you may return — And Oh! May the angel of the Ocean, smooth the waves before you — May the strong hand of the Almighty guard you, and, to our united supplications, once more restore you —

Judith questions Joseph Russell about John's decision to leave.

Letter 591 To Mr Russell of Boston
Gloucester January 18— 1788

… Will you allow me the privilege of a few questions? I know that you will, for humane condescension is yours — Was any skillful Physician consulted, relative to Mr Murray's voyage? What effect was it supposed it would produce upon his imbecile constitution? How as his health and spirits upon his departure? Is it conceived he will from the General Court receive redress? Did he intend to tarry in London, untill he was advertized of the termination of this nefarious business?

The Universalists have signed a petition to the Massachusetts legislature asking them to pronounce John's ministry legal even though, in the eyes of the established clergy, he was not properly ordained. Joseph Russell now becomes singularly helpful in paving the way for John's return to Gloucester.

Letter 608 to Mr Russell —
Gloucester March 22 1788

… I am not ignorant of your indefatigable exertions in favour of our Exile — God bless you Sir — but you are already blessed — for the efforts of good Minds, are never destitute of that accompaniment, which tranquilizes the soul, rendering at the residence of complacency — However the Legislat[ure] may determine — one thing is certain, to the account of gratitude, many items are added, and yet, I am free to own, I wish the Debtor may return….

The Letters

Judith explains John's removal from Gloucester to Catherine Gardiner, along with what the Universalists have endured during the past several years. We learn here that the legislature has ruled in John Murray's favor.

Letter 613 To Mrs Gardiner
Gloucester April 4th 1788

… The reason of the departure of Mr Murray, those gazettes which have come under my observation, have truly assigned, yet, in obedience to your commands, I will render a succinct account of the business — The Universalists in this Town, have for a very long period, regarded Mr Murray as <u>especially</u> their Teacher, and although our number is not large, yet perhaps there is no sect, the adherents of which, are more firmly and uniformly attached to their Leader [—] From the third Article of the Constitution of this Commonwealth, we conceived we derived a right to support Mr Murray, and we imagined we will [be] legally exonerated, from all taxes levied by the authority of the parish from which we had separated — We had built a meeting house, adopted the title Independents and, agreeably to the mode of ordination, established by that sect, consecrated, ordained, and set apart Mr Murray as our Teacher of piety, religion, and morality — The opposite party, however, continued their assessments, and upon a refusal of their demands, entered our houses bearing away a silver tankard from one, spoons from a second, porringers from a third, and a variety of shop goods from a fourth — my Father had his anchor borne from his vessel, when he was on the point of sailing — Those articles were disposed of at public auction, at a very inferior price — The assessors handsomely rewarded themselves, for their wonderful exertions, and conceived they had done mighty well — This act of violence, you will not doubt issued in a judicial process, and, from repeated Juries, as well as judges, we received a most favourable, and, as we believed, equitable award — Thus having obtained a very respectable sanction, and authorized by the most eminent Lawyers — Mr Murray proceeded to perform the ceremony of marriage as often as called upon by those, whom he considered as his particular flock — A new field was now open to his adversaries, and they hastened to avail themselves of his supposed error — A prosecution was commenced, and the decision referred to a special verdict! The result, to the World in general, and to our friends in particular, was altogether unexpected — Mr Murray had solemnized a great number of marriages, receiving the vows of all those, whose attachment to their Minister, rendered them extremely reluctant to apply else when, the adjudication of the honourable judges condemned him to the forfeiture of £50, and as the prosecution was commenced for one offence only, he was liable to repeated penalties doubling of fines, and a most ignominious punishment — The aspect of affairs, you will allow, was now sufficiently formidable! To the clemency of his unnatural opponents in this Town, it would have been madness to have trusted from the justice, and impartial interference of the Legislature, shortly to assemble [—] much was to be hoped, but in the interim prosecutors might be multiplied, and the supreme power was not invested with the right of retrospection — It became necessary Mr Murray should absent himself from this state, and having long wished to revisit England, being often solicited in this respect, by his venerable Mother, he availed himself of so favourable an opportunity of voyage to his native Island — The civil authority have collected, our appeal hath been made, and it appears sentiments the most liberal influenced the Legislature — Mr Murray left in charge with a friend, a petition to that honourable body, and, as I observed, it was subjoined by a prayr from his congregation in this place

The event is happy, full indemnification is obtained — the majority in our favour in both houses of assembly, was prodigious, and an act is now in agitation, which, if passed, will establish that equality, among the various sects, in this our new World, which destroying all subordination to each other, will eventuate, in the establishment of harmony, among the multiplied, and multiplying denominations of Christians....

Judith "opens the door of her heart" to Mary Turner Sargent, reflecting on her first marriage and tracing the evolution of her relationship with John Murray. Judith accurately predicts that her brother Winthrop will oppose her marriage to John. She asks Mary to help change his mind.

Letter 615 to Mrs Sargent
Gloucester April 15— 1788

... I have been more explicit to you, than to any other person — and I will hence forth bid adieu to reserve — I will open the door of my heart, and my candid, my indulgent friend, entering the most [sacred] avenue shall freely expatiate there, nor will I in future acknowledge a thought which to her I should blush to disclose — Allow me then to take a cursory view of my past life — I was early very early united in marriage to a worthy Man — His virtues were many, and I justly esteemed the husband which fate had given me [—] Among his good qualities, probity, and undeviating integrity, were not the least conspicuous, he possessed also a gentle and conceding nature which were the more to be valued as they are so rarely the growth of the manly bosom — Yet, although greatly sensible of his worth, my ungovernable heart, refused to acknowledge the softer emotions — I believed myself incapable of love, as traced by the pencil of the Poet — and far from indifferent, I was rendered happy, by the consideration, that the purest fires of friendship, irradicated my bosom, and that I felt, for no other la belle passion [—] I determined, in the strictest sense, to discharge every obligation, and my perseverance in the path of duty, more than tranquilized my soul — In the misfortunes which involved Mr Stevens, I took my full share, and I lamented with the deepest agony, the melancholy catastrophe of his life — But my serenity returned, and, as I had often thought, and frequently expressed my sentiments, that after having once worn the nuptial chain, and providence had sundered the bond, a subsequent life of retirement, and freedom, was most proper, most ornamental and most dignifying to the female character, so the demise of Mr Stevens, made no change in my ideas, and I still say, if the heart be at ease, a single life is the most eligible, Nay I conceive, if the tender affections were in a first Choice grafted upon esteem, the delicacy of a woman's mind, if it be indeed cast in a feminine mould, will not admit a second election — I did not, however, imagine, I was debarred the pleasures to be derived, from a sentimental intercourse, from sentimental virtuous friendship, and my bosom glowed with an attachment for Mr Murray, which impelled it to recoil from every idea, of relinquishing his valuable society — The World it seems will not allow to a single Woman, an intellectual connexion with an individual of the other sex — but I had determined to brave the world, and conscious of innate rectitude, that my every action, my every thought, relative to Mr Murray would abide the test of the nicest honour, I believed I might be allowed to pursue my course, with tolerable tranquility — I will, however, own, that during the past twelve months, my sentiments partook rather too great a degree of tenderness, and although I became alarmed, yet having marked out to myself a path, pride assisted my perseverance, and I carefully suppressed every rebellious thought — But the event which banished Mr Murray from America, effectively removed the vale, I was solicitous to yield in person that relief, which the balm of sacred friendship might supply, and that I was denied the privilege of sympathizing with a Man, whom I so much esteemed, and revered, was to me an agonizing consideration — Discretion, however, erected her barriers and prudence bound me a fast prisoner in this dreary apartment — In short I could no longer deceive myself, my soul became a scene of tumult, and upon every rising thought, was stamped too sure a confirmation, that I had in fact become a slave, to the most impetuous of all passions, of which I had, erroneously considered myself incapable — Just at this juncture I received a letter from Mr Murray — It informed me that delicate attention to my honour, and feelings, had kept him silent, but driven, by the malice of his enemies, from the Continent, he could not depart without disclosing to me the treasured secret of his soul, since he might thus risque the happiness of his life — he could not but indulge a hope, that domestic felicity might yet be his — he acknowledged he had long loved me, even from the commencement of our acquaintance, with ardour loved me, but that he would have sacrificed his life, rather than have admitted a thought in this regard to me, which my own guardian angel would blush to own, but that, as I had now for many months been released from my early vows, he presumed to calculate upon a favourable hearing, and to supplicate, at least for a continuation of my esteem. I was now, you will allow, furnished with a fresh motive for admiration of him, who had at length avowed himself my Lover — How assiduous, and how honourable, through the course of a number of years, had been his deportment, how unwearied, and how disinterested his exertions — preferring, in every instance, the interest of Mr Stevens to his own, and pointing him out to me, in the most amiable light — How indefatigable were his endeavours to extricate us from our embarassments, to liberate Mr Stevens, and to continue him in his native place, and, after the departure of that unfortunate Man, how zealous to procure the suffrages of his Creditors, for his release — How just, how generous, how next to divine, was this procedure — who would have believed him activated by the passion which he now confesses — Influenced by grateful remembrance, rendered energetic by the then situation of Mr Murray, while the softest sentiments blended with every tender, and grateful recollection, my answer to the letter, which contained a declaration of his attachment, was concurred in terms, as indulgent to the hopes he had formed, in female reserve, and the observation due to my character would allow — and now, why should I hesitate, since the laws of God, nor my country, oppose my union — Mr Murray is derived from a family, which is even ennobled, and although the respectable decision of his venerable Father, forfeited those fortunes, to which it was legitimately entitled, yet, surely, its well earned, and time honoured [name] thus blasted — It will be in the power of Mr Murray, should he be again restored to this Country, to endow me with competency, and is not a competency, when enjoyed with the Man whom love, sanctioned by reason, hath selected, greatly preferable to the possession of affluence, with him we cannot love — The sentiments of Mr Murray are, in every important point, similar to my own, a thousand instances have proved, that our souls are congenial, and surely, it would be highly reprehensible, to reject him, merely because he is an Ambassador of that Prince whose emphatic name, contains salvation, and of whose kingdom, I boast myself a grateful subject — I have long known Mr Murray, and I have been a careful observer of his foibles — I know that his temper is absolutely mean, and impetuous, — yet his acknowledgements are prompt, and generous, and his anger is always chastized by reason — Perfection is not the patrimony of humanity, but our friend has as many virtues, and as few faults, as any of his sex, with whom I have conversed — In short, he is a Man in whom I can confide — Yet there is one consideration which fills me with the most mortal inquietude — the fear of the displeasure of my brother, doth indeed agonize my very soul — hence is derived the anxiety, with a confusion of which, I commenced this detail — Mr Gardiner, from a suspicion of the truth, hath prematurely suggested to my brother, the affair of my heart, and although he hath not explicitly avowed his disapprobation, yet, from the general tenor of his letter, I deduce no very pleasing inference — Peace, from the moment of its reception, hath been a stranger to my bosom, and I am trembling under the apprehension, of the loss, or at least abatement, of the affection of that brother, who hath been, and who will, however he may be estranged, continue to be, the pride of my life — Now then, my beloved friend, is the period for you to exert yourself in my favour — and I shall call upon that friendship, which I have never yet questioned to espouse my cause, to engage warmly on my side, to plead for me, and surely, an advocate so lovely, cannot sue in vain — If you can so far succeed, in conciliating my brother, as to induce him to continue to me his accustomed complacency, I will acknowledge that if I had received from you, no other instance of kindness, this alone, would be sufficient to bind me eternally yours — Alas! you know not, what my affrighted imagination, at times suggests — the present situation of my mind merits your sympathy, your pity, and if you can forward to me any assurance which might soothe my soul, delay not, I entreat, the renovating intelligence — Write however to my dearest brother, let him know the regards of his sister shall, if possible, be augmented and that Mr Murray hath always been, and will still continue to be, among the ... most sincere of his friends and that my only request is, that he will yield me his countenance, and still consent to me, in whatever situation, that fraternal affection and those so essential to my peace....

Judith lets Winthrop know that she plans to marry John regardless of his disapproval. She also tells him that before John's departure, he arranged to transfer his American investments to Judith if he was unable to return.

Letter 617 to my Brother
Gloucester April 18— 1788

... I approach you, my dear Sir, upon this occasion, with even agonizing apprehension — Do not, however, mistake me, I know that the cause I have to plead is marked by equity, but I dread lest he, whom I have so long constituted the beloved, and revered [companion], even of my thoughts, regarding an event, upon which so much depends, in an opposite view from myself, should abate of that affection, which hath for many years been my pride, my boast and a source of the truest pleasure — But, as I said, explicit frankness when thus addressing myself, becomes my character — Know then, and O! regard with a favourable eye a confession, extorted by necessity and by truth, that my heart is indeed tenderly, faithfully, and irrevocably attached, and that I would rather, infinitely rather, pass my days with the person you mention, possessing only that competency, which while his life is lent, his efforts will unquestionably ensure, than to be hailed Empress of the Universe, and doomed to exist, an Exile from his beloved presence — My bosom hath long been actuated by the purest friendship — sentiments of a more tender nature, <u>virtue forbad</u>, and the most secret wish of my soul, was indignant at every improper idea.... Since the departure of Mr Murray, I have received many instances of his marked and disinterested kindness, and should he no more return, he hath made such a disposition of his property, in this County, which amounts to some hundreds of pounds, as will render me the undisturbed possessor — Upon the whole, a supposition that my <u>determination</u> will not be in unison with your feelings, is the only remaining cause of regret — yet this is more than sufficient — like a dark and portentous cloud, it shadows my fairest prospects, intercepting the cheerful light, which tranquility would else diffuse — yet, upon the buoyant wings of hope, I am still borne, and when I reflect, that you are no stranger to my past misfortunes, that the secrets of my life are known to you, and when, an acquitting conscience assures me, that in every relation which I have sustained, I have in every important article, strictly discharged my duty — I cannot but flatter myself, some peaceful hours are yet in reserve for me....

Judith reports to John that she has confided in Anna Plummer, Mary Turner Sargent, and her brother Winthrop about their intention to marry. She also conveys the welcome news regarding the legislature's decision. Now that it is safe for John to return, the waiting seems interminable and news of John's illness is "distressing."

Letter 622 To Mr Murray
Gloucester May 8. 1788

... Upwards of four months since your departure, are at length elapsed, and we are informed we ought not to indulge the smallest hopes of your return, until next Autumn — Well, dear Sir, could [we be assured] of your health, and happiness we would teach our feelings, to accede with your plans — But alas tho arrivals from London are frequent — Scott, in whose ship we were taught to expect you — Barnard, and others have reached Boston, but not a single line from our friend! True it is, that we have gratefully to acknowledge, the receipt of a letter from you by the New York Packet, which administered balm to our hopes, for it informed me, of your supposed arrival, and good health — but how have the pleasures of which that communication was productive, vanished from our bosoms when recollecting its date — February 9th — and comparing it with your address to Mr Russell's son, dated the 24th of the same month, we hear you say, you are confined by illness in Plymouth — Indeed Sir, our sensations are truly distressing, and it would not be wonderful, if our expectations, in regard to you, were totally relinquished — I should have inclosed you the papers you wished by Captain B— but he did not leave Portsmouth until late in March, and I was assured by Mr Russell, it would be in vain to forward them by that ship — he now, however, calls upon me to produce them, and I have selected them with a heavy heart [—] To the benevolent pen of this good Man, having myself not sufficient spirits for the communication, I refer you for an account of the proceedings of the Legislature, he will, no doubt, inform you that the prayr of your petition is heard[,] that you are exempted from all future penalties, and fines, on account of any marriages you may have solemnized, for which a prosecution hath not already been commenced, and, also, that the general government hath referred to the next session, the consideration of an act, which will invest you, and Clergymen of every denomination, with privileges sufficiently extensive — Mr Russell's account will be circumstantial, and his lively page, will afford you superior pleasure while, it is only necessary for me to add that his zeal for your interest, and attention to me is beyond all praise — My wish for you, Sir, is, that your heart may never be experimentally able to judge of that anguish which hath corroded the bosoms of our friends, with your departure — But it is <u>past</u> — Blessed be God that I can say it is past, yes the sorrows of the past four Months, shall no more return — nor shall the bosom that they have tortured, be always doomed, thus to struggle with misfortune…. Taught by Mr Russell to expect your return, in the course of the month of April, I addressed my brother upon the subject of my future prospects — I also unbosomed myself to Mrs Sargent, who hath entered deeply into my feelings, and who tenderly, and warmly, espouses my cause — I have informed them both, that the situation in which you found yourself involved, accelerated declarations, which you had long meditated and that my present determination was in unison with your wishes — The distance from my brother is so great, that I cannot yet expect his answer — I have been thus explicit, only to those two friends, and to our beloved Anna — Anna, I repeat is a worthy child, and the warmth of her attachment to you merits unconditional affection…. Of your ill health I dare not speak, I am struggling with apprehension, it is a precipice to which despair is momently pointing, and I fly from the mournful view, taking shelter in the bosom of hope — yes, you <u>may</u> be in health — yes you <u>may</u> return and I too <u>may</u> live to see it — What then — Why then, I will be truly grateful — discontent shall be no more, and I shall possess the blessings of tranquility…. Our friends have generally collected since your departure — every Lord's day hath witnessed their assembling — I have not failed to join them, so often as my health would allow —

In Letter 625, we learn that John's illness has led him to Bath, England, for that town's famous healing waters. While Judith waits for his return, she attempts to trace John's steps as she receives news of his whereabouts.

Letter 625 To Mr Murray
Gloucester Morning of the 16th of May 1788

Since last I wrote you your letter of March 16 written in Exeter hath been safely wafted to my hands, and I am thankful to the God of my life, for the intelligence which it conveyed — I regard the fond hope which it hath originated in my bosom, as a sweet presage of future good, and gratitude once more predominates in my bosom — I cannot but wonder at your slow progress toward London, especially when I recollect the venerable Matron who with open arms, and a throbbing heart, is waiting to enfold you to her bosom — yet, my dear Sir, I am so far from arraigning your conduct, that I doubt not you have sufficient reason for every step you take — you would long e'er this, have received from many of your American friends a particular account of the award of the Legislature, had they not supposed it hardly possible, the intelligence could reach you in London…. That you are so much beloved, admired, and followed in England is not for me a matter of surprise. We are persuaded you will ever find, or make your Circle of friends, and it is not more true, that you are led by the Redeemer of Men, than you are pursued by the benign ardours of friendship — Report, as usual, hath exaggerated beyond all credibility [—] it hath already placed you in the most affluent circumstances, and it is the recurred opinion of many, that you will no more visit America, nay even your friends are not a little apprehensive…. The two letters which I have received from you, have given tranquility to my bosom, they came by the New York Packet — The first conveyed the intelligence of your safe arrival in England, and the second assured me, you were well, that you were in health, even <u>after</u> the 24 of February, when your information to Mr Russell's Son was dated — with a kind of melancholy pleasure I have endeavoured to trace, upon the Map, the steps of my exiled Wanderer — Falmouth first drew my attention, and, well as I might, I marked the lines — next I applied to Middleton, every word was of importance, its markets, its customs, and particularly its churches, and, upon its distance from London, I dropped an impatient tear — But an account arriving from Mr Russell, bid me search for my friend in Plymouth … and Plymouth took possession of every faculty — But Plymouth hath at length given place to Exeter, and, in that ancient City, melancholy contemplation now loves to dwell — I had its ancient dignities, its religious superiority, its right to be styled the London of the West, with every other etcetera, which can enhance it[s] value. On this privileged spot my last accounts were dated and O! may every thing conspire to promote the happiness of my friend — May the Bath Waters prove indeed a specific, and may you still pursue the purpose of your heart — May you consult <u>abstractedly</u> the wishes of your soul — if they do not lead you again to visit this younger World, may you enjoy the first of blessings in your native land — Adored, forever adored, b[y] the God of our life — we are taught to believe, that in worlds beyond the sky, no separating barriers shall exist.

Finally, John has written about his plans to return. Judith confirms her decision: she is ready to marry him. She tells John that he is "welcome to the soul of [his] Constantia"—her pen name, used affectionately only with John Murray and Mary Turner Sargent.

Letter 627 To Mr Murray
Gloucester May 18th 1788

I now hold the pen, with very different sensations from those which have heretofore agitated my bosom — My dear, my protecting friend is returning, there is no longer a necessity for his banishment, and I shall be — I shall be — in short I shall be very happy — a thousand times a day, do I whisper the tidings to my soul, My heart, my fond heart, throbs with esteem, and gratitude, hourly augmenting, and the pleasing perturbation of the little flutterer seems to render it too big for its enclosure — Not but that fear, often peeps in, from whence is ready, with its cautions, and by Possibility, by way of moderating my expectation, hath a thousand things to urge — I know, Great heaven, too well I know when last you wrote, the wide waters rolled between us — I know the spring is the season, when your complaints assault you, with the most unyielding obstinacy, and I experimentally know, that upon this changeful globe, every thing is precarious [—] Well, what then — still I will say, unto every gloomy apprehension, be ye far from me — I will unwaveringly believe, that I shall yet again meet my friend, and that I shall pass with him, e'er yet I depart to the World of spirits some tranquil days — I am under, to my dearest Murray, eternal obligations, and may the full reward of his extensive benevolence, be his portion — I cannot write, a kind of pleasing tumult takes possession of my soul, destroying that composure, which is necessary for the purpose of arranging my thoughts, with that method, which I am fond of observing — yet I ought to write, and this letter is intended to meet you in Boston — Welcome, then, my dearest friend — Thou art right welcome to the soul of thy Constantia.... Do not, however, believe there is, in my mind, the shadow of hesitancy — No, my determination is unalterably fixed, and although there are many avenues, by which my soul is exposed to sufferings, yet, there is but one, by which the deluging floods of <u>overwhelming</u> misfortune can enter.... Of one thing I am certain — I can never while fate continues to me your friendship, be totally unhappy —

John has written to Judith's mother about his desire to marry her daughter, but Judith still asks her aunt Mary Turner Sargent to keep their plans secret.

Letter 628 to Mrs Sargent
Gloucester May 19— 1788
... I entrusted the secret, which I committed to the faithful bosom of my beloved friend to no other ear, out of this house, my brother's excepted — By Davis however, my Mother hath received a confidential letter from Mr Murray, avowing his sentiments, and soliciting her patronage [—] it doth not appear that he hath incurred the displeasure of my Mother, yet, if our distant Hero looks not with benign aspect what a dark cloud will envelop my future days! [—] As I wish to avoid, as long as possible, becoming the subject of speculation, I know you will still allow the seal of secrecy, which your ever valued friendship emboldened me to affix — Suffer me to breathe a wish, that you may ever find pleasure, in recognizing me, as an affectionate friend since, it is impossible, I should be other than eternally yours —

Explaining her reasons for wanting to marry John, Judith asks her parents for their "blessing."

Letter 632 To My Father and Mother
Boston July 5th 1788
... By this day week I hope to present myself before you — It is at all times my wish to contribute to the happiness of parents, who have, in every instance, discharged to me the duties of the tenderest, the most unabating, and indulgent affection, and I flatter myself, as I am assured their decisions are at all times governed by reason, they will not record the present prospects of their eldest daughter, among the painful events of their lives — I confess to you, my honoured parents, that although affluence, and independence,

may be in my offer, I should consider myself highly reprehensible, according to my ideas of rectitude, where I to avail myself of the lender, while my heart acknowledged a preference for another — Mr Murray is descended from a good family, and, although the religious principles of his Father have divested him of his patrimony, it is, however, in his power, to endow me with a competency and say, my honoured Friends, can doors be necessary, to the mind which is the residence of reason? Vanity is inscribed upon the fleeting enjoyments of life, and, "Earth's highest title ends in here he lies" Is it not similarity of sentiment, is not a union of minds, with an establishment sufficiently easy, infinitely preferable to the most splendid circumstances, w[h]ere a consent of souls is wanting? — Thirty seven years have I been cloathed with mortality — My personal charms, if I ever had any are fading from my view, Misfortunes have impaired my health, the means of sustenance are not within my grasp, my brothers, and my sister, have engagements which naturally supercede their care of me — should death deprive me of my parents, I stand alone in the world, and surely, it is rather late for me, to look abroad for connexions, so recently contemplated and which are, in fact, almost viewless — Can I be wrong to invest with the character of protector, a Man to whom my heart is indeed strongly attached? Upon the whole, dear, and honoured Parents, I ask your blessing, I sue for your indulgence, I solicit your approbation, and I take it upon me to assure you, that no step of mine, shall ever tinge the face of reason, with the blush of confusion —

Judith assures Anna Plummer that she will still have a home after Judith has married John. After many years of struggling, with which Anna is only too familiar, Judith tells her she is finally happy.

Letter 633 To Anna
Boston July 5th 1788

Mr Murray is tenderly attached to you, his bosom glows with all a Father's fondness, Sensible will be the aid which we can offer — but, such as it is — to its utmost limits it shall be extended.... I will own to my young friend, that the manly, and sentimental attentions, which I receive from Mr Murray, possess a power, to soothe my soul; yes my sweet Girl, rational, and refined enjoyments seem now within my grasp — let me mark them with gratitude, and let me cease to refuse although perhaps every eligible, may not be included in my situation....

113

This letter is just one of many in which Judith defends John's character to Winthrop and her decision to marry him.

Letter 634 to my brother
Boston July 8. 1788

… What, my dear brother, are your objections, an easy competency will be mine, and the unanimous consent of the christian World, hath long since given to the public advocates of Religion, a rank, nay even the precedence in genteel society — It is true America knows no dignified Clergymen, but it is as true, she also refuses to acknowledge any order of nobility [—] Mr Murray was the chosen and confidential friend of General Greene, and at the close of every campaign, it was the General's custom, and pleasure, to address our Ambassador, in the language of friendship, and the most unbounded esteem; and those approbating testimonials, received from the illustrious Warrior, are preserved with the most pious care — By the distinguishing kindness of General Washington, Mr Murray was appointed chaplain to three Regiments, an honour not conferred upon any other of his Order — yet, after all it is happy, that Virtue can elevate, that integrity cannot fail of conferring <u>real exaltation</u> — Were it left to the liberal mind, to select the religious sect with which it would stand connected, surely it would not hesitate in acknowledging the sentiment, which precluded not cheerful, and <u>innocent</u> hilarity, the persuasion descriptive of benevolence — Mr Murray, I repeat, is universally respected, the first characters are among the number of his friends, and he is allowed to be a Man of sense, and information — When he, in a late journey, became <u>under your sanction</u>, my Escort — I had the opportunity of observing the attention paid to him, by persons, the countenance of whom, would, in the estimation of the world, stamp a value upon every character — Mr & Mrs Adams, with whom he came passenger from London, are loud in his praises, and I am honoured by those respectable personages, with the most flattering attentions — These informations I have deemed necessary, to convince my brother, that the election of his sister, will not reflect dishonour upon him, and that she is not under the government of caprice, or jocularity — Mrs Adams, after having seen much of the World, recently declared, in a very polite circle, that she thought it impossible for any Lady, whose heart was not preengaged, to put a negative upon the addresses of Mr Murray — Thus much, as I said, may be requisite, to soothe the exquisitely delicate feelings of my Brother — For my own part, I still believe, a <u>union of hearts</u>

and a similarity of sentiments, cemented by a tender attachment, with a decent competency, is sufficient to constitute matrimonial felicity — Mrs Sargent is, to me, an angel of peace, my obligations to her, are eternal, and, in every event, I shall still be actuated by the warmest wishes for her happiness — Fitz William is returned, for this, I bless God — yet both he, and my sister, are enlisted against my hope — No matter — I shall not live always, my honoured Father smiles propitious — my Mother is satisfied, and I ought to be contented — yes and tranquility shall be my continued aim

Despite Judith's view of widowhood as the most proper mode of conduct for a formerly married woman, John seems to have been very persuasive.

Letter 641 To Mrs Pilgrim of London
Gloucester July 31— 1788

… I have always considered <u>second</u> marriages, especially of females as standing in need of an apology — Decorum, I have believed — or at least that delicacy, which appeared to me peculiarly feminine, was thus violated — and, although I was not so arrogant as audaciously to affix a standard, yet I had made up my mind as an individual, according to my own ideas of propriety — There was a time, when had my country offered an Asylum for a desolate Woman, or had my religion allowed a seclusion from the world, within the hallowed walls of a Cloister — I should have hastened to immerse myself in the friendly retreat — Sheltered in so sacred an inclosure, I would have dropped the curtain upon every terrestrial enjoyment, and thus sequestered perhaps have tasted a measure of tranquility, not to be found in the busy scenes of married life — Mr Murray however, appears to have enlisted reason on his side, persuasion, I confess, dwells upon his lips, and, all conquering as he is he doth not easily submit to a negative. New prospects now open upon me, new views unfold, and I am ready to say — Perhaps I have been sacrificing to a chimera, perhaps it may be wrong to relinquish the pleasures in the gift of social life, of a sentimental Hymen, to a glittering idea, which, like an ignis factuus, may very possibly have mislead my judgment — At least while entering a walk, which I do not see that I can avoid, it is necessary to peace, that I thus believe.…

The next letter shows Judith's playful side as she reminds John how much she misses him when he is away.

The Letters

Letter 642 To Mr Murray
Gloucester August 1st 1788

"In all thy humours whether grave, or mellow,
Thou art such a hasty, testy, pleasant fellow,
Thou hast so much of wit, and spleen about thee,
That there's no living <u>with thee</u> — nor <u>without thee</u>."

Positively I experience a degree of inquietude at your absence! — Nay, it is absolutely true, however strange it may seem! — I feel a strong inclination to write you a very long letter, for after all, to tell you a secret, which I presume you have never yet had the audacity to quip, you are, and I foresee you ever will be, absolutely, and bona fide, the impudent, and imperious engrosser of my heart — Hang the stage, I say — it is just setting off, and I am necessitated to suppress the sauciest vein of trifling, which I was ever tempted to indulge — but I must, however, submit.... Adieu, dear Murray, I must, I am convinced I must, be ever, ever yours.

John is impatient for the wedding to take place. Meanwhile, Judith has asked Mary Turner Sargent to help her purchase some new clothing.

Letter 644 To Mrs Sargent
Gloucester August 29— 1788

This dear hurrying Man will not give me time to arrange my thoughts — Let me see — What had I to say — O! I have summoned Gerring, who is disengaged, and if you are not yet supplied, she will, with much pleasure, attend your commands [—] you will be kind enough to let her know your determination, as speedily as possible — you may, my obliging friend, spare yourself the trouble of [sending] out for the shirts to arrange [—] I have come to a resolution to do without them — but I take leave to request you to fancy for me, two dozen of buttons proper for a muslinet, Bath Dress — I have furnished Mr Murray money, so you will please to consider him, upon this occasion, as my Banker....

The wedding day approaches. Because of her siblings' disapproval and to avoid further embarrassment to her parents, Judith and John will take their vows in Salem, Massachusetts, and not in Gloucester.

1

Judith Sargent Stevens's first letter to John Murray appeared on two pages of her first letter book. These images show the damaged condition of the paper, which was probably due to humid conditions in the Natchez, Mississippi, mansion where Judith's letter books were discovered in 1984.

Judith Sargent Murray was approximately fifty-five years old when she sat for this portrait by Gilbert Stuart. By this time, she and John Murray had been married for twenty or so years. In her letters to John, she referred to herself as his "ever faithful and affectionate Wife." He was her "best friend," the "choice of her heart," and the "companion of her soul."

2

John Murray's portrait by Henry Sargent was painted "from life" in 1816 after John's death. Judith called John "an instrument of great good." She once asked him, "Who says that you ought to be second to any in my gratitude, in my affection? Was it not by your mouth that our God, and Father, thought best to show me the way of life more perfectly, and is there not many a denunciation, which being found in holy writ, would have harrowed up my affrighted soul, had not thy irradiated mind ... produced the luminous comment repleat with peace, life, and happiness?"

3

Gilbert Stuart painted this portrait of the only living child of Judith and John Murray when she was fifteen years old. In 1816, Judith wrote to her, "You have been to me the greatest blessing, which heaven, through a long protracted life, has vouchsafed to bestow upon me — Some jars there have been, but the most brilliant sky is occasionally checquered by clouds, and you, my Love, have always emerged with tenfold brightness." Sadly, Julia Maria died young, at the age of thirty-one.

5

4

Epes Sargent (1721–79), one of Judith Sargent Murray's uncles, depicted here by John Singleton Copley, remained loyal to Britain and was forced to leave Gloucester in 1775. But instead of moving to Nova Scotia as so many Loyalists did, Epes refused to leave his extended family. He returned to Gloucester and became one of John Murray's earliest and strongest supporters.

6

Mary Turner Sargent (1743–1813) was married to Judith's uncle Daniel Sargent. She was one of Judith's closest female friends. In her letters, Judith often referred to her as "Maria."

John Murray's childhood home in Alton, Hampshire, England, 7
was dominated by the medieval Anglican Saint Lawrence Church.
Alton was a rural market town, filled with fields of hops and barley
to supply the local bewery.

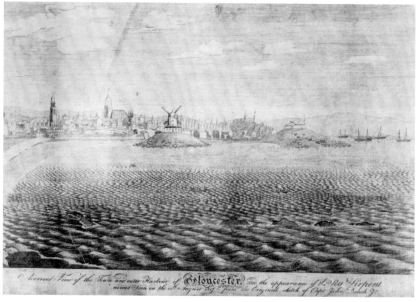

This is the earliest known view of the port of Gloucester, Massachusetts 8
(1817), showing its ships, wharves, lighthouse, and numerous church
steeples. Judith Sargent Murray always referred to Gloucester as her
"dear native place." After their marriage in 1788, Judith and John
Murray lived here until 1794, when John assumed the ministry of the
First Universalist Church in Boston.

Judith lived in this house on today's Middle Street, Gloucester, with her first husband, John Stevens, who built this home in 1782. After his death, she lived here with John Murray until they moved to Boston in 1794. Today, the Sargent House Museum is open to the public.

The Gloucester Universalists dedicated their meetinghouse on Christmas 10 Day 1780, calling John Murray as their pastor. They reordained him here in 1788. This is the first Universalist church building in America.

11

Franklin Place, Boston, also known as the Tontine Crescent (right), was considered one of Boston's most fashionable residences. Built by Charles Bulfinch in the 1790s in the European townhouse style, Franklin Place was destroyed in the Great Boston Fire of 1872. The Murrays moved here in 1794.

The Massachusetts Historical Society and Boston Public Library were housed above Franklin Place's central arch (today's Arch Street). The great urn that stood out front was moved to Charles Bulfinch's grave site at Mount Auburn Cemetery in Cambridge, Massachusetts, before Franklin Place burned down.

12

Judith Sargent Murray's cousin Henry Sargent painted the interior of his townhouse at Franklin Place. Judith's would have looked very similar. In a letter describing her new home, Judith wrote, "The apartments are finished in the modern taste, and they are spacious, lofty, commodious, and elegant[. G]reat attention has been paid to domestic convenience, and we are furnished with almost everything useful as well as ornamental."

13

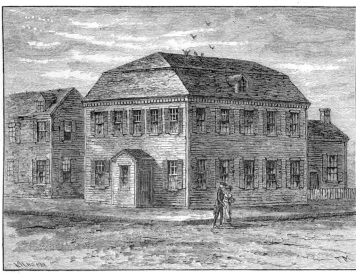

14

Boston's First Universalist Church was located on North Bennet Street in the North End. The building no longer stands, but the site is marked by a plaque.

Judith Sargent Murray is buried in the Bingaman family cemetery in Natchez, Mississippi, alongside her daughter and granddaughter.

In 1837, the U.S. General Convention of Universalists moved John Murray's casket from Boston's Granary Burying Ground to this site at Mount Auburn Cemetery in Cambridge, Massachusetts.

Letter 648 To Mr Murray
Gloucester September 26— 1788

Agreeably to your wishes I will, if nothing prevents, give you the promised meeting — should it be a wet day, do not, however, expect me — should any other accident prevent, I will apprize you — I should have written you by my Uncle, but his departure was sudden, I really think you ought to consult able, friendly and disinterested counsel — should any door be left open, how dreadful will be our situation — should anything render a change of measures I pray you make the communication previous to my departure from home, or meet me this side of Essex Bridge, and as no persons, my beloved Parents excepted, are acquainted with the destination of my journey, I shall not experience the smallest mortification — Consider well — when once we have exchanged our vows, the transaction of that solemn hour will be registered in heaven, and no human authority ought to possess the power, to disannul — once more I entreat you to consult your friends who are learned in the Law — consult your disposition, consult mine — But should you still persist, would it not be best to meet me as early as possible, on Monday morning, between Beverly and Manchester, and there once more discuss a point, to us so all important — If we proceed it will be necessary to engage someone who will assume the paternal characters — I wish this office may devolve upon my Uncle Ollive — but it would be advisable to consult your feelings, consult your heart, and, may that God, who hath the disposal of events smile propitious upon our final determination

Judith lets John know that the wedding plans are temporarily delayed for some unknown reason.

Letter 649 To the Same
Friday evening
Gloucester September 26— 1788

The inclosed letter was written previous to the return of my honoured Father — he has negatived our day, yet I blame not the honoured gentleman — I blame no one — but I am, at times, really ready to view the interdicting hand of fate — October is not my Month — yet, I thus obtain time to deliberate — The course of the ensuing week may confirm my still wavering resolution —

Letter 650 To the Same
Gloucester October 1ˢᵗ 1788

Your several letters my tender, delicate, and indulgent friend are now before me — yet this month of October pleaseth me not, nor would it be to me a subject of regret, were it not entirely erased from our Calendar — Yet, even in the face of superstition, I will give you the promised meeting, I will no longer delay — No new accident intervening, Monday next shall banish suspense from your bosom — And oh May every good Being propitiate the hour, May each benignant spirit smile complacent, and may confiding Love and augmenting esteem ensure to us the rich blessings of tranquility

The "die is cast." They are married! But Judith is still distressed by her brother Winthrop's silence.

Letter 656 To Mrs Sargent
Providence October 13th 1788

Yes, my beloved friend, the die is cast — I have passed the Rubicon, nor can I now refuse the steps I have taken — Well, what then — To you the inmost recesses of my bosom are open — let me therefore whisper to you an opinion for which, were it publickly known, I might be charged with precipotency, undue impartiality, and what not — yet I will hazard a sentiment — I do not repent, nor do I believe I ever shall, of any action in favour of Mr Murray, he is all I wish him, tender, delicate, and manly, and if his life should be continued, my tranquility can only know a pause, when I reflect that the election of my heart, hath not received the sanction of a brother, to whom I must ever continue tenderly and warmly attached — yes, I will confess, that even in the moment when the sacred ceremony was performed the image of this brother, had power to swell my bosom with sighs and fill my eyes with tears, and there are feelings to which I ought to bid adieu, to which I must rise superior, and which in future, I will, as much as possible, suppress [—] I will still hope for his acquiescence, which if I cannot obtain, I will yet remember his acts of friendship, and whenever, or wherever he will allow, I shall rejoice to hail him in his fraternal character.... Had it been possible to have obtained the performance of the sacred rites within the walls of a church our wishes would have been fulfilled more completely, but, by a law extant in this state a Clergyman, who officiates at the matrimonial contract, if the parties be without the pale of his sacerdotal jurisdiction, becomes liable to a very considerable mulet, and many other inconveniences — To imperious necessity we were obliged to submit, and our faith was plighted in a less pleasing, although more legal manner — In other words, an eminent justice, cloathed in his magisterial robes, recorded our vows....

Writing to Anna Plummer, Judith is clearly a happy bride.

Letter 657 To Anna
Gloucester November 7th 1788

... For me, I confess that I am at present in possession of a much larger share of tranquility, than I had hoped would, upon this globe, be my portion, and, I am free to own, that to know myself the chosen companion of the Man of my heart — of a Man of sense, of a cultivated understanding, a strictly moral Man, and in the most extensive sense of the word — a Christian, answers the highest idea which I have ever formed of <u>human</u> happiness....

Judith was never able to meet John's mother, but she corresponded with her regularly. This is Judith's first letter to her mother-in-law.

Letter 660 To the Mother of Mr Murray residing in London —
Gloucester November 17 1788

In some sense indebted to you, dear, and respectable Matron, for the sentimental pleasures which crown my days with tranquility, it is hardly possible I can regard you as a stranger — What though we exist in different Compartments of this Globe yet distance cannot bar the affections of the mind, and souls can hasten to mingle thoughts, and to express the merited, and endearing sensations of heart felt esteem — yes, although a personal knowledge be denied, yet gratitude will animate my page, nor will it fail to furnish, the obliged daughter, with ideas proper to evince her duteous regards to the tender Mother of that Being, who constitutes the prime felicity of her life — Accept, I pray you, honoured Madam, the tribute of duty, and allow me to pen my thanks, and bless the revered hand, which propped my Murray's dawn of being, to hail the wisdom, which with kind indulgence, was the guide of his infant days, and who still watching over him for good, diligently pointed out the path of rectitude — I now claim a rank in your family — I am the chosen, the bosom friend of your first born son, Condescend to receive me among the number of your children, and to present me to your several connexions, with such expressions of regard, as you may judge proper, assure them that I take a deep interest in their well being, and that it is my ardent wish to be viewed by them, as a tender, and affectionate kinswoman — That I cannot in some particulars discharge a daughter's part, is, alas! too true [—] I cannot present myself at your bed of languishment, I cannot smooth your pillow, nor soothe your pained head — I cannot beguile you of those anxieties which years, and misfortunes accumulate — I cannot wipe the tear from your revered cheek, nor periodically alleviate a single pang — But to the God of all grace I can recommend you, and my full soul supplicates for you, the best of blessings — But although deterred the privilege of administering in person to your infirmities, yet I am not to learn, that so glowing are your maternal regards, as to give you to view with complacent approbation, the hours devoted to your son — yes I can watch around his bed of sickness — from his susceptible heart I can occasionally steal the regretting sigh, thus tasting the ineffable felicity of assuaging, for the man I love, the ills of time [—] I am positive it will be to the bosom of a Mother, a consideration replete with satisfaction, when I assure her, that pangs borrowed from her darling son, supposing him thereby relieved, however agonizing they may be wear to my feelings the face of joy, and assume the power to communicate the sincerest pleasure — To such a union, the sanction of a parent will not be denied, and you will not, I assure myself, hesitate to bestow the maternal blessing — Condescend, honoured Madam, to accept the inclosed trifle, accept it as a proof of my attachment, not for its value, for that indeed is small, but as a testimony of what I would do, were the gifts of fortune mine — Once more I request you to present my regards to your children, and I pray you, do me the favour, to view me as a duteous, and affectionate daughter

Judith is impatient with Winthrop's stubbornness.

Letter 665 To my Brother
Gloucester December 21ˢᵗ 1788

Well then my brother, since the idea of your sister has become so painful to you, I shal[l] not in future, at least through her instrumentality be obtruded upon you — yet your sister, conscious of the rectitude, and propriety of her conduct, in regard to you, refuseth to acknowledge that she hath ever yet reflected upon you, the smallest dishonor — she still loves, still reveres you — your image is stamped upon her bosom, and your name will forever be musick to her ears — If, in the confidential <u>interviews</u>, for I cannot call <u>communications</u>, to which you refer, you had condescended to render your reason for the disgust you had conceived, they would have had due influence upon my mind — but, you must recollect, although often requested, you constantly refuseth me this favour, and you know, that warm as my attachment to my brother hath ever been, yet, in no moment did I relinquish my friend — It is true, I remember you cast many reflections upon the temper of the gentleman whom you thought proper to dislike, but, as I have been accustomed to much [condescension] from the individuals of my family, and as I am sensible of the infirmities of my own nature, I have not believed myself entitled, to look for perfection in others — I must confess, that after an almost constant residence of fifteen years, under the same roof with Mr Murray, I had the presumption to conceive myself as competent a judge of his general temper, as any trained observer could possibly be, and, I add, that his deportment to me, both before, and since our marriage, hath been, and still is, sufficiently conceding, manly, and tender — In short, he is all I wish him to be —

Even after they were married, according to propriety, Judith still referred to John as "Mr Murray" in her letters. John is traveling again, but now, when Judith writes to John or their friends, she is free to express her true feelings.

Letter 668 To Mr Murray
Gloucester January 4— 1789

By a single ray of light admitted through the almost closed shutter, I indulge myself by addressing a line to you — My Mother is extremely ill, and I have been through the day a close attendant in her chamber — Greatly doth this most affectionate Parent suffer, her infirmities are not to be found in the common Catalogue of maladies — Is it not exquisitely painful to be necessitated to witness the distress of those whom every principle of duty, and inclination, impels us to regard, with the utmost affection, while we are utterly unable to alleviate in the smallest degree, the agonies of which we are spectators? Your heart, Mr Murray, is the seal of sympathy, you tenderly fill for me, and you will, in all my trials, regard me with blind, and sacred pity [—] May God forever bless you and still give me to merit, and to preserve your continued, and unabating Love — I do assure you, I regard these frequent absences as wearing no friendly aspect to

me — it looks like taking a very large proportion, from the little remnant of time which may remain for us — Yet, ought I to repine, ought I not rather to be grateful that there is a prospect of my enjoying as much of your society, and that upon the least intimation that evil hath overtaken you, can I hasten upon the wings of affection, to attend you — To soothe you in every affliction, and to assuage as far as mortal may, assailing anguish — Well, then let me woo the rich blessings of contentment, let me enthrone tranquility in my bosom, and give the Cherub peace to crown my hours....
I am ever, tenderly, and faithfully yours

Judith confides in John, "I am yours in every sense of the word."

Letter 669 To the same
Gloucester January 9th 1789

Yes, my ever dear, my provident friend, the articles you have enumerated, all of them, have reached me, and, in the very best Order — I cannot express the pleasing and endearing sense I entertain of your affectionate attention — you contrive to invalidate the most respectable testimonies, and the experience of ages notwithstanding, it must be pronounced, that matrimony does not always create a tyrant — that in one instance at least the husband hath continued the Lover — your actions are descriptive of affection, your letters breathe the very soul of tenderness, and as they are doubtless warm from the heart, they can hardly fail of producing, in the bosom of gratitude, a Correspondent effect — Yes, best of Men, I am yours in every sense of the word, and may I cease to breathe, e'er I cease to acknowledge your unvarying, and faithful regards.... May God forever bless you, so prays, with unabating fervour, your tenderly affectionate, and ever faithful Wife

Judith addresses John on their four-month wedding anniversary while he is in Boston. John is apparently becoming impatient with his extended service in Gloucester, and wondering where his energy would be better directed.

Letter 674 To Mr Murray
Gloucester Morning of February 6 1789

Just 4 months will this day elapse, since I became a happy bride — Well, but this you knew before, and Henry says he must carry intelligence — I must write you how I am, every change which takes place &c &c

Why my dear I am very much at your service, quite pleased with my husband, and perhaps as well, all things considered, as can be expected — Poor Wanderer — yet the World is not worthy of you — I wish however you had told me where you did lodge, for from any thing I can gather from you[r] letter you may have taken up your abode in the street — But why, indeed, is my revered friend cast down? Will not He, who does all things well, appoint you your portion, in the very best possible situation — The introduction of the gentleman you mention, is perhaps designed to open the way to your more extensive usefulness. Do you not recollect that there are such places as Philadelphia, and New York, and will not your testimony be as salutary to the inhabitants of those Cities, as to the Bostonians? ... While you are in Boston I am comparatively easy, for I know that in case of accident, a very short time would be sufficient to convey me to you, blessed be the God of my life, both duty, and inclination, would point my way — yet whenever upon deliberate consideration, you are convinced of the propriety of a different arrangement, know, and be assured, that I will cheerfully follow you, even to the utmost extremities of the globe, and although I shall unquestionably experience some natural regrets yet my ultimate, and superior pleasure, will always be to consult your interest, and happiness.... I hope my letter has, or will reach you in safety — it will, I am positive, make you smile, and I am almost as certain, that it will produce upon your manly cheek, the tear of sensibility — your heart is highly susceptible — it is a good, a worthy heart, and it is the chief treasure of your admiring and faithfully affectionate Wife —

Despite John's poor health and the day's "severe" weather conditions, he has left again. In anticipation of his return, Judith has invited Anna Parsons to visit them. Judith wished to expose the young people in her life to John and his Universalist teachings whenever possible, and "Miss Parsons" was engaged to marry Judith's youngest brother, Fitz William Sargent.

Letter 676 To Mr Murray
February 25 1789 Gloucester

I do not recollect that I ever parted with the best of Men, with more reluctance, with a more solemn gloom upon my mind, than that which enveloped it on Friday last — My bosom experienced an uncommon degree of perturbation, and for the best part of an hour, after his departure, I could not restrain my tears [—] I wish my feelings may not have been portentous

— the severe weather on saturday, did not abate my apprehensions, especially as reflection "too busy for my peace" is continually holding up to view the indisposition which hath recently hung about you.... One thing gives me great pleasure, you did not take a water passage, and, as the probability is, that Griffin did not reach the desired port on friday evening, had you been in the boat, during the boisterous winds of that night, and the snow storm on the saturday morning, my soul would have been truly agonized.... Your little family is exactly as you left it — Without you every place looks desolate — I cannot but mourn your absence, but when upon the returning morning, and the closing evening, I no more behold the beautiful order which you established, I sigh for the friend, who hath taught us to begin, and to end our day with wisdom — I shall next week give to Miss Parsons, the proposed invitation — I hope you will return as early as possible, for I would really wish to cultivate in the mind of this good Girl, esteem for my revered Murray, and I know that to be loved, and admired, it is only necessary he should be known [—] Farewell while I have the exercise of my rational powers, I cannot be other than your faithfully affectionate wife —

Once more, Judith chastises John about not taking better care of his health. After all, she tells him, they are expecting a baby—the "innocent stranger" who will need a healthy father.

Letter 677 To the same
Gloucester February 26— 1789

you did exactly right, and I am relieved from a weight of anxiety, by the knowledge that you did not pursue your journey on saturday — Indeed the pressure upon my spirits, had become almost intolerable — but you are a dear, obliging Man, and I love you most devotedly — I am glad you are so considerate, for however mischievously you may have designed your remark, you are absolutely not your own, you have really in taking the vow matrimonial given your self to me, and I pray you to remember that whenever you presume to sport with your health, you are en verity and bona fide sporting with, if not another Man's, at least another woman's property.... I do not, God be thanked, I do not doubt your love, and I know there is but one thing you want — a little more uniformity and if my dear Sir, I should, upon some occasion be considered rigidly frugal — if it be my choice to be so, is there not wisdom in knowing when to spend and when to spare? I am aware our means are small and I also know your health alas! is very uncertain — Besides, why should I blush at the confession — is there not a latent cause? — have we not reason to believe that an innocent, and helpless stranger, will, e'er long, make its appearance in this very bad World, are we not under obligation to provide for the Being, of whose terrestrial existence, we are the authors, and to whom, under God can the little creature look for support, if not to us? Let these reflections properly affect your mind — I know that they do, and I request you, to do the partner of your hopes, and fears, the justice to believe, that they have also penetrated her heart, yet they shall never render me sordid, or unjust, No, to the benign Creator, and preserver of Men, let me rather commit futurity — trusting, in every event, to the all Gracious designations of God, the august Father of my spirit — I admire the conclusion of your last letter, and I would wish you to believe, that so perfect is my confidence in your tenderness, as to stand in no need, at this late period, of additional professions — yes, I assure you, that I regard you as blending the characters of friend, and Lover, of husband, and Protector, and I am, in consequence of this persuasion, and of your other merits, your ever grateful, ever affectionate, ever faithful Wife —

Judith shares her thoughts about their happy marriage.

Letter 678 To Mr Murray
Gloucester March 3d 1789

... It must undoubtedly be confessed, that discretion should ever complete the Trio, with the wedded pair — she is in the matrimonial voyage, a very necessary companion — To her valuable Conductor let us become inseparably attached, let us commit to her the helm, and I doubt not we shall smoothly glide over a stream, in which we might be otherwise engulfed — Sincerely do I believe that a happier pair since the transgression of Adam have never yet enwove the nuptial bands, and the reason is obvious — our sentiments upon points the most essential, are exactly similar....

Judith's loneliness during John's absences never abated, as she confesses to Mary Turner Sargent in the next letter.

Letter 680 To Mrs Sargent
Gloucester march 7th 1789

This day, storms are abroad and I am almost alone.... Yes, my friend, I am right happy, in the refined attachment, and delicate attentions, of the Man I love. In this particular I have no accusation to profer, against my destiny — but do you not see, how many of my hours, are of necessity devoted to solitude — it is surely no small chasm in the enjoyments of friendship, when one half of our days are doomed to a state of separation for the purpose of securing a competency for the remaining moiety....

In a letter to John, Judith reflects upon their six-month wedding anniversary.

Letter 684 To the same
Gloucester April 6th. 1789

This day completes exactly half a year, since we stood before the venerable person, who received our nuptial vows, and yet I have not, for a single moment, regretted the step which on the auspicious 6th of October, 1788 I with such hesitating perturbation consented to take. Pity there is no flitch of bacon, to which I might profer my claim, since I am in so fair a way of making good my pretensions to so honourable a premium — But, cry your mercy honest friend, possibly <u>you</u> might not join me in my petition, and I do suppose, in a case of so much importance, my separate affadavit, would not obtain the celebrated guerdon — Well, perhaps it is best as it is — at least it is as well for me to think, and, upon the whole, I will set myself down contented.... If my expectations are not disappointed, the coming day will present you this line, it will serve to inform you that I am happy in the flight of your indisposition, that I am as well as usual, that I count the days of your absence, that I, however, am solicitous to obey you, by keeping up my spirits, and that you are indeed dear to my heart —

Both Judith and John have difficulty adjusting to long periods of time without each other. Here, Judith tries to cheer him up by suggesting that, perhaps, an old adage is true — that absence makes the heart grow fonder.

The Letters

Letter 686 To the same
Gloucester April 10— 1789

The air of melancholy which pervades the letters of my dearest friend, distresses me exceedingly.... Surely we have many, and great reasons for thankfulness, and how are we certain that the very circumstance of our frequent separation, may not be one of the instances, which evince the kind care of providence, and its watchful guardianship of our peace? ... May not one source of hymenial infelicity be found in the constant association of the married pair, and is it not probable, that short intervals of separation, may give a zest to every terrestrial attachment? — Hitherto we have experienced nothing like apathy — or enui, our pleasures have never palled, for we have constantly blended the charms of expectation, with the more substantial gratifications of social amity — You know that you have derived from Nature, an inclination for varied life — Were you absolutely fixed to one place — the probability is, that a disposition so inherent in your intellectual conformation, would render you discontented, and melancholy — You wished to unite yourself to the object of your affection, you have obtained this wish — you were desirous to have a pledge of your virtuous attachment, and in this very natural desire, you have also every reason to expect gratification — but in the accomplishment of this last wish it was nearly impossible your companion should continue your travelling friend — This was a difficulty which you could not reconcile with your plans....

Winthrop's long silence about Judith's marriage to John continues.

Memorandum — or observation —

May 21— 1789 Four Months, four long months — are now elapsed since my last letter to my beloved brother — yet not a word from him hath met my ear!! I suppose then, that there is indeed a period to an intercourse, which I imagined coeval with our existence — Alas! for me — so often as I reflect upon this subject, my head is agonized — But my husband is every way worthy, he is kind, and most indulgent, I do not repent of the step I have taken — I could not have acted otherwise — For myself, I consider my matrimonial selection as most happy — and may God, I repeat, may Almighty God forever bless my brother —

Judith's delivery day approaches.

Letter 702 To the Mother of Mr Murray London Old England
Gloucester May 26— 1789

... perhaps a very few weeks may present your beloved son, with a little being, who will be entitled to his most careful attention, and who, giving to my bosom a Mother's fond emotions, will furnish me with augmented motives, to love, and reverence, the family from which I derive so rich a treasure....

The primary cause of death for women in the eighteenth century was childbirth. Judith, ever practical, raises the subject with John. What should he do if she does not survive the ordeal?

Letter 708 To Mr Murray
Gloucester June 10— 17[89]

How exquisite are the pleasures resulting from a union with a Man of sense, and sentiment — When the sensations of the heart, generally the offspring of impassioned fervour, are meliorated by reason, and authorized by judgment, how happy, how tranquil is that bosom, which is their retreat — I bless, my beloved Murray, I very devoutly bless the hour which made me yours — I bathe your letters with a flood of tears, but they are tears of rapture — such tears as you, best of Men, have often caused me to shed — Whether I am appointed for life or for death, I have not to complain — I have enjoyed much, my pleasures have been rich, and they have been zested by a hope of the most salutary, important, and divine Nature and I have only to supplicate the God of all grace, the Father of eternity, to slope for you, your remaining steps, May the Redeemer of Men, should He see fit to claim the breath which He hath loaned — give you to soothe your cares, another wedded friend — May she excel in every useful and ornamental accomplishment — May she, by good sense, gentleness, and every blending virtue, render you truly happy, and may she equal in tenderness, your present confiding, and most affectionate Wife — such are my wishes, upon a presumption that the God of my life, should see fit to remove me to another scene of things — otherwise duty, and inclination, sweetly combining, will point my way to every effort, which can promote the felicity of the prime object of my fondest earthly hopes....

The Letters

Tragically, the son they had planned to name Fitz Winthrop was stillborn. Judith, who was thirty-nine years old, nearly died as well. This is her first letter to John since his latest departure.

Letter 722 To Mr Murray
Gloucester November 29— 1789

How many melancholy days, weeks, and months have passed since I last addressed, in this way, my best, my dearest friend — How exquisite have been my sufferings, and how are my maternal expectations buried in the grave with my first born son — yet let me not, by dwelling upon unavailing regrets still more deeply lacerate the bosom of him, from whose tearful eye, I would hide, by the interposing veil of tranquility, every sorrow — I write at my Father's, converged hither yesterday, in the carriage, and the rain coming on suddenly prevented my return — I hope you have obtained relief from your disposition, or that you will make it an object to attend to <u>yourself</u> ... your absence is at all times a source of regret — and that I so much value your society, as to not be perfectly at ease without it....

In May, after Judith recovered, she and John set off on a six-month journey to Philadelphia where John played a central role in organizing the first national Universalist convention. Judith's letters to her family chronicle scenes along the way, places they stayed, people they met, events they attended, and the public's response to John's preaching. This letter, written to Mary Turner Sargent, describes a particularly touching personal moment between Judith and John.

Letter 744 to Mrs Sargent
Hartford May 16— 1790
Sunday morning

... We reached Palmer on thursday — I took up my pen — Mr Murray drew me to the window — see my Love, you are losing a most charming scene — I instantly obeyed the summons — It was all of Nature — Art had not presumed to embelish[,] not a single dwelling was in perspective, but the setting sun, throwing over the Landscape its embelishing and most beautifying radiance, rendered it indeed divine — Mr Murray took my hand and we passed down the activity together — A serpentine River meandered by — its Banks were enchantingly diversified — its surface was brushed by the curling zephyr, and yielded by the parting rays of the setting luminary — The River romantically presenting through a variety of openings, here jutting out and in an ample bend, and there terminating to a point, seemed to lose itself in groves, which apparently intersected its progress, until again gushing out in a number of little rills, it sweetly murmured along the grass grown carpet — In the background a venerable mountain seemed to reach the clouds — and out spread beneath — Thick woods, Vallies, and spacious meadows, were alternately displayed — At a distance a tall tree, single, and independent, seemed stationed the sovereign of the Grove — The tufted Oak, the verdant Pine, the trembling Aspin, and the weeping Willow conspired to variegate, and beautify the scene — The Birds in the branches melodiously chanted their Vespers — the sky was magnificently serene — none but lucid clouds were fliting there — The Mind of Mr Murray is constituted to enjoy, with high wrought satisfaction, the beauties of Nature — Not a songster which spreadeth the party coloured wing, not a flower which blooms but seems capable of inspiring him with an enthusiastic kind of rapture — The surrounding views were well calculated for his meridian, he gathered a bouquet composed of the wild flowers, which adorn the woods, and presented it to me, with a well turned compliment, descriptive of the gladness, and devotion of his soul — he pointed out the names[,] qualities and ability of the objects before me — he expatiated upon the variety and harmony of Nature, and he led my attention from Nature, up to Nature's God — In short the promenade altogether was most delightful....

Judith lets her parents know how affectionately she is received by John's numerous friends. In Philadelphia, she has learned that the Universalists have offered John a well-paid position as their minister. But how could she leave Massachusetts?

Letter 748 To the Same
Philadelphia Arch Street
June 5 1790 — Saturday
   … Mr Murray's connexions croud around me — nothing can exceed their congratulations, and their manifestations of pleasure, at his presence — One of the principal characters in this City, hath offered him a genteel house, for a residence rent free during life, if he will continue here, Previous to his arrival, his friends entered into an agreement to guarantee unto him,

two hundred pounds per annum, besides a number of prerequisites, which they assure him a number of prerequisites will be never failing appendages — Many respectable characters are in the list of my husband's favourers, among whom, the son of Doctor Franklin is the foremost — Could I remove those I so entirely love I could very cheerfully bid adieu to the State of Massachusetts, but strong are the bands which bind my soul, they are indeed interwoven with my existence....

Judith's letter to her cousin Epes Sargent reveals her conflict between wanting what was best for John's career and her desire to live near her family and Gloucester.

Letter 766 To Mr E. S.
Philadelphia Arch street
July 5th 1790

... A removal from Gloucester is an event, which I have never yet realized — I will freely confess to you, my friend, I seriously believe, a residence in this City, would crown the Career of our Murray, with both fame, and fortune — But what are these bubbles — and what is their amount — Indeed if that infant, to whom I loaned so transient an existence, and who for a season enkindled in my bosom the brightest anticipation — had that infant been given to my bosom, I should have deemed it my indispensable duty, to have made every effort in my power, as far as rectitude would have authorized, to have promoted his interest — But as he is, I religiously believe, amply provided for, in the paradise of our God, and as I am couldly debared every rational prospect, of again reiterating those charming expectations, which once so delightfully winged my hopes, what remains, but that I hasten to the world of spirits, there to embrace his airy footsteps — The whole of my plans are now circumscribed, by a desire for a humble competency, and a resolution to pluck as many flowers, as I consistently can, on my way to that hour, which shall unite me to a being — who strange as it may seem, possesses my heart's best affections — Agreeably to this sentiment, I thus argue — Gloucester possesses for me superior charms — My warmest affections hover round the asylum of my youth — There resideth the indulgently venerable forms of my tender, and ever honoured Parents, there dwelleth individuals whom I sincerely love and there apparently stationed, is my select, my sentimental friend, his amiable Companion, and a beautiful little group, the individuals of

131

which, I fondly believe, imbibe with their earliest growth, sentiments of affectionate esteem for her, who most devoutly wishes that for them the path of life may be strewed with the finest flowers, which can bloom in the garden of mortality — I might add, fanciful as it may seem [—] In that spot rests the ashes of my Ancestors — There too sleeps the cold gray tenement of your angel Mother, with many a friend laid low, and there is deposited the little form, which for a season, partook my sufferings — Yet, after all, decision rests not with me — My wishes ought to be formed by the inclinations of Mr Murray — as a Wife, it doth not become me to direct, and as a Christian, I ought rather to say — He who fixeth the bounds of our habitation, will take care to appoint for us a place....

Judith's description of John's preaching truly captures the charisma of the man and his impact on people from all walks of life. She was not the only one who was "beyond expression affected." As John's wife, Judith believed they were acting together "in the path of duty."

Letter 777 To my Father and Mother —
Jersies Mount Place
July 31 1790 Saturday

I apprized you, my beloved Parents, that we were to meet on Sunday, at Du Will's Grove — but I had no idea of the grandeur of the scene, which was to be exhibited — The Grove is about one mile from Mount Place — It is thrown by Nature upon a spacious Green and it is formed by rows of tall, and umbrageous Oaks — The Concourse of people was prodigious — I do not believe there is more than half a dozen houses in view from this dwelling, in any direction, yet, upwards of a thousand persons were collected in the Grove — among whom were, as I am told three hundred Quakers — The Congregation was gathered from more than twenty miles round the Country — They have in this State, much in use, a kind of Carriage, which runs upon four wheels, and is drawn by two horses — its top is solid, and it hath curtains which can be let down at pleasure — it is neatly painted, and lined, and it can accommodate many individuals with great convenience — I think it is called a Jersey Wagon — These Carriages formed a wall round the Preacher — The Circle was widely extended — it appeared to me, there were, in number, at least one hundred — Many attended in their one horse chaises and the horses being taken therefrom, every one kept their seats — which seats on either hand were also placed in this consecrated Grove, and an open eminence, was prepared for the Messenger of peace — Rain is now much wanted in this part of the Country, and just as this vast assembly — the place considered — were quietly disposed, and preparing themselves to listen most attentively, the distant thunder began to roll and the fertilizing shower to descend — I looked, that this circumstance would disperse the people, for the gathering of clouds, appearing through the foliage of the thick, and solemn Grove, wore a most portentous aspect, and there was every reason to expect, heavy, and repeated showers — The Preacher, however arose, and a benevolent smile brightened upon his countenance (—while a handsome Lad, benignity expressed in every feature of his youthful face, held over his head a large umbrella—) and stretching forth his arms to the multitude, thus expressed himself "How seasonable, my beloved friends, is this shower — from the want of a blessing, it is said we learn to estimate its value — how expressive then, must this figure now be rendered — "My doctrine shall descend as the rain, as the fine rain upon the tender grass etc etc["] — The calmness which apparently possessed the bosom of the Preacher, doubtless produced its proper effect, and not a single person left the Grove. The serious attention, in such a place, and from such a throng, made up of people of all descriptions, and in such circumstances, was indeed surprising — The clouds soon broke, the azure sky appeared[,] sun beams began to play, and the birds chanted melodiously — A hymn of praise opened the service, The throne of Grace was addressed — "Although Abraham be ignorant of us, and Israel acknowledge us not — yet doubtless thou art our Father — Thou art the God of the spirits, whom thou hast breathed into these clay built tenements" — The book was opened, the text was worded "The Grace of God which bringeth salvation unto all men, hath appeared — leading us that denying ungodliness, we should live soberly, righteously, and Godly in this present world" [—] In his own animated, energetic, and devout manner, the Preacher proceeded, and every countenance confessed the most solemn attention — The rustling of the leaves, the singing of the birds, were not heard, or heard only as adding to the beauty of the scene — During the intermission of the services of the day, scarce a person quitted the romantically enchanting spot — and the Preacher having stepped aside I listened in enraptured silence, to the various Comments — Serious investigation was now abroad[,] light seemed more than dawning upon the assembly, and I was particularly happy to hear an old Man, utterly deprived of his natural sight, evince by his remarks, that he clearly saw the things which made for his peace — One aged black man, in the midst of the discourse, softly exclaimed to a Bystander, "Blessed God — is there then redemption for a poor slave, as well as for his more happy Master?—" The afternoon service commenced, and the importantly interesting, and divinely affecting subject, was continued — The multitude augmented, but decency, and Order still presided, and, amid admiring throngs, the day was concluded — Mr Murray, in appointing a meeting at the Grove for the following sunday, thus expressed himself — "We will once more assemble in this house of God — yes, my serious hearers, in this house of God — For surely one God is every where, surely the Lord is in this place — He is with us, and will keep us, whither so ever we go — Jacob journeying to Padanarain, resting on his way, in a place where collected stones formed his pillow — where the heavens were his canopy, and the earth his Carpet — yet there counteracted by Jehovah — He said this is now other than the house of God, and this is the gate of heaven" — The scene appeared to me truly august — The solemnly energetic speaker, the surrounding multitude, moved apparently by one spirit — the animated, and correct gladness of their souls standing confessed, and swelling every feature [—] For myself, I repeat, I was beyond expression affected — Tears of transport often trembled in my eye, and I seemed to enjoy a prelibation of that heaven, which is reserved for us — indeed, language must ever be inadequate to delineate, the sensations of a chaste, and tender Wife, as she takes her seat amid the admiring croud, and hangs with the enlightened multitude, upon the hallowed lips of the revered, and beloved Lord of her wishes…. Tea was prepared for us at Colonel Cirkbride's, and we returned home with that kind of conscious complacency which must ever result from an idea that we are in the path of duty….

Despite the fact that New York's churches were "shut against" John, he enjoyed an audience with President George Washington and the First Lady. Following the Philadelphia Convention, it was John's task to present the president with the Universalists' resolutions on governance and doctrine. Later, Judith delighted in her own private time with the "Lady Presidentress," befriending both Martha and the Washingtons' granddaughter Eleanor ("Nellie") Custis. Judith describes the events for her parents in Letter 783.

The Letters

Letter 783 To the Same
New Rochelle
August 14th 1790 Saturday

… The Churches in New York are all shut against Mr Murray, but he met his friends, among whom are some of the most respectable characters, both forenoon and afternoon, in the Assembly room, and the evening produced many Ladies, who did me the honour of calling upon me — On Monday, Mr Murray as the Minister of the Universal Gospel, presented the address of the Churches, professing Universalism to the President of the United States, and was most graciously received — The form of the address, with the answer, will no doubt reach you, in the line of publick intelligence, long before the period, in which this letter is destined [to reach] your hands — While Mr Murray visited at the President's Mrs Washington dispatched a Messenger from her apartments, importing that she should be pleased with a visit from Mrs Murray, that if she — Mrs Murray — preferred enjoyment to ceremony, she need not wait for a Levee day — for Mrs Washington would certainly be at home, whenever it should suit Mrs Murray's convenience, and the President too, deigned to enquire, if my journey had bestowed upon me the blessings of health — all this, you will believe, was highly flattering…. Mr Murray was engaged with Colonel Humphrys, who occasionally regarded me with flattering attention — Thus were we disposed of when General Washington entered the drawing room — My eyes had never before beheld him — but it was not necessary he should be announced — that dignified benignity, by which he is distinguished, could not belong to another — Mrs Washington introduced me[,] I arose, and with a countenance that spoke not my heart, if it were not impressed with affectionate respect, and the highest degree of veneration[, s]lowly bending, in a marked, and expressive manner, I performed my duteous salutations — a smile of pleasure illumined the features of the President, he requested me to be seated, and taking a place by my side, proceeded, with peculiar affability to question me relative to my health, to my brother, to Philadelphia etc etc [—] To discant upon the Virtues of General Washington, however [interesting] the theme, frequently as they have been capatiated upon, and inadequate as I am, I assay not…. The residence of General Washington is in Broad Way, and the edifice which he occupies, presents a superb Front — The drawing room, and the apartments of which we had a view are lofty, and magnificently spacious — the Furniture is rich, but it doth not surpass what I have before seen — The upper end of the drawing room is pierced, with three glass doors, which open into a handsome Balcony commanding an extensive view of the Hudson interspersed with beautiful Islands, and washing, at the opposite point, the Jersey shore — In this Balcony Mr Murray was honoured by a tete a tete with our illustrious Chief, in this Balcony, after we had taken tea, Mrs Washington requested we would walk....

Judith alerts Mary Turner Sargent that John is unwell, exhausted from too many days of traveling and preaching.

Letter 791 To Mrs Sargent —
Norwich September 12th 1790

... My mind is at this moment very much depressed — your gentle spirit will, I dare believe swell a sigh, for in the bosom which goodness bosoms over, the angel pity loves to dwell — Mr Murray is ill — very ill [—] when I closed my journal of yesterday, I indulged a hope that his complaints would pass off — but they are this morning returned, with some symptoms that are truly alarming — you will find in my account of yesterday, that immediately upon his reaching this place, he retired to his bed, continuing there until the evening, when he was enabled to present himself to his expecting friends — I was elated, and upon the wings of buoyant hope I was serenely borne — but this morning the clouds gather — It is really affecting — crouds fill the house, The church doors are thrown open, and they were assured that those hallowed walls, would this day echo the glad tidings of redemption — But, for us, our circumstances might have been much worse. We are in the hospitable Mansion of Doctor Turner — Connecticut doth not produce a more eminent Physician — his benevolence is unquestionable — His Lady and family are precisely what I would wish them — Well then I will essay to pierce the dun obscure, and once more endeavour to bask beneath the sunny beams of genial hope

Judith is relieved to report to Mary Turner Sargent that John has recovered. But apparently preaching one moment, and returning to his sickbed the next, was not an unusual pattern of behavior for John.

Letter 792 To the Same
New London September 15. 1790

... Quitting you last sunday, I endeavoured in vain to tranquilize my bosom — That balmy Hope, which I had presumed to arrogate, became regardless of my advances, and pervading glooms continued to enwrap my soul — Until twelve O clock every appearance was against me, when a medicine skillfully administered, began its salutary operation — Mr Murray declared himself better, much better, and avowed a resolution to answer the expectations of the people, by meeting them in the afternoon — I have often known him to pass from his bed to the church, and to return to it again immediately after the close of the service, and I have learned not to remonstrate — The effort last sunday, was manifestly advantageous; the spirits, and the health of my husband, were surprisingly restored — and my satisfaction was proportioned to my previous inquietude....

Judith and John are finally returning home to Gloucester. John evidently understands Judith's attachment to her "native state" and to her family.

Letter 805 to my Father and Mother,
State of Massachusetts Taunton October 16 1790
Saturday Evening

... And now my best, my parental friends we have attained the bounds of our native state — I speak, you will observe in the plural — for Mr Murray obligingly tender, unites so effectually in my hopes, my fears, and my wishes, as to render it hardly possibl[e] to recur to the circumstance of his not being a native of that remote spot, which gave me birth — We expect to reach Boston the last of next week — The ensuing sunday must of necessity be devoted to the congregation in that Metropolis — but upon the following Monday, with hearts beating with expectation, we shall commence the last, and most pleasing stage of our journey, and if the weather corresponds with our wishes, tuesday noon, will produce us once more in Gloucester....

After over a year of silence, Judith has finally heard from her brother Winthrop. From what Judith wrote in Letter 807, he seems to have relented in his opposition to John.

Letter 807 To my Eldest Brother
Boston October 24th 1790

With unequaled joy, I once more recognize the hand writing of a beloved brother — of a brother, whom my agitated mind, represented as forever lost to me, as forever estranged from all the sweet, and social offices of fraternal love....

John is traveling again, and Judith confesses how much she enjoyed his daily company during their recent journey together. She also continues to mourn the loss of their baby.

Letter 120
Gloucester November 6th 1790

... I do not know, my Love, in what light [your] absence may appear to you, but I confess that it is a very formidable foe to my peace — Upon our late tour to Philadelphia, constantly with you for six pleasing months, the returning evening, which hath been accustomed to present you, now materially add to the cloud, which fate hath ordained, a heavy, and melancholy weight, upon the life which for one little period, enjoyed as much, as mortally could give ... for me — alas for me! happiness and your Constantia have long since shook hands — It was upon the fifth day of August, 1789 that I bid adieu to the charming fair — she took her flight from my bosom in the form of an infant Cherub, and I am sometimes ready to think, that I shall not again meet even her semblance, upon this side the celestial abodes.... I wish you could make it convenient to let me know on what day you purpose to return to Gloucester, because as you will not come alone, it may, and undoubtedly will, be useful to make some few arrangements — The letters that you wish me to forward are not yet written, but tomorrow's sun, agreeably to your wishes, shall see me commence this business — would it were in my power to gratify every wish of your soul — but at least I can boast of an unalterable attachment, of an unabating affection for you — at least I can boast that I am your friend, your wedded friend nor have I ever written to you a line, with a heart glowing with a more sincere, and tender Love, then at this moment swells the bosom of your faithful, although sorrowing Constantia —

The Letters

Traveling during New England winters could be treacherous. Judith always feared for John's safety during the "winter months," telling him to be safe rather than risk a much-desired reconciliation.

Letter 121
Gloucester January 1st 1791
Saturday Night

What shocking, shocking weather [—] Oh that I could be assured you were safe housed, during this inclement season, in some hospitable dwelling, Many have lost their lives in passing from one neighbor to another [—] If you have attempted to go to your lodgings — what may have been the consequence!! but surely no one would suffer you to go out upon such a night — I am solitary, melancholy, and distressed — yet it would be madness in you to brave this storm — but I fly reflection — I will give up my pen — I will hope the best —

This is an early and amusing indication that John had difficulty managing money. Judith tended to take the lead on financial matters, as she does here.

Letter 123
Gloucester January 29th 1791

Your attention to me, my dear, when ever I am called to mourn your absence, from the first moment of our acquaintance, hath been uniformly, and pleasingly marked, hath ever been unremittedly tender, and by consequence I regard the proof, which was this evening presented me on my return from my Father's, where I tarried untill ten O'clock, but as a continuation of your wonted indulgence — Accept, my best friend, my sincere thanks, and believe that I can never be ungrateful — the quills are excellent, and they came very opportunely.... One thing I ask, that you will purchase for your self a genteel outside garment — half the money for which you sold your horse, will certainly procure it, and you ought surely to allow your self the decencies of life — since I am upon this subject ... suffer me to add, that I regret that you are not more uniformly attentive to your interest — at times you appear anxious, and sufficiently economical — but you seem to have no fixed plan — If you have an account open with Mr R— or any other person, let me conjure you to adjust such accounts — and if there are arrearages, let us think of some method of discharging them.... Now, my dear, if you do not return with a resolution to sift this business, I shall think it will be incontrovertible proof, that you are in deed, and in fact, remarkably deficient, in worldly wisdom — Having thus ended my lecture, and the night being pretty far advanced, I will only add — that I wish you the most peaceful, salutary slumbers and that I am &c &c

The Boston Universalists are pressing John to accept their offer to become their full-time minister. Judith decides she will go along with whatever decision he makes. Initially, John arranged to divide his time between Gloucester and Boston and serve both congregations.

Letter 125
Boston March 11th 1791

... I trust that you will think it advisable to call your friends together, and to obtain from them a fair, and candid hearing of your cause, with some fixed resolution in regard to your future establishment — It is certainly time that we came to some conclusion.... I should certainly wish for a residence in my native place — but if this must not be — my mind shall bend, accommodating itself to exigencies which may be unavoidable....

Nothing like a little teasing to spice up a marriage. One wonders who "Mr T—" was!

Letter 126
Boston March 14th 1791

... By the way — Do you know that Mr T— hath fallen violently in Love with me?

John has been worried about Judith's physical well-being, and she longs for his return.

Letter 128
Gloucester May 24th 1791

Yes, I have been really ill — but I write now with my own hand, to convince you that I am indeed, and in truth, greatly relieved — So, my poor apprehensive friend, you may set your anxious mind at ease.... I received your kind letters by Mr Hall, and I once more pronounce you the best of men — I know that I am not enough sensible of the worth of the husband, whom a benignant God hath given me ... let me see you as soon as your duties will permit. Let me see you with a smiling countenance, and a tranquil mind — and I will then love you better than any body else in this world forever, and ever — that is if memory is continued so long — Farewell, I am your ever tender, ever faithful Constantia —

After many weeks of confinement, Judith has recovered enough to write to John about how pleased she is with her choice of a husband.

Letter 129
Gloucester Morning of Saturday June 18th 1791

I am, upon this charming morning, the daughter of hope — I quit my bed, refreshed by a night of the sweetest slumbers — I seat my self in my chair — I can almost say that I am without pain — that I am surprisingly relieved is certain, and I hasten to communicate to my best friend, intelligence which I doubt not will diffuse over his manly bosom, the most pleasurable glow. Right glad am I, that the husband whom God hath given me is so wholly mine, that his attachment to me is entire, and that I can at all times confidently assure my self, that a knowledge of my welfare, cannot fail of yielding him the sincerest pleasure

John is on his way home, and Judith's "heart gladdens."

Letter 131
Gloucester July 25th 1791

The week which is to mark your return to Gloucester, once more opens upon me — my heart gladdens at its approach, that heart which glows with love and friendship for thee — for thou art in truth far dearer to my soul, than it is in the power of language to describe — Although I wrote to you yesterday by Mr G— I cannot forbear indulging myself by penning an additional line for the stage — it will advertise you that I have written, it will apprize you of my continued health, and it will acknowledge the receipt of yours by Captain L— Was you my Love aware how alarmingly you expressed yourself in your last — I wish you had informed me from what source the sufferings of which you complain proceeded — but you seem not, in the moment of writing, to have recollected the pain of suspense, or how wide a [departure] when cut by fertile imagination, are the territories of conjecture — yet having of late acquired a habit of resolving every thing into that Vortex, <u>self</u> I impute your distresses to a concern for me, and I am by this consideration eased of many apprehensions which would otherwise torment my mind.... I would scribble on, but the stage hath this moment passed — Do we not have charming weather — May God forever bless you —

Judith's recent "illness," described here, was, in fact, a successful pregnancy. On August 22, at the age of forty-one, Judith gave birth to Julia Maria Murray. Mother and daughter had a difficult time of it, and neither one would be terribly well again. Still, Judith had realized her greatest desire. In this letter, Judith tells John she hopes fatherhood will keep him at home more often.

Letter 132
Gloucester November 4th 1791

The last time — near four months since — that I penned a letter to my best friend, I was struggling for that composure which the prospect then opening to my views, was but ill calculated to bestow — now, what a blissful reverse — I press my lovely infant to my transported bosom, and I am ready to characterize myself the happiest of Women — upwards of two months has the little voyager been to me an exhaustless source of felicity, nor can I ever be satisfied, with contemplating the heavenly innocence of her Cherubic countenance [—] Yet, that the avenues to pain are still unbarred, I yesterday feelingly experienced — No sooner had you left me, then the descending storm commenced, and I am really grieved at heart — The obligation which is upon you to take these winter journeys is truly vexatious, nay, seriously distressing — would that we could hit upon some expedient to obviate this difficulty — Yet, if we were thus fortunate, would not some fresh subject for regret, in some unknown cause originate? doubtless it is best, in whatever state we are in, to be therewith content — yet how difficult a lesson to learn — We have received much from the hand of our common parent — this we acknowledge, and yet, ungrateful as we are, we become peevish, that the grant of any of our wishes are denied us! Every day encreases the captivating charms of our little Girl — well, this is to me inexpressibly pleasing — but then again I am ready to murmur, that her Father cannot every day watch her gradual improvement — It is true that her Father still lives — that I am still happy in the husband of my choice while many a female has to mourn through life her widowed hours and to bedew the cheeks of her fatherless offspring with the tears of anguish — The probability is that a few days will restore to me the parent and the husband and possibly too these short absences may encrease his zest for his little home — yet, perverse as I am, I have dared to lift even to the throne of the Almighty a repining, a guilty eye and because every circumstance corresponds not exactly with my wayward wishes I tacitly arraign the wisdom of God! Is this true — am I thus rebellious mortal? A moments reflection assures me that I am! A moments reflection originates a train of ideas and I throw by the pen to weigh, ponder and arrange.

At long last, thanks to John, Judith is a "happy mother."

Letter 419 — To my Mother
Boston September 22d 1791

... Well my Mamma — how good is the God with whom we have to do — hardly for a single moment did I dare to indulge a hope of the blessing which is now in my possession — I stand amazed at the event which hath taken place — at times I can hardly believe myself awake, and I am fearful that the coming moment will arouse me from my dream of happiness — yet when I press my child to my bosom — when her infant form is with each returning morning presented to my view — surely I cry this is substantial enjoyment — surely, this is real felicity — my wishes are at length crowned with fruition, and I am now indeed a happy Mother....

Judith tells their friend Mrs. Woodrow about Julia Maria's first words and first steps.

Letter 432 To Mrs W— of Philadelphia
Gloucester 13th of June 1782

... The tender appellations Papa, and Mamma, already trembles upon the infant tongue of my daughter — by the assistance of a finger, which she grasps for safety, she can go all over the house and — and — in short she is a very lovely child....

During a new indispostion, John is still an "enraptured father."

Letter 444 To Mrs W— of Philadelphia
Gloucester March 8th 1793

... I had hoped to have made a journey to Philadelphia the coming May, but the engagements of Mr M— are of such a nature, that I am apprehensive it will be impossible for him to gratify me in this respect — he is at present very unwell, but I persuade my self that the approaching renovating season will fan the vital flame, and by renewing the lamp of life, restore the health and spirits of him, on whom my dearest earthly hopes depend — yes indeed, Mr M— is a truly enraptured Father, and, precisely as you suppose, tears of luxuriant pleasure, often chase each other down his cheeks, our daughter still continues a healthy and truly desirable child, the morn of life is always pleasing....

John is very sick, and Judith contemplates the challenges she would face in the event of his death. She is frustrated that current laws and customs prevent women from earning and managing their own money—a regular theme in the essays she wrote from 1790-8 in the Massachusetts Magazine *and her three-volume book,* The Gleaner.

Letter 445 To Maria
Gloucester March 16 1793

... Mr M— hath been, ever since his return from Boston, really ill, his health hath been for some time apparently declining, and the probability is that the lamp of life is by the uncommon exertions which he hath unintermitedly made, may be nearly exhausted; should he be thus prematurely summoned to receive the reward of labors, which have been almost uninterrupted, I shall not only be called to witness a termination of that social intercourse with which I have so long been indulged, I shall not only behold the tender friend, in whose bosom I could repose my joys, and sorrows forever torn from my view; the cutting of this source of refined delight, however distressing, will not be the only cause of my perturbed regrets, all my plans, and the hopes that I had formed for her, for whose dear sake I would brave the worst of horror, will be buried in the grave of him, to whom she owes her being! Scanty as is our income, I make it a rule to lay by every week a trifle of that little, in order to defray the expenses of an education, which from the result of our most sober deliberations, we have elected as the most eligible for our child, but when Mr M— pays the great debt of nature, every pecuniary emolument that moment ceases

— reservations are no more, and we become the needy dependants, upon caprices which chance may render most unpropitious — Would it were the custom to qualify Women for exertions, which would enable them to bring forward, even in a state of widowhood, the children whom they had introduced into being — but, alas! by the kind of instruction to which we are limited, we are in many respects unwarrantably degraded, and we are left, in every situation, to struggle with all the mortifications incident to artificial imbecility....

The Murrays' move to Boston is imminent while John searches for a residence. While Judith will miss Gloucester she realizes that Boston is closer to her native place than Philadelphia.

Letter 484 To Maria
Glo[u]cester July 14th 1794

... I thank you for the interest you take in our establishment in Boston [—] our present situation is indeed gloomy, and embarrassing [—] Mr M— despairs of obtaining a house — I do not know what will be the consequence — but, let me whisper my Friend — I am suspicious that these difficulties, which we find it impossible to surmount, in our pursuit of a residence in Boston will terminate in fixing us in Philadelphia — In the City of Philadelphia a very genteel house hath been offered us rent free — during the life of Mr M— and, added to this, his income would be beyond its present amount — Let this intimation be considered in confidence....

The Murray family has moved to Franklin Place in Boston. A British-style curved row of brick townhouses built by the renowned Boston architect Charles Bulfinch, Franklin Place was one of the most fashionable addresses in Boston and within easy walking distance of the Universalist meetinghouse in the North End. Judith immediately wrote to relatives and friends urging them to visit. Judith and John always enjoyed hosting house guests, especially young people. Writing to Dorcas Babson Sargent in Hampstead, New Hampshire, Judith encourages Dorcas to let her children visit soon. In fact, over the years, these young cousins were regular visitors to Franklin Place.

The Letters

Letter 490 To Mrs S—
Boston Franklin Place September 19th 1794

... For me, I have to say that beds, tables, chairs, looking glasses, pictures &c. &c. having all received their respective stations — we begin to be a little at leisure, and we are earnestly looking out for the promised evening when you will pop in upon us, in the way which you permitted us to hope — Our situation is pleasing, and even rural, our apartments are convenient, and we shall enjoy every privilege with a higher zest if we can be permitted to partake them with our friends — The young ladies I hope will remember their promise of which I shall expect the fulfillment with anticipated satisfaction — I shall with pleasure take care of the parcel you mentioned for Charles, and both he and his brothers — will ever be received by me with sincere affection. Mr Murray unites with me in tender salutations — and I am with affectionate esteem ever yours

One Sunday morning in church, John bends the rules of conduct to present Judith with long-awaited letters from her brother Winthrop.

Letter 160
Franklin Place May 30 1795

How cheering in the gladsome ways of the morning after a night draped in uncertainty, and apprehension. Delightful is the beam of intelligence, and right precious is the voice of health from a far Country — Yesterday was Sunday, and I presented myself in the house devoted to the worship of our God [.] Mr Murray, previous to the communion service, descended from the pulpit, he approached our pew — I was astonished at a movement so unusual — but he could not suspend the pleasure he proposed to himself in relieving a heart which he knew had been so long burdened — A friend on his way to Church, had given him yours of the 30th of March — and he put the letter into my hand. I recognized the well known characters of my Brother, and my soul was at peace

Judith entertains Epes and Dorcas Babson Sargent's children in Hampstead with a glimpse of the Murrays' family life with four-year-old Julia Maria. Julia Maria's father, whose flowers and vegetables she mentions, was an avid gardener from a very young age in England.

The Letters

Letter 529
To the children at Hampstead
Boston Franklin Place June 22d 1795

My dear young Friends

Julia Maria, you know, cannot write — I wish she could — it will give your Aunt Murray great pleasure that she should be fond of her Cousins Epes and Dorcas and that she should be so good a girl as to deserve their love in return — I hope you will write above a hundred letters to each other, and that every letter will be better and better [—] Meantime, the paper is before me, and she shall speak for herself — Come hither Julia Maria — What have you to say to your dear Hampstead friends — mind I shall write down exactly what you say — Here beginneth Julia Maria's letter "You must write down that I will come and see them — you must make a sweet letter just like theirs — you must write down that I am going to send it by the Concord Stage — that is pretty to write down, is it not? I like Boston very well [—] May I say that Mamma? as soon as I write my letter may be they will send us another — Do they know how to write? how fast you write Mamma — Why cant you tell them that I will come to see them — write down to Epes that I should be very glad that Dorcas and Epes would ride clear to Boston to see me — you must write two or three verses down, you must tell them if they will come to see me I will give them something — have you write down just what I told you? now you must tell them that I will come to see them as soon as possible, and bring Mamma with me — you must write that it is a very handsome present that I shall give them — tell them that my Pappa has got a sweet little garden, a very pretty garden indeed, and there is flowers in it — all blown — you must write them word that yesterday, sabbath day, I had some strawberries out of Pappa's garden to eat — there is Sweet Williams in Pappa's garden — but you must write two letters Mamma — write them word that I am sick up chamber because they dont know it — tell them when they come to see me I shall show them all my house — write word how fast it rains to day — write Our Father who art in heaven — well I do not know what else to say" [—] Here endeth all that I can get from the little Prattler — but, trust me, my sweet Cousins, she is an affectionate little creature, and she will love you very dearly, and that both she and her Mamma, will rejoice to see you in Boston — I am your sincerely attached relation, and friend, etc.

The Letters

Disease in Boston keeps John busy presiding over funeral services.

Letter 533 To my Sister E—
Boston Franklin Place July 24th 1795

... It is indeed very sickly in Town at present, a contagious fever, and putrid sore throat, are spreading devastation — there is hardly a day on which Mr Murray is not summoned to attend a funeral, and the progress of the disorder is generally very rapid, particularly among children, and young persons....

John's congregation has voted to send him to the General Convention of Universalists in Vermont. Meanwhile, Judith is increasingly uneasy about their finances and Julia Maria's future.

Letter 538 To Mr S
Boston Franklin Place August 31st 1795

... my wishes are frustrated by a vote of our congregation, which is a mandate for the departure of Mr Murray to the state of Vermont — to which place he will soon commence his journey, and he will be absent about one month.... you are kind enough to express a wish to be informed of every circumstance by which we are affected whether well, or ill — know then, my dear Friend, that in consideration of the advanced price of the necessaries of life — the congregation to which Mr Murray administers, have unanimously voted him an addition of twenty shillings per week, to the five pounds which he has been accustomed to receive, and they have also agreed to procure for him twenty cord of wood for the present year — so far — so good — but on the other hand our rent is raised from eighty, to one hundred pound per year — you will see, however, that the balance is in our favour ... and, if Mr Murray is continued to his family, my patrimony, what ever it may be, will serve as a provision for my child....

John returns home from Vermont with a tumor in his side.

Letter 543 To my Sister E
Boston Franklin Place October 30th 1795

... It is my determination to come to Gloucester on Thursday ... that Mr Murray shall be able to beguile the time of my absence by visiting his friends but God only knows whether this will ever happen — Doctor

Lloyd is apprehensive for his life — a mortification has actually taken place and it is with difficulty that he sets up while his bed is made — his journey hath been attended with truly melancholy effects — Well — Well the last hour will arise upon me Also — I can no more always be your affectionate Sister —

In 1795, Judith's first play, The Medium, or Happy Tea-Party *(later renamed* The Medium, or Virtue Triumphant*), was performed at the Boston Theatre on Federal Street, making Judith the first American playwright to be so honored. Her second comedic play,* The Traveller Returned, *was produced in 1796. Initially, Judith kept her playwrighting secret from John, hoping to prevent his "agitation" if her plays were rejected. But her second comedy experienced production delays, and Judith had to confide in John after all. He immediately found a way to help her, as Judith explains here to Epes Sargent.*

Letter 555 To Mr S—
Boston Franklin Place January 9th 1796

Mr Murray has given you, my dear Sir, a wrong idea — The Medium has not received a new cast — and being fully satisfied with your approbation, I am confident that I shall in future attempt an alteration — Yet I have been much elated only, as it should seem, to give me an opportunity of tasting the poignancy of disappointment — Before I had received your remarks on the Medium, I had written another Comedy which I entitled The Traveller Returned — This play was calculated with a view to stage effect, and its production was a profound secret even to Mr Murray…. The play was put into Rehearsal, and was published for presentation, but before the arrival of the appointed evening, the Manager received the to him distressing intelligence that he was dispossessed of the Theatre — he became totally deranged, and although engaged to take the part of Rambleton, quiting Newport, in the moment, he immediately set of for Boston, the company was disperced and my hopes in my original plan entirely lost — for a long time, however, I cherished an expectation that the Manager would be reinstated, or that a coalition with Col Tyler would be produced, and under this persuasion I was to confine my anxiety to my own bosom — for it hath ever been my wish to conceal from Mr Murray, every thing which can agitate, or in other words whatever is involved in uncertainty. But all prospects, of a reconciliation, or a reinstatement, at length vanishing, I unbosomed my self to my husband — you will not doubt that he partook my mortification — he did so — but he was, according to custom, charmed with my piece — he advised me to apply immediately to Mr & Mrs Morton, and to solicit, under a seal of secrecy their patronage — Thus then I am at present circumstanced....

In a letter to Anna Parsons Sargent, we learn that John has presided over a wedding ceremony while his proud wife looked on.

Letter 557 To the same
Boston Franklin Place February 12th 1796

... Mr Murray received the vows of the affirmed Lovers in a manner peculiarly animated — his addresses to the throne of grace in their behalf, were uncommonly elegant, and fervid, and he pronounced the benediction in a voice, meliorated by affection, and elevated by devout sincerity — need I say, that I was not, in that solemn moment, ashamed of my husband — The conversation, after the ceremony had passed, took a general turn, and Turkeys, hams, tongues, Plumb Cake, Cheese, Punch, and Wine, in great abundance, succeeded in course....

In 1794, when Judith first moved to Boston, she was approached by the editor of The Federal Orrery, *one of Boston's weekly newspapers, to publish a column. She submitted five entries of "The Reaper" before refusing to send more and telling Thomas Paine, the publisher (not the patriot) that his editing was excessive and insulting. For the next few years, Paine used his newspaper to criticize Judith's work and accuse John of writing her plays which caused the Murrays personal and public embarrassment.*

Letter 563 To my Sister E—
Boston Franklin Place March 28th 1796

Mr Paine, as you have doubtless seen by the papers, has used me cruelly — his malice in regard to Mr M— and myself, has been wholly unprovoked — nor can I at all account for the illiberal abuse which he has so copiously produced from his pen. Many persons insist that he is urged by envy, that he is offended by the uncommon applause with which the Traveller Returned was received, and that having it in contemplation to produce upon the stage a Play of his own, he conceives that I have monopolized to great a share of that praise, which is due only to his superior abilities — However, I, myself, do not admit this explanation [—] I will confess to you, my dear, that I am deeply wounded — I am not accustomed to disregard the opinion of the world, and although it is a general observation, that his malice will defeat itself and that he will be incapable of injuring me in this Town — yet his papers travel far, and wide, and there is no saying what conclusions may obtain in many minds.... Mean time, I am terrified by what Paine may yet achieve — finding he had publicly charged Mr M— with falsehood, I wrote to him, informing him that my address was not intended for the public eye, but simply for his private information, and to prevent further misrepresentation — This billet he declares shall make its appearance in his Orrery, and, if he should publish it entire, I shall have nothing to fear — but the mischief that he will select such parts as suit his purpose, and make them up in a manner which will not fail of making me ridiculous — You will judge, my dear, that, thus circumstanced, the situation of my mind must be truly perturbed....

Thomas Paine's bizarre behavior continues, as Judith explains to Epes Sargent. Judith even had reason to fear for John's safety one night, and was forced to venture out late in the evening to find him. She could "command no language" to describe her anguish.

Letter 564 To Mr S—
Boston Franklin Place April 2d 1796
... My feelings in the course of the news paper altercation, and as often as I reflect thereon, are beyond expression painful — To behold the Man, to whom I am united by indesoluable ties, the Father of my child, of the rectitude of whose life I am hourly witness — to behold him once more dragged to public view, with the opprobrious charge of falsehood, so unjustly affixed to his name, to observe all this, and to conceive of myself as some sort the cause, was productive of more heartfelt anguish, than I had conceived was yet in store for me. There is one circumstance, which marks the conduct of Mr Paine with peculiar inhumanity — Two days before the Traveller Returned was presented, I myself informed him, while he was, in all the freedom of apparent friendship, seated by our fire side, that it was my opinion, if Mr Murray's congregation were prevailed upon to believe he had written a play it would totally ruin his interest among them — Mr Paine never supposed Mr Murray the Author of The Traveller Returned — I have strong reason to believe he well knew from whence the production proceeded. What hath originated his rancour I pretend

not even to conjecture — It has been said that he has three plays ready for presentation, and it hath been conceived the indignation which he has manifested, was occasioned by the favorable reception given to a piece, which he supposed the offspring of inferior abilities, imagining that the applause, which ought to be reserved as the reward of his superior talents, had been thus monopolized, or forestalled — I, however, am not a convert to this opinion — But whatever is his motive he hath inflicted upon me much heartfelt sorrow — he accosted Mr Murray, on the afternoon previous to our periodical lecture, at the door of our dwelling, in a very insulting way — throwing out some ambiguous words, in the form of a threat! I was then confined to my chamber with my daughter, who was ill with the measles — Mr M— was necessitated to attend church — Mr Paine boards in the home of Mr Wallach, who has under his command a number of soldiers — it is believed that there is no action however atrocious, which Mr Paine would not attempt, provided he was sure of personal safety — for from the time of his patiently submitting to be horse whiped by the son of Doctor Jarvis in State Street, his character hath received the indelible stamp of cowardice — but I knew not what masked Man might be prevailed on to attempt upon Mr Murray, who still continues obnoxious to many individuals — I continued in agonies untill his return from church which was not till eleven in the evening — but this was not enough [—] Mr M— went out the ensuing morning, at eight O'clock, he had intended to have returned immediately — but those attentions which he was necessitated to pay to many sick friends, and others of his congregation, unexpectedly detained him — not impressed by those frightful apprehensions which tortured my bosom, he neglected to apprize me of his movements, and I neither saw, nor heard of him again, untill near twelve o'clock at night! The day wore gloomily away — when the solitary candle was light for the evening, my spirit seemed to die within me — scarcely could I draw up a breath [—] When the clamorous bells proclaimed the hour of nine — but what were my sensations when the clocks from the neighboring steeples announced ten, and eleven — and no husband!!! — I can command no language which is sufficiently comprehensive to describe the anguish of my spirit — We sallied forth in quest of our Wanderer — but this, in this Town of Boston, without a male Protector, was a perilous enterprize, and where to direct our steps we knew not — Fortunately, however, we had not proceeded far, when we met the object of our care, returning home, as tranquil, as integrity, and an unconsciousness of having given occasion of sorrow — could render him — his cheerful greetings banished our apprehensions for the night, but for many succeeding days they returned with more or less force, as the situation of my mind assumed a perturbed, or placid aspect....

John is off again, she tells Winthrop.

Letter 184
Gloucester October 13th 1796
... Mr M— too has been absent from this Metropolis on a visit to Portland....

Judith contemplates publishing her letters and allowing the Reverend Robert Redding to reissue The Gleaner *in England. John has an accurate perception of his wife's motives!*

Letter 598 To the Reverend Robert Redding Truro England
Boston Franklin Place December 14th 179[6]
... I should my dear Sir find a superior pleasure in presenting you the letters written to my beloved parents, which you have done me the honor to request, did I not contemplate, as leisure may permit, the copying [of] them with some degree of accuracy, as a legacy for my daughter: my manuscripts are multiplied, Mr M— says I am ambitious of shining as an Author, I need not add that Mr M— has penetration, and perhaps my ardor in the pursuit of fame, is unwarrantably fervid. With regard to publishing my letters, I do not possess the means, if I did, I have thought that letters addressed to private individuals, should be preceded by a production which may announce, and give a degree of eclat, or importance to the Author: I have flattered myself the Gleaner would produce this effect....

The developers of Franklin Place lost most of their money on the venture. For a while, it was unclear what would happen to the building's residents. Luckily, Judith confides to Epes Sargent, she and John were able to borrow enough funds to purchase their apartment. I suspect that "Mrs S— of G—" is Anna Parsons Sargent, Judith's sister-in-law and the wife of her brother Fitz William. Judith and John had borrowed money from them before, and in Fitz William's absence during one of his frequent ocean voyages Anna might very well have handled such a transaction.

Letter 629 To Mr S— and Lady
Boston Franklin Place March 14th 1797

... The business which caused us so much anxiety is now brought to an issue, a legal division of the property in Franklin Place is obtained, Mr M— is secured in the peaceable possession of the tenement we now inhabit, and he is to pay for the three remaining shares thereof, twenty six hundred, and twenty-five dollars — this money we are to take up from Mrs S— of G— for the use of which we are to pay annually six percent, placing in her hands a mortgage deed of the house, with a policy of insurance, and we have liberty to reduce the original sum every six months.

Judith's brother Winthrop had by now removed to the Northwest Territory where he served as secretary of the Ohio Company, the group of investors who expanded the country to the west. With regular accounts of "Indian" attacks reported in the local newspapers, Judith feared for his life. In this letter, we learn that Winthrop has told Judith about his illegitimate daughter, Caroline Augusta, his "little Cherub." Winthrop wanted Judith to raise and educate her in Boston. Naturally, John needed to agree to this plan as well, which he did.

Letter 195
Boston Franklin Place August 1st 1797

... I must confess I should view with pain any circumstance which rendered you finally stationary upon the banks of the Ohio. May your contemplated ascension of the River, prove pleasurable, and advantageous, both to yourself and the people of those counties, whose boundaries you are to describe — May the little Cherub you will visit, originate in your bosom those transports, which sacred Nature can alone bestow — and which render so delightful the duties she imposes — if your resolution in regard to the dear child, may place her in the arms of your sister, my satisfaction will be exquisite — My duty, as a Wife, rendering it necessary I should, upon every important occasion in which he may be essentially concerned — consult my husband — it became incumbant upon me to name the lovely stranger to Mr M— to him therefore, and to him only have I announced the birth, and my communication hath been made under seal of the strictest secrecy — he is perfectly with me in sentiment [—] he wishes, passionately wishes, she may prove a sister to our daughter [—] he presses me to be importunate with you upon this subject, and I repeat that she shall come into this house under whatever name, or upon whatever conditions, shall best accord with your feelings, and, while I continue in this abode of mortality, I will discharge to her, in every respect the duties of a Mother....

While John was away in Portland, Maine, Judith wrote to the Boston Universalists to plead for John's salary. This won't be the first time. Despite their sumptuous residence at Franklin Place, Judith and John struggled to make ends meet. At one point, described here, John told Judith to stay in Gloucester. He literally could not afford to support her.

Letter 678 To Mr J. G—
Gloucester September 5th 179[7]

Respected Sir

I persuade myself that the subject of this address will plead its apology — Involved in a situation, which gloomy apprehension, in the most melancholy moments of conjecture, never admitted as possible, I feel impelled to make application to a person, whose benevolence I have experienced, and whose acts of kindness to me have been most obligingly repeated. When I quitted my native place, where our situation was in many respects eligible, I confidently believed that as long as it should please heaven to bless me by a continuance of the life of my husband, I did bid adieu to uncertainty, in regard to pecuniary aid, and that an easy competency would be the coeval of his abode in mortality. Reflections upon the ability, and punctuality of our Boston friends, hushed my every fear, and futurity arose grateful to my imagination, nor was it untill last may, that I admitted a possibility of my expectations being frustrated.

Mr Murray, willing to divest himself of embarrassing attentions, consigned to me the care of our little property, and the pleasure I derived, upon every revolving week, from appropriating the stated stipend, in a manner which should answer our various exigencies, none but those who are attached to order, will conceive — But since the above mentioned period — alas! alas! how hath the scene been changed — debts have accumulated upon us — we are deeply in arrears, and we cannot determine whether or not our expenses have out run our income — Once, my dear Sir, in connexion with a man of sorrow, I was doomed to drag the Debtor's lengthening chain — and hence perhaps proceeds the horror with which I shrink from the most remote resemblance of my former misfortunes. Our cares are not confined to our immediate family — Mr M— has a Mother, who is aged, and infirm, and precipitated by a state of widowhood, from that independence, in the gift of competency, that marked her better days [—] she has long received her sole support from her two sons — My husband's brother, with whom our parent resides, has a large and still encreasing family, and his circumstances are narrow — we are in the habit of making remittances to this dear, and worthy Mother; and we have been particularly careful that supplies should reach her in season to render cheerful her Christmas holydays — but if our affairs are not adjusted, the ships must sail this Autumn without a filial memento!! The past summer has been dreadfully embittered — Mr M— has marked each evening by his sighs, deeply lamenting that after spending his prime of life in speaking peace to an extensive Continent, he should be doomed in the Autumn of his days to suffer want, or supply his exigencies by borrowing, which last expedient, he has been absolutely necessitated to adopt.

I have assayed to soothe the mind of my husband, by pointing his views to better days — to a period when things would revert to their accustomed order, but I have seldom been successful, and indulging a melancholy despondency, he has looked for relief only from his departure out of time!!

It is true we are the nominal Proprietors of the house in which we live but besides that this will not supply our board with provision, and that only a part of this house has been paid for by interest accruing to me, from the Estate of my Father the whole tenement is mortgaged as security for money taken up to purchase the remaining moiety, nor have we yet been able to appropriate a shilling, toward paying even the interest of that sum, which will in a very few weeks be due — and in addition to these considerations, Mr M conceiving that while he has health, he ought to support his family, refuses to accept the little pittance arising from my patrimonial inheritance, which he considers as a sacred deposit reserved as the source of calamitous exigencies, or for the emolument of that infant, whom, his years considered, he may probably leave, at an early period of life, an orphan —

It was but yesterday I received a letter from Mr M— requesting me not to return home, as it was impossible for him, in his present situation, to support his family!! — Judge, my dear Sir, what must be my feelings upon this occasion!! We do not ask from the society additional sums — a punctual fulfillment of the contract made in April that is a regular advance of our weekly stipend — and a payment of arrearages due to us — will supply all our wants and every difficulty will vanish — Or if there is a radical inability to perform stipulations so cheerfully entered into, let information thereof be given, and we will, although with pangful reluctance, again embark upon the wide Ocean of contingencies — We supplicate, Sir, your advice — if you think proper, show this letter to the Committee, of which you are a member — or make whatever representations your unquestioned friendship, and good sense may dictate — Our wishes, our ardent wishes, are to be placed in the situation in which we were, previous to last April or May, and having perfect confidence in your attachment we earnestly solicit your aid —

I am, Sir, with respectful esteem your most obedien[t]
Humble servant
J.S.M.

John's recent ocean voyage to Portland was a life-threatening decision on his part. Judith describes her state of mind to Anna Parsons Sargent.

Letter 691 — To my sister S—
Boston Franklin Place October 20th 1797

Mr Murray is not yet returned — your friendly expressions relative to his journey are like yourself, benignly good — Its commencement was truly distressing — He left Boston upon the 4th instant — the wednesday afternoon preceding the violent storm which you may perhaps recollect — he took passage for Portland in an eastward bound vessel, and as I had been kept awake the preceding night, by a variety of careful attentions, untill the dawn of day, I retired to rest early in the evening with the child — and slept untill between ten, and eleven o clock — When I was roused by a sound resembling the solemn knell by which we mark the departure of our friends, and instantly the bellowing winds with frightful violence shrieked around our dwelling, sleep was banished from my eyes, and quitting my pillow, in an agony beyond description, my bosom became the seat of the most heart affecting apprehension — I passed the night in alternately traversing up and down the apartment, and clasping to my bosom my sleeping infant, whom I addressed as a bereaved, and helpless Orphan — The morning however presented a number of kind friends, who endeavoured to soothe me by the strongest assurances that I had nothing to fear — but both the male, and female relations, of those who had friends on board the same vessel, crouded upon me with looks of terror inquiring if I had heard any tidings, and this circumstance was more than a balance to the well meant effort of those, who took an interest in seeking to calm the tumult in my soul — but no words can delineate the anguish of my spirit, when the Centinel on saturday morning gave information that many vessels eastward bound, were on wednesday night cast away in winter harbor, and a number of lives lost — at noon however my Cousin Henry — dispatched by his Father, as an angel of peace, hastened to me with the tidings that the vessel in which Mr Murray had embarked was seen on friday making her passage to Portland — yet still I rejoiced with fear and trembling, untill tuesday's post brought me a letter written by his own hand, and containing the assurance of his safety — It is true he has suffered much — The vessel was filled with passengers of both sexes — and it was old, and poorly fitted to contend with the horrors of the night — They proceeded however on their way below Bakers Island, when they concluded that perseverance was inevitable destruction and they in the same moment became sensible of the utter impossibility of returning to Boston — yet the result of incredible exertions placed them in Nantasket road, where they rode out the storm, and where with returning day they had the distress of beholding a vessel in their neighbourhood reduced to an entire wreck! — Mr Murray observes that he never before passed such a night — The shrieks of the distressed Women during the swelling of the pityless storm, was indeed truly agonizing — His own individual hardships in such a vessel — and on such a night, will produce him an Invalid through the winter — But peace ingratitude — Surely I have reason to sing of mercy, inmingled with judgment — They continued in Nantasket road untill friday morning, the Captain judging the wind too high to proceed untill that period, and on their arrival in Portland, they were regarded as persons arisen from the dead — I make no apology for engaging your ear upon a subject so near my heart — you are my sister, my affectionate sister — and your tender attachment is abundantly reciprocated, by your truly grateful &c &c

Fever spreads throughout Boston. John must care for his congregation. Judith won't leave his side and risk losing him, which she explains to Anna Parsons Sargent in the following letter.

The Letters

Letter 762 To my sister S—
Boston Franklin Place August 7th 1798

Accept, my dear sister, my grateful thanks for your kind attention to me, evinced in your letter of Thursday last — The progress of the fever, from which you seem to apprehend so much, is neither so rapid, nor so alarming, as is represented — and indeed were it as contagious, and as fatal, as is reported — I should on no consideration leave Boston — for as I cannot take Mr M— with me, the probability would be, that the first intelligence I received relative to him, after my quitting Town would apprize me that he had bid adieu to time — Providence has stationed my husband in this place, and his parochial duties necessarily render him particularly conversant with the sick — he has in no instance declined attending the bed of languishment, and while I cannot but applaud the consistency of his character, in this respect, I am impelled not by propriety, and the dictates of his affection, to continue with him in every hour of danger [—] But, my dear, I am not at present called to any extraordinary effort — the sufferers are, I do assure you, comparatively few, and in no instance has the disorder been communicated by the sick — It is said to originate in a collection of offensive, or putrid substances, contaminating the atmosphere — together with a predisposition in the constitution occasioned by a redundancy of bile — If my information is accurate, Doctor Danforth has not lost a single patient, and many of those who are deceased were the victims of imprudence, rather than the malignancy of the disease — a few days will determine relative to the further progress of the disorder, and I persuade myself I shall soon be permitted to visit Gloucester, divested of those apprehensions, that by corroding the pleasures which I anticipate from my contemplated excursion, would render me a burden to myself, and to my sympathizing friends....

John has apparently persuaded Judith to visit Gloucester as she did every summer. She goes, but plans to return soon despite the lingering fever in Boston.

Letter 774 To Maria
Gloucester September 17th 1798

... your wishes that I may continue in Gloucester untill salubrity is restored to your atmosphere are sufficiently kind — but as the fatal epidemic whose career hath given death to numerous victims, was not the procuring cause of my absence from Boston, neither will its progress delay my return

159

— a part of August and September is the portion of time which I allot to my friends in this place but had any of my near connexions been visited by the virulent invader of our devoted Country, I should have hastened to the chamber of sickness, and of death, nor can I think any place too hazardous where Mr Murray resides....

John tells Judith it is too dangerous for her to return; she should stay in Gloucester. Judith is not at all happy about being so far away from him.

Letter 775 To the same
Gloucester September 24th 1798
... This air my friend is not salubrious — a dysentry of the most mortal description is now prevalent among the children, and I tremble for my daughter — I had determined to return home on fryday next, but I have received a letter from Mr M— urging me to suspend my purpose, and the language which his affectionate anxiety for me has dictated amounts in my view to a prohibition — and while this prohibitory letter remains in force, I am of course stationed to this spot — For my self I have not a single fear — Did the plague, with all the malignancy incident to the fatal disorder, rage in Boston — I should conceive that my duty lead me to the abode of my husband — and duty is a path in which she who would ensure tolerable tranquility, must be careful to be found....

Finally, it is safe for Judith to leave Gloucester for Boston.

Letter 777 To Maria
Gloucester October 1st 1798
... As Mr M— hath withdrawn his prohibition, I should now return home....

Judith and John are happily together again at Franklin Place.

Letter 781 To my Sister E—
Boston Franklin Place October 19th 1798
... I reached home in safety; that I found Franklin Place exactly where I left it — No. 5. standing erect, and guarded on either side, and my good Man immeasurably rejoiced at my return....

The Letters

But only a few weeks later, John is off for Philadelphia.

Letter 785 To my Brother F W—
Boston November 5th 1798
... Early on Monday morning next Mr M— will set out for Philadelphia....

John's visits to Philadelphia kept him away for months at a time.

Letter 791 To Miss E. S. of Hampstead
Franklin Place December 11th 1798
... Mr Murray has been absent, on a tour to Philadelphia, nearly five Weeks....

Julia Maria is very ill from her recurring "throat disorder." Meanwhile, the Universalist congregation is behind in its payments again. One of the reasons John accepted so many invitations to preach outside of Boston was to supplement his income.

Letter 798 To my Sister E—
Boston Franklin Place December 21st 1798
... alas! a rapid succession of events, many of them truly painful, hath totally deranged my views, and rendered me, at times, incapable of the smallest exertion — The illness of my poor Girl, by throwing my domestic arrangements into disorder, gave them an additional claim to my attention, and they necessarily engrossed a large proportion of my time — in this situation, company, which in other circumstances would have contributed largely to my enjoyment became a source of embarrassment, and the neglect of Mr Murray's hearers, in paying those sums which they had pledged their honour to pay, combining with other commanding motives, reduced him to the necessity of taking, at this inclement season of the year, a journey to Philadelphia, and thus was the most pleasing hope I had formed for the winter, unexpectedly cut off, and the whole burden of providing for my family, thrown upon me, with no other assistant than an aged person, whose time of life, and abilities, are barely suited to the common duties of her station....

The Letters

While John was away, Hosea Ballou, a young Universalist preacher, delivered a sermon in John's pulpit that Judith and many other parishioners found objectionable—even blasphemous. Ballou had strayed from traditional Trinitarian Rellyan Universalism, offering a more Unitarian view that caused confusion and dissention within John's congregation. In an unusual role for an eighteenth century woman, Judith found herself explaining Universalist doctrine and defending her husband's views. In this letter, she expresses her anger about Ballou's interference to Epes Sargent, who was himself an ardent Rellyan Universalist.

Letter 800 To Mr S— of Hampstead
Boston Franklin Place January 11th 1799

… I said I was uncertain when Mr Murray would return, and I add that his presence was never more fully necessary — I think he gave you, some time since, in very strong terms, his sentiments of a Mr Ballo, a young Man who is an itinerant preacher. Without assigning motives for the conduct of Mr B— it may suffice to say, that there appeared an entire revolution in his sentiments — I heard him deliver five sermons in Gloucester, the doctrines of which were, in my opinion, strictly correspondent with the genuine truths of christianity — In my letters, written from Gloucester, to Mr Murray, I laboured to remove the unfavourable ideas which he had entertained, and as it was rational to suppose, the mind of a young Man open to conviction, and early susceptible of impressions, I the more easily succeeded, and Mr M— engaged Mr B— to supply his place in his absence, who for a time went on to general satisfaction gaining over the minds of the people a considerable ascendancy — his natural powers appear respectable although their want of cultivation is strikingly apparent. Whether he estimated his influence too highly or whether regardless of consequences he was under the direction of principle I pretend not to determine, but in the afternoon of last sunday he came out with a "Now my heaven I will tell you the truth and let me persuade you not to reject it because it is new — this exordium was followed by the most blasphemous deital discourse I have ever heard from the pulpit…. The weather was extremely cold, and for the advantage of the fire, we pressed to the vestry — My connexion with Mr Murray, pointed me out to the agitated people, and while solicitous for my opinion, they pressed around me, with more warmth, than prudence I asserted that I had never attended a public exhibition of sentiments so deritical and blasphemous — They requested me to name the reprehensible particulars

— the vestry became every moment more thronged, I trembled excessively, my voice faltered, it was with difficulty that I uttered a word, when good Deacon Faxon appearing to my relief, informed me that his sleigh waited to take me home — Some members of the society have since called upon me, to whom I have given copies of the inclosed writing — They inform me, that there are not more than four persons in our connexion, who are not forcibly struck with the unscriptural ideas of Mr Balloo, but it cannot be concealed that these four are influential persons, and, strange as it may seem, they insist that Mr Balloo is exactly in sentiment with Mr Murray! Mean time, the general voice is, that nothing can restore their tranquility but his return....

Judith informs her aunt Lucy Saunders Sargent that John's congregation is in disarray, and no one knows when he will return. Judith has not received a letter from John in weeks.

Letter 808 To Mrs L Sargent of Sullivan
Boston Franklin Place February 4th 1799

... Mr Murray is not yet returned, and it is an addition to my regrets on this account, that his congregation is in a very disarranged state. The young Man who he engaged to supply the pulpit, and in whom he confided, has introduced doctrines which, to the christian ear, sound very much like blasphemy — he denies the perfection of the individual character of the Redeemer! and asserts that his death was not the procuring cause either, of our redemption from misery, or of our eternal life!! — for sentiments so derogatory to the character of the World's Saviour, he was, by a respectable member of our Church, publicly opposed, and immediately dismissed, since which, we have had no public preaching, and the pulpit has already been vacant four sabbaths! — By some strange misconduct, although we receive letters from Mr Murray, ours do not reach him, and he, remaining entirely ignorant of this unfortunate event, while he supposes the people completely satisfied, the more readily yields to the solicitations of his southern friends, who earnestly entreat him to prolong the time of his sojourning among them....

Finally, John arrives home in Boston.

The Letters

Letter 813 To my sister E—
Boston Franklin Place February 26th 1799

... Mr Murray's return, although a much desired event, involves its appropriate cares, as well as pleasures — In short, in short — I have frequently been reduced to the necessity of declaring, that during the course of a long life, there is no want which I have so forcibly, and so invariably experienced, as the want of time....

John is ill again with another painful tumor. Judith warns her sister, Esther, that it is unclear if he will survive.

Letter 827 To my sister E—
Boston Franklin Place
April 17th 1799

Late at night

Depressed in mind, and fatigued in body, by the anxieties, and labours, consequent upon attending the bed of a sick husband, I permit myself the indulgence of inquiring after the health of my dear sister.... Mr Murray has been confined to his bed several days; the effects of repeated colds are now heavy upon him, but his principal distress proceeds from a large tumor under his left arm, from which he endures most exquisite pain, and which we have been endeavouring to reduce, our physician still flatters us that it will be scattered, but I do not look forward without apprehension, and anguish. He was not able to attend meeting on sunday, but he indulges a hope that he may be conveyed thither in a carriage, upon the approaching sabbath — yet, it appears to me that even the effect would be presumptuous — his torture, particularly during the night, is indeed excrutiating.... Good night, my dear, may all good angels guard you — and may God forever bless you....

In another letter to Esther, Judith reports that John insists on preaching despite his lingering illness. Immediately afterward, he returns to his sickbed.

Letter 828 To the same
Boston Franklin Place May 1st 1799

... Mr Murray is indeed very ill, he is confined through the week, altogether to his chamber, and almost wholly to his bed. Upon the last, and upon two sabbath days, he was prevailed upon to suspend his pulpit labours — but last sunday, ill as he was, he was conveyed in a close carriage to church, from whence he returned immediately to his chamber, and to his bed — his sufferings are beyond description — the tumor is neither [distressed], nor does it approach to supperation; it is hard, distinct, and prominent — possibly it is of the scirulus kind! — even his physician admits this idea — my spirit seems to die within me, at the view of a calamity so pregnant with evil; so fatal in consequences!! Yet have I not enjoyed much, and by what right can I plead an exemption from the ills which are incident to humanity....

At last, Judith tells Epes Sargent, John is "restored" after a painful operation.

Letter 832 To Mr S— of Hampstead
Boston Franklin Place June 13th 1799

By the pen of your amiable son, you are, I presume, informed of the progress of a calamity which hath inexpressibly afflicted us. In his faithfully recording page you have traced the pangful days, and nights, which have been appointed for us; his sympathy hath much endeared him to us, and we should regard a separation from virtues, so impressively engaging, as a very distressing event — From the same source you are acquainted that Doctor Lloyd has laid open the absess, that it discharged copiously, and that we flattered ourselves, with having attained the period of our sufferings — But alas! the anguish which hath succeeded is far beyond any thing which he had previously endured, Of all these particulars you are doubtless in possession, and it is at length reserved to me, to announce the more agreeable tidings of returning health, and peace. Mr Murray has got abroad, his spirits charmingly restored, and although he has now an open wound nearly three inches in his side, as this wound is at length in a state of healing, past sorrows [have] taught us to regard this as a very inconsiderable evil....

As a prominent couple, Judith and John were often invited to the homes of leading political, religious, and literary people. In this case, they have visited their friends John and Abigail Adams in Braintree, Massachusetts (now, the Adams National Historical Park in Quincy, Massachusetts).

Letter 838 To Mr S— of Hampstead
Boston Franklin Place July 31st 1799

... Last wednesday, escorted by Mr Murray, I did myself the honour of paying my devoirs to the distinguished patronage whom you mention ... by Mrs Adams, and her illustrious friend, we were received with a degree of cordiality, and condescension, far beyond our merit, or our expectation....

Judith has encouraged John James Sargent, the son of Epes Sargent, to view John as a role model and a source of inspiration. Both Judith and John were very attached to the young man, and enjoyed his company at Franklin Place. Sadly, less than two years after this letter was written, John James became ill in Boston and died in Hampstead at the age of twenty.

Letter 841 To Mr John James S—
Gloucester August 24th 1799

... I am happy that you appear so fully sensible of the value of those views, which through the instrumentality of my best friend, you have received. No reflections can more abundantly enhance the correct, and virtuous pleasures, even of the present scene, than an assured prospect of future, and never ending felicity. you will ever find Mr Murray a real friend — he hath endured much in life; and the retrospect of the past, and anticipation of future misfortunes, frequent arrests that equal flow of cheerfulness, which his natural vivacity would otherwise give him, uniformly to exhibit. "but take him for all, in all, we shall not look upon his like again...."

George Washington's death profoundly affected Americans; Judith and John shared a mutual admiration for the former president. As commander of the armed forces during the Revolutionary War, Washington had supported John at a time when the established clergy considered him a threat. In this letter, Judith describes the Universalists' service for her sister, Esther, and her own emotions.

Letter 869 To my Sister E—
Boston Franklin Place January 18th 1800

... on entering the broad aisle — awed, and softened, by the solemnity of the scene, I melted into tears, my emotions were spontaneous, and nearly ungovernable, and it was with difficulty that I suppressed their audible manifestation [—] Mr Murray assayed to sketch the life of the departed

Chief, but, overwhelmed by his feelings, he was necessitated to say, "And the noble acts which he did, and his greatness, they are not, and cannot be written, for they were very many["] — Mr Murray preserves a strong sense of the favours which, as an individual, he hath received from the beatified deceased — and the confidence reposed in him by the then Commander in Chief, when he appointed him the ecclesiastical guide to three regiments, while other Clergymen were confined to one, can never be forgotten....

Judith confides to Esther that the Murrays' financial "prospects" are increasingly "gloomy."

Letter 881 To my sister E—
Boston Franklin Place March 24 1800

... my pecuniary prospects are at present rather gloomy — we have recently received accounts from Philadelphia, which gives us reason to expect the total loss of our property there — Mr M— finds it extremely difficult, to obtain from his hearers, his customary dues, they are many hundreds of dollars in arrearage to him, and whether they will ever discharge this debt must be regarded as extremely problematical [—] it [is] easy to see, that if they cannot fulfill their contract for last year, they will find it still more difficult to answer the double demand for the present, and Mr Murray will never litigate with them, for his dues — the consequences of their deficiency are, to us, extremely painful, we are necessitated to obtain credit for almost every article which we procure, and the whole of the fuel, which we have consumed during the past winter, is yet unpaid for — Mr Murray has a mother, a very ancient, and worthy woman, who depends almost entirely upon him for support — did he neglect her, he would take rank with those sons who are as the most abhored blots of humanity....

John is unwell again, and Judith is unable to make plans with Mary Turner Sargent or anyone else. Meanwhile, the New York Universalists have offered John an attractive position as their minister.

Billet to Maria Evening of January [26] 1801

... The expectation of meeting you at the Spanish Consul's, invests the prospect with new interest — Motives, similar to those which determined you to accept the invitation, influenced my wishes to join the party; but I have not yet returned an answer — the situation of Mr M— occasions my indecision — he has been hardly able to set up a single hour, since sunday evening last — he is now, however much relieved, and should his indisposition continue to abate, I may be able to give my responses in the affirmative. We had last evening a letter from New York, containing a pressing solicitation to Mr M— to remove to that City, together with an assurance of two thousand dollars per annum, and a positive engagement for prompt, and regular payments — Mr M— hesitates — What are your sentiments upon this, to me, important subject?

John has apparently declined the offer from New York. He is on his way back to Philadelphia where he was always treated well and handsomely paid.

Letter 939 To Miss N. P.
Boston Franklin Place October 19th 1801
... He is now absent on a journey to Philadelphia — I do not expect his return until January....

After John returns from Philadelphia, he falls ill again.

Letter 953 To my sister E—
Boston Franklin Place January 26th 1802
... my head, and hands were never before so increasingly occupied — The situation of Mr Murray's health requires the most critical attention....

Many months later, John appears to have suffered a minor stroke, leaving his writing hand useless. On his behalf, Judith addresses a letter to Eleanor Custis Lewis, George and Martha Washington's granddaughter. She thanks "Nellie" for the lock of Martha's hair she sent upon Martha's death.

Letter 956
To Mrs Lewis Granddaughter of Mrs Washington
Boston Franklin Place February 12th 1802

Madam

Had Mr Murray been less susceptible, or less grateful for your condescending responses, to your petitioning letter, written some weeks since, his acknowledgements had not been thus long delayed — To say truth, his continued ill health seems to envelop in clouds, a mind once

irradiated by uniform cheerfulness, and the warmth of those energies, which lately induced an opinion, that whatever he ardently wished, was certainly attainable, suffers no inconsiderable abatement. Thus, although an irresistible desire to possess a treasure, impelled him to address you, as if astonished at his own presumption, he shrinks from a reiteration, of what he terms temerity, and appealing to a right hand, rendered nearly useless, he pronounces decisively that he ought not again to appear before you upon paper ... he commands me to transmit to you, those assurances of respectful esteem, which are most unquestionably your due — We behold with mingling pride, and pleasure the requested lock of hair....

That spring, John traveled once more to Philadelphia.

Boston Franklin Place
June 15th 1803
... Mr Murray has been absent many weeks, on a tour to Philadelphia....

John has returned, Judith tells Winthrop, and life has returned to normal.

Boston Franklin Place
July 30th 1803
... Mr Murray has returned, we are again alone, our domestic arrangements revert to their accustomed order and I am once more seated at my writing desk....

Judith describes the challenge of taking care of her sick husband to Winthrop and his second wife, Mary McIntosh Williams Sargent.

Boston Franklin Place
Morning of November 21 18[0]3
... Mr Murray has been confined to his chamber, and to his bed, by severe illness, and as this distressing event took place, when my maid Catharine was absent, on a visit to her Gloucester friends, and as I had no other assistant in my domestic duties, and in my attendance in the sick chamber, than my little Girl Sally, who you will recollect is not the very best of all possible Girls, Catharine not returning until the day that Mr M— quitted his chamber, my hours, by consequence, were barely

sufficient for my avocation — Mr M— however is now restored to health, and a recollection of the past enhances the pleasures of the present.... I rejoice greatly that I have at length leisure to pen my responses....

Judith confesses to Winthrop that she is resigned to John's need to travel.

Boston Franklin Place
January 31st 1804
... I thank you, most cordially, for your affectionate congratulations, on Mr Murray's restoration — Heaven seems to have designed him, an itinerant promulgator of the doctrines of revelation, and it becomes me to acquiesce....

In another letter to Winthrop, we learn that John is gone again as soon as his health is restored.

Boston Franklin Place
March 31st 1804
... Mr Murray has not yet returned from Philadelphia....

Judith is dismayed that the children of Fitz William and Anna Parsons Sargent have heard John denounced by his detractors in Gloucester. Judith urges her brother and sister-in-law to allow the Murrays to have more exposure to their nieces and nephews in order to counteract this prejudicial influence.

Boston Franklin Place
February 26th 1805
... They receive the attentions of their Uncle, with marked reluctance, and, with a kind of peevish frigidity, which they do not even attempt to conceal! They frequently throw out severe remarks upon his religious sentiments, with their ideas of which, they seem to have connected every error, that has been imputed to him — I do not blame the children for these appearances — they are associated with the declared enemies of Mr Murray, and thus those seeds of prejudice, are early sown in their young minds, which, it is more than probable, revolving years will never eradicate. I repeat, that it is for this reason, among many others that I am desirous of seeing them daily, thus seeking, if possible, to counteract impressions most unfriendly to my peace....

The Letters

Judith tells Winthrop there are more divisions within the Boston congregation. She has even tried to mediate with some of their parishioners.

Boston Franklin Place
July 6th 1805

... Politics having created an alarming schism in our church, and the effect produced upon the mind of Mr Murray being truly deplorable, I was induced, by his wishes, to a personal intemperance, urged by sympathy, by interest, and above all by religion, I visited the parties[,] reasoning with them, with all the energy and pathos which I could command — I bless God I have reason to be satisfied with the results of my embassy, that the Crisis has passed, and that the calamity is subsiding....

Judith attempts to reason with a member of their congregation on John's behalf, staunchly defending her husband as she has had to do for decades.

Boston Franklin Place
July 17th 1805

... What took place yesterday between Mr M— and yourself, has placed another dagger in his bosom — you can have no conception of the anguish of his spirit — Mr Murray has had but one object in view — Peace among the members of his society — Considering his hearers, as the individuals of one collected family, he regards them with the eye of a Father, if he has mistaken his path, since he has not intentionally erred, can it be right to persecute him with unbending vigor? ought he not rather to be forgiven? Should he not, at least, be heard before he is either judged, or condemned? Mr Murray knows not that I write to you, it is my desire that it may not, at least for the present, come to his ears — My object is to pray, to conjure you, in the sacred name of Christianity, and for the dear sake of the Redeemer of Man, that you will hasten to pour wine, and oil, into the wounds of him, who has so long administered to you, in the precious truths that regard your everlasting salvation — Excuse this interference, a wife is always in the way of her duty, when promoting, by every justifiable expedient, the happiness of her husband — My heart is the heart of sorrow — Will you not contribute to lighten its pressure? Do you ask how you can do this — I answer, by speaking to Mr Murray, when ever you may chance to meet him, the language of friendship and consolation....

The Letters

John is traveling again. Judith has returned from her annual visit to Gloucester to face an empty house. She describes her feelings to Anna Parsons Sargent, whose home she has just left.

Boston Franklin Place
October 7th 1805

A painful kind of languor pervades my spirits, my dejection is indescribable, and my efforts to surmount those regrets, which are consequent upon my separation from my very dear friends, have hitherto been unsuccessful. Mr Murray's multiplying connexions will not allow him to abide in his own house, and I look in vain for those smiling countenances, on which, for many weeks past, my eye has delighted to rest....

Judith struggles to pay bills, borrow money, and collect John's income. Here, again, she asks a member of their congregation for John's salary.

Monday morning 14th of July

Sir

Troublesome as my frequent applications to you may be the necessity which impels them, is, I assure you, equally painful to me. It is a truth, which my situation obliges me to repeat, that the whole of Mr Murray's salary, is barely sufficient, in the present advanced prices of the articles of living, to answer the exigencies of his family. I have received from you, since the departure of my husband, thirty five dollars, and, as I have already informed you, I have been obliged to pay to Mr Mc Gibbon a debt of thirty four dollars, and sixty one cents. Mr Mc Gibbon is an industrious artist, whose demand I could not with propriety refuse — Fortunately I obtained a small loan from a friend, which loan is expended, and I stand in debt to Mr Wright for my last two days marketing. Thus, Sir, you see I am reduced to the mortifying necessity of once more soliciting you to pay to my daughter, who will hand you the request, the entire sum which has this day become due to your most obedient &c &c J.S.M.

John is back home, but he immediately takes to his sick bed. Judith has been invited to a social function, but she declines.

The Letters

Boston Franklin Place
April 13th 1807

My Dear Ladies
... Neither duty nor inclination allow me to leave Mr Murray in his present debilitated state....

In October, Judith decides to accompany John to Philadelphia rather than endure another lengthy separation. This time, sixteen-year-old Julia Maria is old enough to join them. John's many friends fill his days with preaching engagements, as Judith explains to Sarah Wheat of New London, Connecticut, a Universalist friend.

Philadelphia
November 6th 1807

Dear Madam
... We are passing on, from Friend, to Friend, from whom we receive, and to whom we seem to give real pleasure. The connexions of Mr Murray in this City are almost countless, and the consequences are unavoidable — we have scarce a moment to ourselves....

Winthrop's stepdaughter Anna Williams, who lived with the Murrays for several years while she attended a female academy, has returned to her home in Natchez, Mississippi. She has dutifully written to John, but he is physically unable to respond. Judith asks Winthrop to explain his predicament to Anna.

Boston Franklin Place
April 11th 1808
... Mr Murray is highly pleased with Anna's letter, he says if he held the pen of a ready writer, he would not delay his responses, but he is an old Man, and he is sure the dear creature will excuse him....

Winthrop urges Judith, John, and Julia Maria to visit Natchez and consider establishing a permanent residence there. Judith doubts such a journey will ever be possible.

The Letters

Boston Franklin Place
June 26th 1808

... Mr Murray is more and more enfeebled — No, he will never visit your Country — and of course it is decreed — I can never but in vision become your guest ... it is my part to acquiesce in the allotments of Providence....

Judith has agreed to board Adam Lewis Bingaman, the son of Winthrop's friends in Natchez, while he studied at Harvard. Adam's father sent $500 for his son's tuition and for the Murrays' expenses. Judith will keep their portion of the money in savings for emergencies—and as a surprise for John. She asks a financial adviser for his assistance.

Franklin Place
Morning of August 17th 1808

... Mrs M— has received from a friend the sum of five hundred dollars, with a request that it may continue subject to her control; she is desirous of rendering it as productive as possible, and, in this view, she respectfully solicits Mr Parkman's judgment and advice.... Mrs M— requests this application, or any transaction it may originate, may be considered as a secret, even from Mr Murray, as her plan is, in a day of adversity, to surprise him with an unexpected resource....

Judith reports to Winthrop that John is well enough to travel again—this time, to Portsmouth, New Hampshire, where he has preached since the 1770s.

Boston Franklin Place
May 27th 1809

... Mr M— is absent on a visit to his friends in Portsmouth, his health, during the past winter, has been comparatively good, and we flatter ourselves that his days of usefulness may yet be multiplied....

Judith lets Anna Parsons Sargent know that she will probably have to forego her annual visit to Gloucester that summer due to John's absence from home and the costs involved in closing their house for the season.

Boston Franklin Place
June 5th 1809

... Mr Murray has been for more than two weeks on a visit to his friends in Portsmouth, he has enjoyed through the past winter, much better health than usual, but the spring months have, according to custom, affected him rather unpleasantly [—] I do not, my Love believe, that I shall be able to visit you this summer — Mr Murray contemplates a journey to Philadelphia, and it would not be convenient for us to leave home together, except we were to shut up the house, which, as we are at present circumstanced, we cannot well do....

This time, it was Judith's turn to collapse.

Boston Franklin Place
June 24th 1809

Again I am raised from the gates of the grave! ... the infirmity to which I have so long been subjected assumed a most distressing appearance, and I was thrown, as I then believed, upon the bed of death — a violent nausea, high fever, and strong delirium, were, in my situation, most alarming symptoms, my husband, and my poor girl, were in despair — nothing could exceed their agony; but, by the mercy of my God, and the instrumentality of my very meritorious physician, I am again a convalescent....

Judith's appeals to John's congregation never seem to end. She hopes to gain their sympathy by explaining her failing health and their domestic needs. But, more importantly, she asks, doesn't John deserve their support after all he has done?

Saturday Morning
August 5th 1809

Dear Sir

Strange as it may seem, I am really a distressed Woman, I cannot even purchase bread, because I have only Coos and Penobscot bills! Our society are exceedingly tardy in handing in the sums for which they stand pledged ... we always owe more than we receive, this is extremely unpleasant, surely "the Labourer is worthy of his hire" Would it not become the affectionate attachment which the friends of the truth, as it is in Jesus, avow for

Mr Murray to put his allotted stipend, into some currency, which they can guarantee, at least for one month? As things now stand, my way of living is extremely burdensome, and as I accumulate years, and my health is broken, while the whole weight of our domestick arrangements rests solely upon me, we must absolutely relinquish our present situation....

After years of John's travels and irregular health, he has suffered a debilitating stroke that has left him bedridden and "helpless as an infant" for the rest of his life. Judith explains what happened to Winthrop. While his mind would continue to be alert and he could still speak, the right side of John's body was paralyzed. Befitting John's prominent stature, the Boston Universalists have promised to hire a nurse, provide "watchers," and continue paying his salary.

Boston Franklin Place
November 19th 1809

... For myself, alas! dark clouds gather round me, this day completes one month, one sad month, since my long beloved husband received what Physicians term a paralytic stroke! He left his bed at midnight, and in attempting to recover it, fell prostrate upon the floor since which period, he has continued totally helpless! The whole of his left side is as useless as if it made no part of his frame, he could not move a finger if he might thereby gain the Universe, and two persons are necessary to take him up or even to turn him in his bed: yet, nothwithstanding the decision of the ablest Physicians which our Metropolis can boast, would fain give to his disorder a less terrified name than the numb palsy, and, I ground the hope which I presume to indulge, upon the following circumstances, no part of his frame is so sensible to the touch as his useless limbs, his hand is frequently much more swoln, if, in moving him, we chance to bear the least weight on his disabled shoulder, his torture is extreme, and he often complains of excrutiating pain both in his ancle, and shoulder, add to these facts, that his intellectual vigour is in no sort diminished, that his mind is perhaps more clear, and elevated than usual, that he defends his favorites tenets, with all the force of argument, strength of reason, perspicuity, and commanding pathos, which distinguished his happiest moments — He has been visited by almost every Clergyman in Boston, and when they interrogated him respecting his readiness to depart out of time, he uniformly replies, his greatest struggle would consist in obtaining sufficient resignation to acquiese in the mandate which may prolong his stay! One Clergyman observed, that he thought he possessed every thing which could render the present life eligible — he fervently rejoined — "Every thing which humanity can bestow, Yes, a dear and precious wife, a meritorious daughter, many worthy friends, and a pecuniary competency; but my family I leave to God, they will be reunited to me in heaven, and my spirit pants to repose upon the bosom of its Father." He exhibits a perfect pattern of patience; his hearers frequently thronging round his bed, gaze upon him with love, renervating love, I had almost said with adoration, and seizing his helpless hand, they impress upon it the most filial kisses, and bathed in tears, retire to give place to a succession of weeping friends. The society have addressed to me a letter, in which they guarantee their services as Watchers, so long as their venerable pastor shall need their assistance. They have engaged, and are to compensate a faithful, and able Woman in quality of nurse, who is a member of our church, and who attends upon us, with all the affection and assiduity of a sister, and they have promised that the stipend allowed us, shall not be diminished....

Judith writes to her sister, Esther, about John's stroke and her longing for the companionship of her siblings.

Boston Franklin Place
November 27th 1809

... There is, my long, and tenderly beloved sister, nothing to be done for the restoration of my husband, for which I so ardently wish, as once more to see my poor, afflicted, suffering brothers, and their very meritorious wives. If the scattered individuals of our family were once more collected, where they might reciprocally console and aid each other, I think I could bear the rude buffeting of time, I think I could submit to the storms which assail the winter of my life, nor would my composure, my firmness, be thus prostrated. But, when I view one Brother distanced near three thousand miles, and the other as effectively removed from my sight, as if he too were a dweller in the Mississippi Territory, when I view my distressed husband, helpless as an infant! I will confess to you, my sister, that my mind is shaken as by a mighty tempest that the waves of affliction nearly overwhelm me, and that there are times, when I am ready to sink beneath the burden of existence.... I bless God that the mind of my husband invariably reposeth upon the rock of his salvation, or, if a murmer at any moment escapes his lips, it originates in the disappointment he has experienced, relative to a speedy departure out of time.... It is nearly seven weeks since the poor sufferer has been able to raise a finger on his left hand, he could not change his position in his bed a single inch, if he might thereby obtain the Universe! Yet in the whole of his left side although totally useless, so exquisitely sensible to the touch, that during the operation of moving him, his anguish is greatly augmented — Christmas is approaching, dear appointed hours! where are all those sacred pleasures, which during those highly interesting holy days we had taught our spirits to anticipate? Dark clouds gather round me! God knows whether we shall ever meet again, and I know, that I ought to be content, the ingredients of my cup of life have been far sweeter, far more enriched than I have merited, nor have I any claims to make upon the Author of my existence....

Judith fears the Murrays' approaching financial "adversity" which she confides to Winthrop. They are now almost solely dependant on the good will of John's not particularly wealthy congregation.

Boston Franklin Place
January 20th 1810

... the dread of pecuniary embarrassments, is an addition to the melancholy glooms of the present scene. Mr Murray is not associated with his congregation as other ministers are, his contract with the people is annually renewed, and on the first day of the approaching month of April it expires. He depends upon the will of his hearers whether the connexion be again resumed. Our society are not rich, and they are already considerably burdened, having been, since the nineteenth of October last reduced in the necessity of supporting another Minister. For us, it is a fact, that in the best times the utmost economy has been requisite to confine the expenditures of the week, within the allowed stipend. At this period, our expenses are vastly accumulated, a person in the quality of a nurse, is added to our family, she is a member of our church, and we are constrained to treat her as a visiting Lady. Two watchers occasionally, and every night one, are to be entertained, additional fire, and candle light, are of necessity consumed, and our apothecary's bill amounts to six dollars per month. Thus circumstanced, although we have not yet experienced the want of any article proper to our situation, it becomes us to consider, what arrangements can be made for the purpose of meeting those exigencies, which too probably await us.... I have been in possession of your note for

seven hundred and eighty-five dollars.... If I have not miscalculated, the interest upon this note amounted on the 14th instant to two hundred and fifty-one dollars and twenty two cents.... I have no immediate call for this property, but I feel that my day of adversity is at the door....

Judith tells Fitz William that John is only able to leave the house with considerable assistance.

Boston Franklin Place
February 17th 1810

Mr Murray ... during his very debilitated state has been wrapped in a bed blanket, and placed in a chair borne by four men, has been conveyed to a Hackney coach in which he has been carried as far as Roxbury....

Judith hopes for the best from John's congregation.

Franklin Place
February — 1810

My Dear Sir

At an early period of Mr Murray's illness, I was told by an influential member of your Committee, that it was unanimously agreed, to defray every extra expense incurred by his melancholy indisposition! Our hearts were expanded by gratitude, at this assurance, and we did homage to the benevolence which called into action such abundant generosity.

The inclosed bill, which I have not the means of discharging, was sent me some days since, and this is the second time it has been tendered, I do not often hear from the Collector....

In the following letter, Judith complains to Winthrop about the Universalists' ongoing negligence. Since John is no longer an "able minister," what will happen to them? It is evident that John neglected the business affairs of his ministry, but will the Universalists really abandon him or, to exaggerate the point, force him to commit suicide as the only way out of debt?

The Letters

April 23 1810

... I informed you, I think it was in November last, that the congregation over which Mr Murray presided, had health very honourably by him, that they had voted undiminished continuance of his salary, and a disbursement of every extra expense. But alas! this pleasant dream has vanished, and thick clouds envelop our future prospects [—] The establishment of our Clergy is generally for life, but my beloved husband, never possessing world wisdom, ran a long career before he would accept the smallest compensation for his labours, and when at length the calls of his family compelled him to become stationary, and to receive a certain stipend, he would only consent to an annual contract, to be renewed on the first sabbath of every returning April. But, you will say, fetters are not forged for rectitude. True, most true, and we hoped every thing, and believed every thing — The congregation met on the first instant, when it appeared there had been a mistake in the statement made to me; that they had passed no vote to defray extra expenses, and that while we imagined we had hundreds of dollars to receive, we had consumed every cent in fuel for our fire, which has continued unextinguished through the whole of these long wintry months, which have, in their tardy revolutions, been most dreadfully tedious. But this is not all, they proceeded to Vote twenty two dollars per week, the sum they were accustomed to appropriate to Mr Murray, while, instead of naming him, they directed it should be subject only to the controul of their Committee, who were ordered to procure therewith an able Minister to supply the pulpit. Mr Murray is no longer an able Minister, and it follows that this Vote can in no view take consequence of him. But they have voted us twenty cord of wood, and were suicide a christian virtue, it would seem they had thus given us a broad hint to light up one great bon-fire, and mounting the pile, entertain the Town by a grand funeral exhibition... It is impossible to deny that their Pastor, by his long performance of official duties, without claiming remuneration, and his diligence in his stated administration, has earned a liberal support, even though his natural life should exceed his usefulness, during many revolving years. Upon this foundation, hopes are based, that something may yet be done, but in the mean time we are in a state of torturing suspense....

A month later, Judith is able to report to Winthrop that they will receive short-term assistance from John's congregation.

Boston Franklin Place
May 8th 1810

... our society came last sunday to a determination to allow Mr Murray, for three months, commencing from the 18th of last March, twelve dollars per sunday, thus reducing his income from twenty two dollars per sabbath to twelve, and refusing even this pittance longer than the 26th of June next! They, however, give hope that they will meet at that period, and consider what is proper to be done. Mr Murray apprehends they will then still further curtail the provision they have already rendered so scanty or perhaps cut him off entirely!

John has urged Judith to visit Gloucester, where her brother Fitz William lay dying. She goes, but soon writes to Julia Maria to inquire about her father's health.

Gloucester
May 18th 1810

My beloved Child

... The circumstances attendant upon the severe indisposition of your dear Uncle, have not been exaggerated.... your indulgent Father was truly kind in urging me upon this visit, had I not made it, I might have added new thorns to a pillow already sufficiently planted with the piercing ills of life.... How are you my dear? How is your beloved Father? Every moment which I pass out of his chamber is for me a moment of apprehension. His patience is wonderful and his general conduct truly exemplary. May God continue unto him that portion of resignation he hath hitherto possessed. Give unto him my heart's love. In writing to you I do in effect write to him, tell him I say so, and that he is in possession of my esteem, of my veneration, and of my affection....

Judith's letter to Winthrop announces the Boston Universalists' appointment of a new minister, Rev. Edward Mitchell of New York. Despite illness and the cost of transportation, John insisted on attending Mitchell's installation and shaking his hand as a gesture of welcome. Meanwhile, Judith has been contemplating a removal to a much less expensive "rural retreat." She describes the current state of John's health for Winthrop in the next letter.

The Letters

Boston Franklin Place
October 1st 1810

... Mr Murray, having still the use of his right hand, was enabled at the installation of ... his Successor, to give public testimony of his approbation, by extending to him, in a very solemn, impressive, and affecting manner the Right Hand of Fellowship. But even the indulgence of attending Church, is, to the apprehensive mind of my dear invalid, strongly tinctured with alloy, he cannot ride out, he cannot go to church, without paying one dollar per time, if he is carried to church forenoon, and afternoon, it is two dollars per day, and if he attends the evening lecture, it is three dollars, and this, as often as he recollects our reduced income, he regards as a very high tax. These embarrassing facts induce me again to solicit your advice, upon this, to us very important subject. should we take up our abode in the interior of the country, we may command the necessary articles of living at a much less rate, and for the rent of this house, we shall receive six hundred dollars per annum, it now only affords us shelter, a very agreeable shelter it is true, would our income permit the indulgence, but may not our continuance here, in the present state of our finances, subject us to the accusation of extravagance? The rent we should receive, would, as I said, united with other little resources invest us, in some rural retirement, with a competency. To a common observer, the helplessness of Mr Murray's situation, is inconceivable. His appearance, when seated in his chair, indicates little more than slight indisposition, but he could as well have stood alone in the first moment of his existence, as in the present, and as he cannot move his left hand, and indeed has totally lost the whole of his left side, crutches are not of the smallest use. He is borne to, and from his bed, upon a wheeled chair, and if he be turned, or even moved a single inch, we must quit ours to perform for him this necessary office....

Despite John's long and mutually frustrating confinement, Judith's love for her beloved husband is unshakable. She writes to him from Gloucester, assuring John that they will always walk "hand in hand" whatever may lie ahead.

The Letters

Gloucester October 9th 1810

My Dear, my beloved, my venerable sufferer

Who says that you have not been made to me an instrument of great good? Who says that you ought to be second to any in my gratitude, in my affection? Was it not by your mouth that our God, and Father, thought best to show me the way of life more perfectly, and is there not many a denunciation, which being found in holy writ, would have harrowed up my affrighted soul, had not thy irradiated mind, by dispersing the clouds, produced the luminous comment repleat with peace, life, and happiness? Are you not the Father of my child? Is there, can there be a more excellent thing, do I not in her enjoy that desideration for which my soul long languished, and which I have hailed as heav[e]n's best gift? Away then with every recurrence to accidental evils, to the thorn in the flesh, to human frailties, from which no mortal is exempt. What are the fading evils of time, to the substantial felicity in possession, and reversion, of which you have been made to me the beloved medium. Talk not of forgiveness, of offences, or of pardon, but let us mutually bear, and forbear, and let us hand in hand pursue the rugged path, which yet remains, until we arrive at that beatified state, where sin nor sorrow will no more invade, and where we shall be completely blessed. I am happy to find your approbation of your child so unreserved, she does indeed merit every effort which we can make in her favour, and I persuade myself you will, in every particular, discharge to her the whole duty of a Father. I rejoice your airing in the carriage was so refreshing, and I trust my poor, way worn sufferer, will find many resting places on the road, in which he can sincerely say it is good for me to be here.... May God forever bless you [—] I am truly your faithful and affectionate Wife

John is impatient to die, Judith tells Winthrop.

Boston Franklin Place
November 6th 1810

... The situation of my venerable husband continues stationary, his appetite is tolerable, and his countenance good, but he is utterly helpless! He regards his remaining days as a blank, and frequently speaks of the 19th of October 1809 as the day of his death. To say truth his patience is nearly exhausted nor can it be matter of wonder....

The Letters

Judith asks a cousin in Gloucester to help her find a new nurse for John.

Boston Franklin Place
December 16th 1811

... you have perhaps heard the distressing situation to which Mr Murray has been reduced. For more than fourteen months he has been, by a stroke of the palsy, deprived of the use of his limbs, in all which time, he has not borne the smallest weight upon his feet! Another Minister is settled in his pulpit, and whenever he is carried abroad, he is borne in a chair to a Hack, in which he is placed. Circumstanced as he is, I am of necessity almost wholly confined to his chamber, and of course stand in great need of a steady person in my family. I can obtain no good help in this town, and I am told you have been instrumental in procuring assistance for your friends in this Town, and I feel assured you will exert your self in my favour in This line. Thus I introduce my request [—] Procure for me, my dear, if possible, a young, or middle aged Woman. Let her be steady, honest, neat, industrious, healthy, good natured, and willing to be taught. Let her understand washing, ironing, and plain cooking, and I will pay her every saturday morning, one dollar in cash....

To solidify John's place in Universalist history and to generate income, Judith and John edit a number of his letters and sermons for publication. They published Letters and Sketches of Sermons *in 1812. Judith thanks Winthrop for selling book subscriptions to his friends.*

Boston Franklin Place
June 11th 1811

... Mr Murray is highly obliged by your disposal of so large a number of the copies of his intended publication, and he observes with gratitude, that for a patronage so liberal, he is principally indebted to you....

Judith has to inform "Mr B of Philadelphia," a Universalist, that John will "never again" be able to visit their city.

184

The Letters

Boston Franklin Place
January 28th 1812

Sir

Our dear, and venerable sufferer, has been from day to day, indulging a hope, that he should gather sufficient organical strength to reply to your truly affectionate, and filial letter, with his own pen but this cheering hope, the soothing voice of which so frequently proves fallacious, he is at length compelled to surrender. He however bids me to say, that while his chilled limbs are rendered useless by the icy influence of unyielding palsy, gratitude is nevertheless warm at his heart.... No Sir, Mr M— will never again, while tenanted in clay, visit your City; but when he shall spread his glad wings, and soar away to regions of eternal bliss, he will probably glance, with benign complacency, on those Philadelphian haunts, where he has so frequently been indulged with the feast of reason, and the flow of souls. His depressing indisposition does not in the smallest degree abate, nay I rather think he loses ground; his passage out of time is lingering, and gradually sloped: he is, as he frequently observes, the Lord's prisoner, and consequently he is a prisoner of hope.... He is not greatly exercised with pain, although he is at present afflicted by a severe cough, but this we hope will abate, and in the interim I do not believe his patience has often been surpassed. Twenty seven months confinement, without the power to move a single inch, is no common trial. He receives, with great delight, and enthusiastic gratitude, the attention of his friends. your letter, and the present which accompanied it, gave him high pleasure [—] the article with which you have furnished him cannot be obtained in its highest state of perfection in this Town, and there is nothing upon which our dear invalid feels with so much pleasure....

War with Great Britain interrupts American trade and causes the Murrays' investments to fail. The Boston Universalist congregation, meanwhile, has voted to reduce John's salary. Judith communicates her fears to Winthrop whose concern for his sister must only be growing. As a former military officer, Winthrop knew full well the dangers of war and British invasion.

Boston Franklin Place
May 8th. 1812

... Such is the state of Commerce reduced to the last extremity by non intercourse and embargo laws as to preclude all hope of a dividend from the Suffolk funds on July next, January last gave us not a cent, and our prospects do not brighten. Upon me as an individual thick darkness gathers, a darkness which is literally felt. Our Society have made a new arrangement until the 20th of March last they allowed Mr Murray 12 dollars per week and 20 cord of wood per year but from that period they have voted by a fearful majority to pay him only ten dollars per week and not to furnish him a single stick of wood. Mr Murray continues the same....

The Washington Monument Association has called upon John for a financial contribution. He was unable to receive them, and only capable of contributing a small amount of money. Judith writes to them on his behalf.

Written for Mr Murray

Mr Murray takes leave respectfully to observe that being, in consequence of a sleepless night particularly indisposed on the day the Committee from the Washington Monument Association did him the honour to call upon him, he is persuaded he did not receive the gentlemen in a manner becoming their characters or his own. Every faculty of his soul most devoutly wishes unbounded success to all those attempts which are calculated to illustrate, or to commemorate the peerless virtues, and achievements of the venerable Father of these American Federal, Republican States. Had he millions he would rejoice to evince his high sense of the unrivalled merit of Columbia's Chief, by contributing in full proportion to his possessions. As it is, he humbly begs permission to offer the inclosed trifle, trusting that it may serve to evince what he would do, did not niggard fortune confine within very narrow bounds, the operation of those feelings which however he still delighteth to indulge.

Franklin Place May 27th. 1812
Honourable William Sullivan Esquire Corresponding Secretary
of Washington Monument Association.

A Universalist friend, Mrs. Terrell, has been profoundly affected by John's book. Her letter reminded John that despite the debts incurred by his project, Letters and Sketches enabled him to be "made the instrument of speaking peace" to a wider audience.

Boston Franklin Place
February 27th 1815

... Mr Murray had looked to his publication as a support during the number of his days but the failure of his Printer obliged him to have recourse to loans for the purpose of redeeming the work from the hands of Creditors, and hence, in a pecuniary view, it became a real loss — But you discovered your high estimation of the promulgator of glad tidings, together with his writings, by purchasing a copy at more than double the price demanded, nay more, you pointed us to a period when you might be instrumental in assisting us to dispose of a number of copies, thus enabling us to obtain emancipation from a debt, which will exonerate us from a most heavy pressure, and do you not think that gratitude has raised for you an altar in our bosoms, do you not think we gladly do homage at the shrine of beauty, virtue, and benevolence — Mr Murray would have answered your obliging favour with his own hand, but alas! he can experimentally say although his spirit be willing, his corporeal powers are indeed weak — yet your letter has afforded him abundant consolation, while such testimonies as it contains, give him thus to behold the travail of his Redeemers soul, his satisfaction cannot but be complete. In whatever pecuniary embarrassments his publication may have involved him, while he is made the instrument of speaking peace to the redeemed world, through the emphatic name of Jesus, he cannot but be most devoutly glad and rejoice, he cannot but bless God manifest in the flesh, the Saviour of sinners, the beatified head of every Man....

Anna Williams, one of Winthrop's stepdaughters, has married Mr. Thompson. Judith shares her views on marriage with Anna in the following letter, in words that neatly describe her own marriage to John. In earlier years, Judith published these ideas in her essays.

The Letters

Boston Franklin Place
February 14th 1814

... Marriage is the highest state of friendship — let your husband enjoy your undivided, unreserved confidence. Little dissentions wound a common amity, but they too often inflict a mortal stab upon wedded love — Love is, as I believe, an evanescent passion, but well earned esteem, cherished by discretion, will be the coeval of your existence. The married pair should never be rivals; they should be friends, Husband and Wife should not be considered as terms synonimous with Master and slave — Equality should be the motto of wedded life, and the only contention of friends, thus affianced, which should most largely promote each other's happiness....

Judith asks Winthrop's advice about changing the will she and John had written years ago. She wants Julia Maria to have sole control over her inheritance, but while John is alive Judith is powerless to act on her own. Julia Maria married Adam Lewis Bingaman in 1812 after he graduated from Harvard. Adam soon returned to his native Natchez, Mississippi, leaving his new wife and infant daughter, Charlotte, behind. For unknown reasons, his family refused to pay Judith the money they owed her. Winthrop intervened on his sister's behalf to have the debt paid and Adam reunited with Julia Maria. When he failed on both counts, he barred Adam from his home which created an even more difficult division between Judith and her son-in-law. Judith did not trust Adam to take care of her daughter. She wanted Julia Maria to have her own resources.

Boston Franklin Place
April 15th 1814

... I have contemplated a disposition of our property, which would give the sole controul of our interest in the event of our demise to our daughter, I suggested the idea to her, when, after declaring that such an arrangement would give a mortal stab to her domestic peace, she absolutely seemed to gasp for breath. Her concurrence, however, not being necessary to such a transaction, an instrument might be drawn without her knowledge. But difficulty stares me in the face at every step. Previous to Mr Murray's distressing indisposition, a will was made putting me in possession at his death, of the whole of our little property — This will, Mr Murray signed and sealed in presence of witnesses, and as no other has since been written

I suppose it is still good. While Mr Murray lives I know I am powerless — I can make no will, and were I to propose the business to him, who only can make the wished for disposition, it would agitate him beyond description, he seems to have abhorrence of property, and of all questions relative thereto. [He has] no memory, or rather no discriminating memory — he mentions every thing to every body just as it happens to occur and there is by consequence no safety in making him any communication — God help me — I am at a loss how to act but from your exertions my ever dear brother I expect much....

The threat of British troops occupying Boston caused Judith great distress. Enemy soldiers had already invaded Washington and burned many buildings to the ground. She turns to Winthrop for advice.

Franklin Place
September 8th 1814

My beloved brother
   ... Before this letter can possibly reach you it will be proclaimed in your territory that the British have been in possession of Washington[,] that all the public buildings are laid in ashes and that our whole seaboard is threatened! But will not the arm of Omnipotence proportion our strength to our day — It will be difficult to remove Mr Murray and if Boston is destroyed where shall we find safety?

More financial embarrassments prompt this letter to one of Judith's aunts.

Boston Franklin Place October

My best Aunt
   ... Our society are either unable or unwilling to pay us the stipend they had allowed, they are in arrears since the month of June last. My eldest brother's funds in the state Bank, and in the Suffolk office are for the present totally unproductive, and, to the kindness of my youngest brother, we have long been indebted for a loan, and many little gratitudes, and whatever we might be inclined to offer for sale, of our own small property, would be nearly sacrificed. When I can hear from my eldest brother, whose sons are under my care, my difficulties will be in some

measure removed, but, in the interim, necessitated by the distressed situation of my husband, together with other circumstances, to retain a large family, you will readily conceive my embarrassment....

Judith no longer wishes to "sanction by her presence" the theological change that has taken place at Boston's Universalist church. She announces her decision to the Reverend John Sylvester John Gardiner, the rector of Boston's Episcopal Trinity Church and the grandson of her cousin Catherine Goldthwaite Gardiner Powell.

Sunday evening
April 23d — 1815

Rev. & Respected Sir

The cloud which during the protracted period of five years, and upwards of six months, has enveloped my once brighter prospects, looks with a peculiarly melancholy aspect upon those holy days of which for the first fifty years of my life I was a constant attendant upon public worship — I cannot enter the house where I have been accustomed to unite with those of the persuasion of my adoption, without the intrusion of reflections painful in the extreme. When my eye is fixed upon the pulpit of my afflicted husband, the comparison of his present situation with what it was in the days of other times, obtrudes upon my sorrowing mind, originating regrets almost too potent to be endured — Feelings of this nature it would, however, be my duty to surmount, had it not unfortunately happened, that the person offitiating in our church, varies essentially from more than one of the fundamental principles in the faith which I have embraced; and I cannot believe it consistent, to sanction by my presence, in the congregation of Universalists, sentiments which my reason, and my conviction disdain, and thus am I, almost necessarily, precipitated upon the practice, of forsaking the assembling with those who ostensibly collect for the worship of Deity — It is almost superfluous to add, I regard this circumstance as a real misfortune....

Finally, after patiently enduring almost six years as an invalid, John Murray died. The Universalists held two services for him, one in Gloucester and the other in Boston, where he was interred in the Sargent family tomb at Granary Burying Ground. Judith details the events for Winthrop.

The Letters

Boston Franklin Place
September 11th. 1815

My beloved my sympathizing my brother

Many weeks, in the estimation of calamity years, have passed on since I last addressed you. During this period I have watched the expiring moments of my long suffering, my venerable, my now beatified husband. His demise took place on Lord's day morning 3d instant, at 6 oclock, and as the interment of his precious remains, could not be delayed, he was entombed on the following monday evening 4th instant, with all the ... arrangements, and honours, which his now mourning and deeply penetrated congregation, could bestow. My respectable husband died as he had lived, bearing unequivocal testimony to the grand, and fundamental truths of revelation ... and thus have been laid in the grave a Man, to whom from sentiment and from principle, my heart, my soul was engaged, and thus is your sister once more a widow — A Widow — desolate sound — but I too shall soon lift my head on high, for my deliverer, my Redeemer still lives, and the time of my emancipation draweth nigh.... I will yield to the remonstrances of an aching heart, a swimming head, and trembling fingers, which are momently stimulating me to relinquish my pen [—] I am, most devotedly, your affectionate and deeply affected sister

Judith captures John's final moments for Edward Mitchell.

Boston Franklin Place
September 13 1815

Dear and Rev. Sir

Strange as it may seem, your letter of the 9th instant reached me only a few minutes since. Yea, Verily, my venerable, once deeply afflicted husband, now reposes upon the bosom of God his Creator, his Father, his Redeemer — Of his last moments I would speak — but no language is adequate a description of my feelings — I had entertained a persuasion that an exit from this vale of tears, would be granted me previous to the departure of my husband — consequently I was unprepared for the stroke. Time had reconciled us to the arrangements of providence, and, it is a fact that the last six years, lacking only a few days, of the life of the deceased, was more replete with tranquility, and consolation — taken as a whole

— than any previous six successive years, since I was blessed with his society — This he frequently remarked — I am the Lord's Prisoner, he would say — and by consequence a prisoner of hope. But it cannot be denied that he frequently evinced great impatience to be gone, and after recovering from any little indisposition, he would reply to congratulating friends — It is as if, when I believed I was voyaging to my native country, where health, happiness, and peace, and abundance awaited me, borne upwards by gales the most propitious, and supposing myself almost in the moment of obtaining the long desired, when suddenly driven back by some envious circumstance, instead of being soothed by condolence, I am [shaken] to the soul, by the discordant voice of congratulation — you Sir have often heard him express himself to this effect, and the months which have revolved since you saw him, have furnished no additional motives for complacency in the present state of being. It was about four O clock on Lord's day morning, August 27, that he was violently seized — We were however, so far from apprehending danger, that we rather believed his illness would have a salutary effect upon his constitution, through the approaching wintry months. We summoned the aid of a physician, who was of our opinion — yet the honoured sufferer himself, occasionally observed — Who knows — perhaps the hour of my emancipation draweth nigh — On tuesday evening 29th. ult. his complaints evidently abated in so much, that while the features of his strongly marked face expressed the deepest mortification, he exclaimed, am I then once more thrown back, the melancholy subject of alternate hope and fear — on wednesday evening his symptoms encreased, I sat by him through the night, he obtained little rest, but hope manifestly triumphed in his bosom — On this evening we called in another physician, whose doubtful answers to the questions we put, gave us the first alarm — he seemed to consider nature as surrendering her offices — In the course of thursday 31st. ult. he repeatedly, and earnestly said, "I cannot be sufficiently thankful to God my Saviour, that I suffer no pain either of body, or mind["] — My daughter sat by him on Thursday night, and observing toward morning, a kind of wildness in the looks of her Father, she tremulously questioned — "Dear Sir do you not know your child?" — Yes, my Love, he returned, and I delight in her — Bless me, oh! my Father, with a supplicating voice she rejoined bless your child — I have, I do bless you, already you are blessed in the Redeemer of your spirit, who will never forsake you, whose faithfulness can never fail — At daylight, friday morning, September 1st, I approached the bed — Do you not know that I am your Wife? — yes indeed I do and I greatly rejoice in this knowledge — These two replies were satisfactory instances of sanity, but as the day advanced, his derangement became unquestionable; from Friday morning until saturday evening, a little after sunset, he continued with few intervals, repeating, in an incoherent manner indeed, the glorious and fundamental truths of our most holy religion, his right hand constantly in motion — When any one approached, whatever might be the question — The answers were ready — "To Him," said the expiring Man of God "shall the gathering of the people be, and his rest shall be glorious, glorious, glorious — I am blest with all spiritual blessings in Christ Jesus — Nor I alone — Christ hath tasted death for every Man &c &c &c" These God honouring, Man restoring truths, were audibly articulated, while voice and strength continued, and when speaking only in a whisper, I applied my listening ear to his moving lips, I had the satisfaction to witness, that the same consolatory appearance dwelt upon his tongue — Thus the luminous points upon the noble, the capacious mind, had so long reposed, beamed refulgent through the scattering fragments, then dissolving, which until this had constituted the tenement embodying the immortal tenant [—] Almost immediately after sunset, he ceased to speak, his right hand no longer moved, and he continued in the position in which his ever kind friend, Mrs Leonard, had placed him, until 6 o clock Lord's day morning, 3rd instant when, without a sigh, or a struggle, or a single distortion of countenance, he expired — He did not appear through the whole of friday and saturday, to have suffered a moment's pain, except when an attempt was made to move him — his breath grew shorter and shorter, like the sweet sleep of a tired infant, until we could no more distinguish it — Only a minute previous to his departure, without a supposition that he was so near his end, I introduced a tea spoon full of cordial recommended by his Physician, into his mouth with a request that, if he loved me, he would assay to swallow it — He instantly made the attempt, and succeeded, I heard it pass — I hesitated whether I should add another tea spoonful, his lips being evidently parched, but before I could fill the spoon, he had escaped — And I also shall quickly follow, the time of my emancipation is at hand — I pray you to commend my daughter, and myself, to your family, and to your congregation — We ask your united prayrs, and we cordially thank you, for every favour, conferred upon us, and upon the venerable deceased — I am, with much gratitude Most respectfully yours &c &c

Judith tells Winthrop she is overcome by deep "melancholy" after losing her best friend and husband.

Boston Franklin Place
September 26 1815

My beloved brother

Upwards of three weeks of my melancholy widowhood are gone past and so irrational is my unquiet spirit, that it spontaneously exclaims, could I behold that white, that venerable head, once more an occupant of the window which, with so much dignified patience, he was accustomed to fill, the view would greatly mitigate every misfortune....

Universalist friends have approached Judith to complete and publish John's autobiography which he had abandoned in 1774. Judith asks Edward Mitchell for assistance. Now, with John's death, income from the Boston congregation is once again in doubt. The book will reenforce John's leading role in Universalist history and, perhaps, raise much-needed funds. Judith published the book in 1816, with a sketchy "continuance" by "a friend," meaning, herself. Sadly, only John's earliest years were chronicled in depth.

Boston Franklin Place
September 28 1815

Rev. and Dear Sir

Late last evening your kind letter of the 23d ultimo, was handed me from the office.... It gives me pain to neglect, or even to delay compliance with any request of yours, but a prevalent confusion or swimming in my head, together with great depression of mind, has not, for many weeks (in my Computation years) allowed me sufficient calmness to examine the papers, relative to the dear, and honoured deceased which await the hand of method, to prepare them for the public eye — Application has been made to me to publish those papers — they comprize details that include the infancy, and a variety of anecdotes, relative to the life of my friend, until some months, perhaps years, after the commencement of his public labours in America — I am bound by a promise, of very long standing, to give publicity to these sheets — The work may be entitled Records of the Life of Rev. John Murray, Minister of the Reconciliation, written by himself, until a late period, and continued until the closing scene, by another hand — The detail you request might interfere with the proposed sketch — yet your long acquaintance with the meritorious deceased, possessing, as you do, a superior, and penetrating mind, will enable you to give so masterly a delineation of the Man, and his manner, as will questionless meet the wishes of his most partial admirers — Permit me to say, I look for this from you — a disciple whom our friend so greatly loved — His eulogy would come with a better grace, and abundantly more propriety, from any lips than mine. The character which you may draw, I shall beg leave to insist in the proposed Volume, either in your name, or as a portrait furnished by a friend — Proposals will probably be shortly issued, copies of which will be forwarded to you — The society have buried their Minister, but their arrangements did not include mourning for his family. They have also voted to pay the salary, which would have been due, if their vote of 1815 had been similar to that of 1814, and they include Lord's day September 3d— 1815 — am I never again to see you in this Town? — I never so ardently wished to see you as at present — With regards to Mrs M— and family I am &c &c &c

Winthrop's refusal to allow Adam Bingaman into his home makes it impossible for Judith and Julia Maria to consider residing with Winthrop. As it is, Judith prefers to die in Boston, in the bed she shared with John.

Boston Franklin Place
November 16th 1815
... My brother I am old, I am feeble, I am a woman — my health is broken, my mind is depressed — I am unequal to any uncommon exertion, I am changed by sorrow. I shall not again lift my head yet, a little while, and I shall be here no more — Previous to the receipt of your last letters, I had arranged my plans [—] I had decided to retain this house, and to lay my dying head in the same spot, and upon the same pillow, which received that of my departed, of my venerable husband, My daughter, and her infant, are still more endeared to me, since the demise of their Father, they are all that is left of him — and they are more precious to my soul, than the virtual stream which warms me to existence — I cannot voluntarily separate myself from them, and the improper conduct of my son in law, is a bar to their residence in your family....

The Letters

Judith explains her concern regarding Adam Bingaman's legal hold over Julia Maria to Winthrop.

Gloucester January 27th 1816

... I am afraid of A.L.B. because the Law has placed the destiny of my only child, and now of a darling grand child, in his power — he can, if he pleases, remove them forever, from my view — is not this fact enough to fill me with the most dread apprehension? — God only knows how much the fear of a separation from my children, harrows up my soul....

Despite Adam's lengthy silence, Judith writes to him hoping to prevent Julia Maria's removal to Natchez.

Boston Franklin Place
October— 1816

... Why my dear fellow are you so silent to our repeated letters — I confess I should prefer you as a dweller in this Mansion to any other person and you may take up your abode in Franklin Place in whatever may best accord with your wishes and feelings....

The Boston Universalists have begun construction on a new meetinghouse. In a moment of wishful thinking, Judith hopes they will name the church after John and call Edward Mitchell as their minister, which, she tells Mitchell, would serve as a "bright gleam" at the end of her life and a proper tribute to John.

Boston Franklin Place
March 18. 1817

... Did you hear we were to have a new meeting house built in this Town, for the purpose of promulgating the grace of God our Saviour, who gave himself a ransom for all to be testified in due time.... This Temple is to be reared and consecrated by the uniform adherents of my deceased friend, and it will no doubt be completed during the coming summer — If it could be distinguished by the name of the Murraytanian Church, and if Mr Mitchell, or some able consistent Gospel Preacher, could be established in the pulpit, I should be inexpressibly gratified — and one bright gleam of settling life, would thus eradicate my parting hours....

The Letters

Edward Mitchell has advised Judith against pressing her case with the Universalists. She agrees, but her desire to keep John's memory alive is strong.

Boston Franklin Place
March 22d 1817

... Arrangements for the completed Church are in train, and it is expected the structure will be completed in the course of the coming summer — your remarks upon the new Association, and upon my wishes relative to the designating appellation of the Church to be reared, are in every view, correct: they are stamped by reason, and by propriety, and yet my love for the name of the deceased, induces the strongest complacency in whatever may rescue it from oblivion....

At the "consecration" of the new Universalist meetinghouse, Judith tells Edward Mitchell that John's name was barely mentioned by the presiding minister, the Reverend Thomas Jones, their friend from Gloucester. Ironically, the Boston Universalists built their new church in close proximity to where the Reverend Andrew Croswell, one of John Murray's strongest detractors, had denounced and accosted him in the 1770s (see "Introduction").

Boston Franklin Place
October 22d 1817

... On thursday last the new meeting house was consecrated, with scarce a reference to the venerable founder of Universalism in this Country — The sermon was preached by Mr Jones, a Man at this moment reaping the fruits of my husband's patronage, and what renders the little respect paid to the memory of the deceased, more extraordinary, is, that the New Temple is erected, not ten yards from the spot, upon which he suffered so much contumely, from Mr Crosswell, and his adherents....

Judith is so dissatisfied with the new Universalist minister in Boston, Hosea Ballou, she contemplates moving to New York to be near Edward Mitchell.

The Letters

Boston Franklin Place
May 7th 1818

... I am more and more dissatisfied with Mr Ballou, you will greatly oblige me if you will tell me, as accurately as possible, how much it would cost me annually to become a housekeeper in New York, or, in other words, whether I might not live as cheap in your City, as in this Town [—] It is my wish to be in the vicinity of a minister of the reconciliation, and that my dying hours should be solaced by the soothings of a preacher of glad tidings....

Denouement

On August 14, 1818, Judith penned her last letter from Boston. She did not move to New York, nor was she able to die in the bed she had shared with John during their marriage. Instead, when Adam Lewis Bingaman journeyed to Boston that summer to accompany his wife and daughter to Natchez, Judith moved with them, taking up residence at the Bingaman mansion, Oak Point.

Among the papers Judith packed with her belongings were twenty letter books—blank volumes into which she had copied her letters to family, friends, and, of course, to John.

It is possible she brought John's private letters along with her. It is also possible she burned them before leaving Boston at his request. While John's business letters are easily found in libraries and historical societies today, his personal letters—especially those written to Judith—have for the most part disappeared.

Selected Resources

Websites

Judith Sargent Murray Society: www.hurdsmith.com/judith
Sargent House Museum: www.sargenthouse.org
Unitarian Universalist Association: www.uua.org
Andover-Harvard Theological Library: www.hds.harvard.edu/library
Dictionary of Unitarian Universalist Biography: www.uua.org/uuhs/duub
Conference Center at Murray Grove: www.murraygrove.org

Books, Monographs, and Essays

By Judith Sargent Murray

Murray, Judith Sargent. *The Gleaner: A Miscellaneous Production.*
　　Boston: I. Thomas and E.T. Andrews, 1798.
　　Reissued by the Union College Press, Schenectady, 1992.
Murray, Judith Sargent. *Massachusetts Magazine.* Poetry as "Constantia,"
　　1789–91; Essays as "Constantia," 1790–4; Essays as "The Gleaner,"
　　1792–4.*
Murray, Judith Sargent. *Federal Orrery.* Essays as "The Reaper," 1794.*
Murray, Judith Sargent. *Boston Weekly Magazine.* Poetry as "Honora
　　Martesia," 1802–03.
Stevens, Judith Sargent. *Some Deductions from the System Promulgated
　　in the Page of Divine Revelation: Ranged in the Order and Form
　　of a Catechism Intended as an Assistant to the Christian Parent
　　or Teacher.* Portsmouth, New Hampshire, and Norwich,
　　Connecticut, 1782.*
Stevens, Judith Sargent. *Gentleman and Lady's Town and Country
　　Magazine.* Essay as "Constantia," 1784.*
*Essays and catechism reissued by Bonnie Hurd Smith, Cambridge,
　　1998–9 (www.hurdsmith.com/judith).

By John Murray

Murray, John. *Letters and Sketches of Sermons.*
　　Boston: Munroe and Francis, 1812.
Murray, John. *Records of the Life of the Rev. John Murray.*
　　Boston: Munroe and Francis, 1816. Reissued many times.

Resources

On John Murray and Universalism

Bisbee, Frederick A. *From Good Luck to Gloucester.*
Boston: The Murray Press, 1920.

Cassara, Ernest, ed. *Universalism in America: A Documentary History of a Liberal Faith.* Boston: Skinner House, 1971.

Cleaveland, John. *An Attempt to Nip in the Bud, the unscriptural Doctrine of Universal Salvation, and some other dangerous errors connected with it; which a certain stranger, who calls himself John Murray....* Salem: E. Russell, 1776.

Croswell, Andrew. Mr. *Murray Unmask'd, in which among other things, is shewn, that his doctrine of universal salvation, is inimical to virtue, and productive of all manner of wickedness; and that Christians of all denominations ought to be on their guard against it.*
Boston: J. Kneeland, 1775.

Eddy, Richard. *Universalism in Gloucester, Mass.*
Gloucester: Proctor Brothers, 1892.

Howe, Charles A., ed. *Not Hell, But Hope.* The John Murray Distinguished Lecture Series, 1987–1991.
Lanoka Harbor: Murray Grove Association, 1991.

Howe, Charles A. *The Larger Faith: A History of Universalism in America.*
Boston: Skinner House Books, 1993.

Miller, Russell E. *The Larger Hope: The First Century of the Universalist Church in America, 1770–1870.*
Boston: Unitarian Universalist Association, 1979.

Relly, James. *Union, or, A Treatise of the Consanguinity and Affinity between Christ and His Church.* London, 1759.

Skinner, Clarence R. and Cole, Alfred S. *Hell's Ramparts Fell.*
Boston: Universalist Publishing House, 1941.

On Judith Sargent Murray

Branson, Susan. *These Fiery Frenchified Dames: Women and Political Culture in Early National Philadelphia.* Philadelphia: University of Pennsylvania Press, 2001.

Dykeman, Therese Boos. *American Women Philosophers 1650–1930: Six Exemplary Thinkers.* New York: Edwin Mellon Press, 1993.

Emerson, Dorothy May. *Standing Before Us: Unitarian Universalist Women and Social Reform, 1776–1936.* Boston: Skinner House Books, 2000.

Resources

Gibson, Rev. Gordon J., "The Rediscovery of Judith Sargent Murray," in *Not Hell, But Hope*. (*See* Howe, Charles A.)

Harris, Sharon M., ed. *Selected Writings of Judith Sargent Murray*. New York: Oxford University Press, 1995.

Kerber, Linda K. *Women of the Republic*. Chapel Hill: University of North Carolina Press, 1988.

Kerber, Linda K. and Dehart, Jane Sherron. *Women's America: Refocusing the Past*. New York: Oxford University Press, 1991.

Moynihan, Ruth Barnes, Russett, Cynthia, and Crumpacker, Laurie, eds. *Second to None: A Documentary History of American Women*. Lincoln: University of Nebraska Press, 1993.

Norton, Mary Beth. *Liberty's Daughters: The Revolutionary Experience of American Women, 1750–1800*. New York: Little, Brown and Company, 1980.

Rossi, Alice. *The Feminist Papers*. Boston: Northeastern University Press, 1973.

Sargent, Emma Worcester, arr. *Epes Sargent of Gloucester and His Descendants*. Boston: Houghton Mifflin, 1923.

On Gloucester history, with references to John Murray and Judith Sargent Murray

Babson, John J. *History of the Town of Gloucester, Cape Ann*. Gloucester: Proctor Brothers, 1860. Reissued by Peter Smith, Gloucester, 1972.

Garland, Joseph E. *The Fish and the Falcon*. Charleston: The History Press, 2006. A reissue of *Guns Off Gloucester*.

Hurd, Hamilton D. *History of Essex County, Massachusetts*. Philadelphia: J.W. Lewis & Co., 1888.

Pringle, James R. *History of the Town of Gloucester, Cape Ann, Massachusetts*. Gloucester: published by the author, 1892. Reissued by the Gloucester City Archives, Gloucester, 1997.

Ray, Mary, comp., Dunlap, Susan V., ed. *Gloucester, Massachusetts Historical Time-Line, 1000–1999*. Gloucester: Gloucester Archives Committee, 2002.

Index

Page numbers in italics refer to recipients of the letters. For more information on these individuals, see "Recipients of the Letters." However, a number of people to whom Judith wrote, or to whom she refers in her letters, are unidentifiable at this time. They are listed by the first initial of his or her last name, as Judith did in her letters. Names appearing in quotation marks include those for whom only partial information is known at this time, or pen names.

Relatives of Judith Sargent Murray and John Murray have been identified as far back as grandparents, and as far forward as nieces and nephews. Judith's cousins (including those by marriage) and their children may be assumed by the last names of Ellery, Elwell, Goldthwaite, Odell, Ollive, Osborne, Parsons, Plummer, Prentice, Sargent, Saunders, Stevens, Turner, Walker, and Webber.

Specific references to "God," "Jesus," "Christ," etc. are not indexed as they appear with great frequency when Judith concluded her letters. Where more substance was involved on these subjects, readers may refer to "Murray, Judith Sargent, spiritual development and theology of" or "Murray, John, spiritual development and theology of."

Key
JSM: Judith Sargent Murray
JM: John Murray
JMMB: Julia Maria Murray Bingaman

Adams, Abigail, 7, 13, 28, 114, 165–6
Adams, John, 7, 13–14, 28, 114, 165–6
Adams National Historical Park, 165
The African (JSM's play), 8, 15
Alton, England, 20, 22
America, 25, 31–2, 50, 93, 104, 110
   class structure in, 114
   clergy in, 114
   government in, 28
   playwrights in, 149
   publishing in, 14
   trade in, 185
   Universalism in, 7, 11, 56
American Revolution, 10, 27, 38, 62
   Continental Army, 16, 20, 27, 30, 38–9, 50
Anglicanism/Anglicans, 22
Annisquam River, 3

architecture, 3, 135–6
Arlington (mansion), 18
Arnold Arboretum, 36
Atlantic Ocean, 3, 71, 98

"Mr B of Philadelphia," 33, 184, *185*
Bakers Island, 158
Ballou, Rev. Hosea, 15, 21, 29,
    162–3, 197–8
Barrell, Jonathan Sayward, 35
Bath, Eng., 109, 111
Beach, Clementine, 8, 15
Beverly, Mass., 3, 117
Billerica, Mass., 15
Bingaman family, 16–17, 188, 198
Bingaman, Adam Lewis (JMMB's
    husband), 8, 16, 21, 33, 174, 188,
    195–6, *196*, 198
Bingaman, Adam Lewis, Jr., 17
Bingaman, Charlotte (JMMB's
    daughter), 8, 16–17, 21, 188,
    195–6, 198
Bingaman, Julia Maria Murray, 8,
    16–17, 148, 153–4, 156–7,
    172–3, 175, 181, *181*, 183,
    188, 192–3, 195–6, 198
    birth and childhood of,
        13–14, 21, 29, 142–3, 144
    death of, 17, 34
    description of, 33, 143, 146–7
    health of, 152, 161
    marriage to Adam Lewis
        Bingaman of, 8, 16, 21, 33,
        188
    as mother, *see* Bingaman,
        Charlotte
Binney, Dr. Barnabus, 39
Binney, Mary Woodrow, 39
Bisbee, Frederick A., 31
Blanchard, Joshua, 81
Boston ("Metropolis"), 28, 33,
    50, 56, 59, 61, 72–5, 79, 83,
    92, 96, 98–9, 111–13, 122,
137, 140, 143–9, 151–4, 157,
    159–89, 190–1, 194–8
    burials in, 191
    church bells in, 152
    clergy in, 26, 176, 180, 190;
        see also Ballou, Rev. Hosea;
        Dean, Rev. Paul; Murray,
        Rev. John
    currency in, 175–6, 189
    dangers for women in, 152
    description of, 13, 29, 152
    disease in, 148, 158–60
    domestic help in, 184
    Federal Street Theatre, 8, 14, 149
    female academies in, 8, 33, 39,
        173
    First Universalist Church in
        Boston, 21
        see also Universalists, in
            Boston
    Franklin Place
        see Franklin Place, Boston
    Granary Burying Ground
        see Granary Burying Ground
    harbor/port, 27, 30, 98
    Loyalists in, 10, 36
    newspapers in, 150
        see also The Federal Orrery
    North End, 145
    public buildings in, 39
    residents of, 35–7, 56
        see also Universalists,
            in Boston
    State Street, 152
    trade in, 186
    transportation in, 182
    Trinity Church
        see Trinity Church, Boston
    Universalists in
        see Universalists, in Boston
    war in, 185, 189
Boston Weekly Magazine, 8, 15
Braintree, Mass., 165

Index

Bristol, England, 24
Britain, *see* Great Britain
Bulfinch, Charles, 145
Byfield, Mass., 44

Calvinism/Calvinists, 22, 32, 51
Cambridge, Mass., 21, 31, 76
Catholicism/Catholics, 32
Chandler, Rev. Samuel, 26
Chebacco Parish, Ipswich, Mass., 10, 46
childbirth, 12–13, 16–17, 128–9, 142
Christianity/Christians, 103, 119, 132, 163, 171
Christmas, 55–6, 92–3, 101, 156, 178
Cirkbride, Col., 134
Columbian Centinel, 158
Concord stage, 147
Connecticut, 26, 39, 58, 69, 89, 136, 173
"Constantia,"
    see Murray, Judith Sargent, as "Constantia"
Continental Army,
    see American Revolution
Coos and Penobscot "bills," 175
Cork, Ireland, 22
Croswell, Rev. Andrew, 26, 197

Danforth, Dr. Samuel, 159
Dawson, Capt., 45
Debtor's prison, 11, 78, 85–6
Derry, N.H. 48
Dixwell, John, 36
Dorchester, 8, 15
Du Will's Grove, N.J., 132

Eddy, Rev. Richard, 17
Ellery, Esther Sargent (JSM's sister), 6, 92–3, 95, 115–16, *148*, *148–9*, *150–1*, *157–8*, *160*,

161, *164*, *164–5*, *166–7*, *167*, *168*, *177–8*
    description of, 33
Ellery, John Stevens (JSM's brother-in-law), 33
Ellery, John ("Jack") Stevens Jr., 33, 92–3
Ellery, Sarah ("Sally"), 33, 92–3
Elwell, Jacob, 39
England/English, 4, 9, 12, 20, 23, 27–8, 32, 71, 83, 98, 103, 109–10, 128, 146, 153
    Universalism/Universalists in, 4, 35, 38, 70
    see also Great Britain
Episcopalians, 33, 56, 190
Essex Bridge, 117
Essex Gazette, 26
Essex, Mass., 46
Exeter Academy, 37
Exeter, Eng., 110
Exeter, N.H., 15

Falmouth, Eng., 110
Fatherland (plantation), 17
Favourite (ship), 88
Faxon, Deacon, 163
Federal Orrery, 13, 150–1
Federal Street Theatre,
    see Boston, Federal Street Theatre
female academies,
    see Boston, female academies in
The Feminist Papers, 18
Field, Vena Bernadette, 17
First Parish Church in Gloucester
    see Gloucester, First Parish Church in
First Universalist Church in Boston
    see Boston, First Universalist Church in; and Universalists, in Boston
food and diet, 4, 64, 66–8, 76
    meals, 3, 44, 60, 62, 93, 134, 136
    events, 150

Forbes, Rev. Eli, 26–7, 76–7
Foster, Capt., 72
Foster, Col., 69, 70
Fowle, Daniel, 58
Franklin, Benjamin, 131
Franklin Place, Boston, 8, 13, 15–16,
    33, 146–51, 153–7, 159–89,
    191, 194–98
    description of, 145–6, 154
French/France, 32
From Good Luck to Gloucester, 31

"Col G—," 56
"Mr J. G—," 33, *155–7*
Gardiner, Catherine Goldthwaite,
    see Powell, Catherine Goldthwaite
    Gardiner
Gardiner, Rev. John Sylvester John,
    33, 190, *190*
Gardiner, Dr. Sylvester, 34, 95, 106
*Gentleman and Lady's Town and
    Country Magazine*, 7, 12
Gibson, Rev. Gordon J., 18
The Gleaner (JSM's book), 8, 14,
    18–19, 35, 144, 153
Gloucester, 7, 31, 41–2, 44–9, 51–5,
    57–9, 61–67, 69–72, 74–77,
    79–80, 84–98, 101–3, 107–8,
    110–12, 115–129, 131,
    137–45, 148, 155, 159–60,
    166, 169–70,
    174–5, 181–3, 190, 197
    church bells in, 53–4
    clergy in, 5
    descriptions of, 3, 9–10, 67–8
    domestic help in, 184
    Eastern Point, 67–8
    First Parish Church in, 7, 9–11,
        20–1, 26–7, 51, 74, 76–7
        see also Universalists, in
            Gloucester, law suits of
    Middle Street, 28, 32
    port/harbor, 36, 52
    residents of, 4, 8, 10, 20, 26–7,
        33, 36–9; *see also* Universalists,
            in Gloucester
    smallpox in, 47
    war in, 10, 27, 38, 45–6, 52
Goldthwaite, Catherine
    see Powell, Catherine Goldthwaite
        Gardiner
Granary Burying Ground, 16, 21,
    30–1, 190
Great Britain
    war with, 10, 16, 30, 62, 185,
        189
    see also England
Greene, Nathaneal, 114
"Mr. Gregory," 38
Griffin, Capt., 124

Hampstead, Eng., 35
Hampstead, N.H., 36–7, 145–7,
    161–2, 166
Hancock, John, 28
Hand-in-Hand (brig), 25
Hartford, Conn., 129
Harvard College, 9, 16–17, 33,
    36–7, 174, 188
Hawley, Eunice, 37
"Honora Martesia"
    see Murray, Judith Sargent,
        as "Honora Martesia"
Hope (warship), 45
Hough, Benjamin Kent, 88–9
Hudson River, 136
Humphreys, David, 135

Independent Church of Christ,
    Gloucester, 20, 27, 31
    see also Universalists, in
        Gloucester
"Indians," 154
Inns, 49
Ipswich, Mass., 10
Ireland, 20, 22–3

Index

Jarvis, Dr. Charles, 152
Jersey wagon, 132
Jones, Thomas, 29, 197
John Murray Distinguished
    Lecture Series, 31
Judith Sargent Murray Society, 18

Leonard, Mrs., 193
Letters and Sketches of Sermons
    (JM's book), 8, 16, 21, 30,
    184, 187
Lewis, Eleanor ("Nellie") Parke
    Custis, 34 134, *168–9*
Limerick, Ireland, 23
Little family, 20, 23–4
Lloyd, Dr. James, 148-9, 165
London, 22, 24, 34, 101, 108, 110,
    114–15, 119, 128
    Tabernacle, 23–5
    Universalists in, 20, 24, 70
Lowe/Low, Jonathan, 79
Loyalists, 10, 35–6, 43–4

Maine, 35, 37, 155
Manchester, Mass., 3, 117
Maryland, 26
Massachusetts, 15, 26, 36, 39, 48,
    56, 89, 130, 131, 137, 165
Massachusetts Constitution, 38, 102
Massachusetts legislature, 12, 28,
    101, 103, 108, 110
Massachusetts Magazine, 7–8, 12–13,
    18, 144
Massachusetts Statehouse, 39
Massachusetts Supreme Judicial
    Court, 11, 20, 27, 74
McGibbon, Mr., 172
medicine, 64, 88, 137, 178, 193
The Medium, or Happy Tea-Party
    (*The Medium, or Virtue
    Triumphant*; JSM's play),
    8, 14, 149
McIntosh, James, 37

Methodism/Methodists, 20, 22–5
Middleton, Eng., 110
Miller, Russell, 32
Mississippi, 17, 37–8
    see also Natchez, Miss.
Mississippi Department of Archives
    and History, 18
Mitchell, Rev. Edward, 15–16, 30,
    34, 181–2, 184, 191, *191–3*, 194,
    194–5, 196, 196, 197, *197*, 198
Mr. "Mountford," 61
Morton, Perez, 150
Morton, Sarah Wentworth Apthorp,
    150
Mount Auburn Cemetery, 21, 31
Mount Place, N.J., 132
Murray Grove Association, 31
Murray Grove Conference Center, 31
Murray, Fitz Winthrop (son of JSM
    and JM), 7, 12, 20, 28, 124,
    128–9, 131–2, 138
Murray, Rev. John, *41–2, 42–3,
    44–5, 45–6, 46, 47, 48–9,
    50, 50–1, 51, 52, 53, 54–5,
    55, 56, 56–7, 57, 58,
    59–61, 61–2, 63–4, 64–5,
    65–6, 66, 67–8, 69–70, 72–3,
    73–4, 74–5, 75–6, 76, 77,
    79–80, 80–4, 84–5, 86, 86–7,
    87, 88, 89, 91, 92, 93, 96–7,
    97–8, 98–101, 108–9, 110–11,
    111–12, 116, 117, 118, 121–2,
    122–3, 123–4, 124–5, 125,
    126, 127, 128, 129, 138, 139,
    139–40, 140, 140–1, 141–2,
    142–3, 146, 150–1, 160, 174,
    182, 183*
    accused of writing Judith's work,
        61, 151–2
    admiration and support of JSM
        of, 70–1, 149–50
    as advocate for John Stevens,
        78–80, 86–7, 89, 91

206

as Army chaplain, 10, 27, 45–6,
114, 167
arrival in America of, 20, 25,
31–2, 91, 93; in Gloucester, 3,
10, 20, 38, 42
birth and childhood of, 4, 20,
22–3, 119; heritage, 32,
105–6, 113
death of, 8, 16, 21, 30–1, 72,
144–5, 183–4, 190–5
description of, 5, 88–91, 99,
105–6, 113–15, 118–19, 121,
127–8, 130, 132–4, 136–7,
140–1, 146–7, 150–3, 168–9,
173, 176–9, 181–5, 188–9,
191–3; love of Nature, 130;
self-doubt, 52–3, 59, 62–3,
91–2
education of, 22–3
as Eliza Neale's husband, 20, 24–5
as father, 25, 28–9, 113, 124,
128–9, 142–4, 183, 192;
surrogate father, 154
financial difficulties of, 14, 24,
29–30, 139, 154–6, 161, 167,
179–81, 186–7; salary, 148,
156–8, 161, 172, 175–6,
177–81, 185–6, 194–5
see also Murray, Judith Sargent,
financial difficulties of
as grandfather, 188
health of, 8, 15–16, 21, 23, 27,
29, 30, 34, 50, 56, 58–61,
69–72, 76, 87, 90, 96, 98, 101,
123–6, 136–7, 141, 144,
148–9, 167–70, 173;
depression, 22, 62–4; tumors,
148, 164–5; strokes, 168-9,
176-88
as JSM's boarder, 57, 83, 121
as JSM's friend, 5–7, 11, 20, 26,
41–117

as JSM's husband, 6, 12, 20,
27–8, 118–90, 196–8;
marriage proposal, 98, 105,
115; wedding, 117–19;
anniversaries, 122, 126; fears
for JSM's health, 140, 141, 175
legacy of, 30–2, 194–7
letter writing of, 27, 54, 56,
58–9, 61, 65, 68–9, 73, 76,
82, 89, 97, 100, 108, 110, 112,
123, 125, 127–8, 140, 163,
198
portrait of, 37
preaching and ministry of, 3–5,
8, 12–13, 20, 22–5, 27–30, 32,
34, 42, 46–7, 51, 53, 56, 71,
89, 93, 101, 110, 118–19, 123,
130–4, 136, 140, 144–5, 148,
150, 152, 156, 159, 161–7,
171, 173–4, 179–80, 187;
opposition to, 11–12, 20, 23,
26–7, 42–3, 51, 53, 76–7,
89–90, 91, 93–4, 98, 101–3,
105, 134, 135, 170–1, 197;
job offers, 24, 26, 29, 130–1,
167
as role model, 34, 58, 166
reading of, 23, 61–2
spiritual development and
theology of, 20, 22–5, 61,
176–7, 191–3
see also preaching and
ministry of
travels of, 10, 13, 15, 20–1, 23–5,
27–9, 39, 57–8, 62–3, 68–71,
73, 75–6, 88–91, 96–111,
114–16, 122–3, 129–30,
131–8, 140–2, 148, 153, 155,
157–8, 161–3, 168–9, 170,
172–5, 179, 183, 185
writing of, 8, 16, 21, 25–6, 30,
32, 59–60, 184, 187, 194

see also *Letters and Sketches of Sermons* and *Records of the Life of the Rev. John Murray*

Murray, Judith Sargent
  advice to John Murray of, 59–61, 63–4, 76, 92, 124–5, 139–40
  birth and childhood of, 7, 9, 137
  birthday of, 64–5
  as "Constantia," 7–8, 12–13, 112, 138
  conversations of, 44
  death of, 8, 16, 128, 195, 198
  description of, 4, 113
  domestic cares of, 63, 76–8, 138, 161, 164, 169, 173, 175–6, 178, 184, 189–90, 198
  domestic help of, 49, 161, 169, 176–8, 184
  education of, 9, 23, 38
  as educator, 8, 11, 15, 17, 71
  as early Universalist in Gloucester, 7, 11, 12, 26
  financial difficulties of, 14–16, 77–89, 91, 96, 107, 144, 148, 155–6, 161, 167, 172, 174, 178–82, 185–6, 188–9, 194–5; views on women and money, 144–5, 188–9
  as "The Gleaner," 13
  see also *The Gleaner*
  as grandmother, 16, 188, 195–6, 198
  health of, 12, 28, 64, 86–9, 96, 129, 140–1, 175; smallpox inoculation, 47; aging, 66; depression, 86–7, 96, 100, 164, 176–7, 191, 194–5
  as "Honora Martesia," 8, 15
  houseguests of, 36–7, 145–6, 166
  as JM's defender, 18, 42, 50–1, 53, 55, 76–7, 162–3, 170–1, 179–80
  as JM's friend, 5–7, 11, 20, 26,
41–117; loneliness during JM's absences, 57, 63, 99–101, 109, 115–16; fears for health, 50, 58, 69–74, 79, 87, 99, 108–9
  as JM's wife, 6–7, 12, 20, 27–8, 118–193; marriage proposal, 98, 105, 115; parents' blessing, 112–13; opposition to, see Sargent, Winthrop (JSM's brother), opposition to JSM's and JM's marriage of; wedding, 117–19; anniversaries, 122, 126; loneliness during JM's absences, 123–7, 129, 139, 142–3, 172; views on marriage, 104–6, 113–15, 122, 124–5, 127, 132, 134, 171, 187–8;
  as John Stevens's wife, 7, 10, 12, 103–4
  letter books of, 7, 16, 17, 18, 198
  letter writing of, 5–7, 9–10, 16–18, 34, 36, 39, 41–2, 54–5, 61–2, 69–70, 73, 87–8, 91, 96, 121, 129, 138, 140–2, 147, 168–70, 186, 191
  as mother, 7–8, 12–13, 29, 34, 124–5, 127, 129, 131–2, 138, 142–3, 147–8, 183, 188–9; as surrogate mother, 7–8, 11, 15–16, 33, 35, 37, 55, 71, 154–5, 189
  see also Bingaman, Julia Maria Murray; and Plummer, Anna
  reading of, 9, 61–2, 68
  philosophy of, 43–4, 48, 50, 59–61, 65–6, 104, 128, 142, 165
  see also views on marriage
  shopping of, 49, 72–3
  spiritual development and theology of, 5, 9, 34, 41–3,

51–3, 100, 106, 128, 131,
142–3, 156, 183, 190–1
travels of, 13, 44, 48–9, 52, 67–8,
74, 88–93, 97, 114, 129–38,
155, 159–60, 172–3, 181, 183
as widow, 12, 16, 95–7, 104, 115,
191–4
writing of, 7–9, 11–14, 16,
18–19, 29–31, 35, 47–8, 57–9,
71, 149, 153, 184, 187, 194–5;
criticism, 14–15, 17, 59, 61,
150–2; self-doubts, 59; tributes
to, 14, 17
*see also The African; Boston
Weekly Magazine; Federal
Orrery; Gentleman and Lady's
Town and Country Magazine;
The Gleaner; Massachusetts
Magazine; The Medium,
or Happy Tea-Party; The
Traveller Returned;* Federal
Street Theatre, Boston; and
Universalist catechism
Murray, Julia Maria
see Bingaman, Julia Maria Murray
Murray, "Mr." (JM's father), 22–3,
105, 113
Murray, "Mrs." (JM's mother), 27,
34, 98, 103, 110, *119–20, 128,*
156, 167

Nantasket Road, 158
Natchez, Miss., 8, 16–18, 33, 37–9,
173–4, 188, 196, 198
Neale, Eliza, 20, 24–5
Newburyport, Mass., 36, 48
Newport, R.I., 35, 90, 95–6, 149
Newton, Mass., 36
New England, 3, 10, 13, 28–9,
32, 139
New England General Convention,
21

New Hampshire, 15, 26, 34, 36–7,
48, 58, 174
New Hampshire Gazette, 58
New Jersey/Jersies, 25–6, 93,
132, 136
New London, Conn., 39, 91,
137, 173
New Massachusetts Universalist
Convention, 32
New Rochelle, N.Y., 135
New York, 15, 25–6, 28, 30, 34, 123,
134–5, 197–8
"Broad Way," 135
description of, 135–6
Universalists in, 167–8, 181
see also Mitchell, Rev. Edward
New York Packet, 108, 110
"Mr Noble," 50
Northwest Territory, 38, 154
Norwich, Conn., 58, 69, 136

Oak Point (mansion), 16, 198
Odell, Polly, 7, 11
Ohio Company, 38, 154
Ohio River, 154
Ohio Territory, 14
Ollive, John Barnard, 117
"Miss Osborne," 75
Oxford, Mass., 20

"Miss N. P.," 34, 168
Paine, Thomas, 13–14, 150–2
Palmer, Mass., 129
Parker, Mary, 34, 72
Parker, Noah, 34, *58–9, 69*
"Mr Parkman," 35, 174
Parsons, Capt. Thomas, 36
Parsons, Sarah Sawyer, 36
Pearce, David, 38
Pennsylvania, 26
see also Philadelphia, Penn.
"Mrs Perkins," 56

Philadelphia, Penn., 13, 21, 28–9,
33, 39, 71, 96–7, 123, 129–31,
134–5, 138, 143–5, 161, 167–70,
173, 175, 184–5; Arch Street,
130–1
physicians, 12, 64, 71, 87–8, 136,
148–9, 152, 159, 164–5, 175–6,
192
Pilgrim, Mary, 35, 70, *71, 115*
Pill, Eng., 24
Plummer, Anna (JSM's niece), 7, 11,
35, 55, 58, 88–9, 109, *113, 119*
Plummer, Caroline, 17, 92–3
Plummer, Dr. David, 75
Plummer, Mary (JSM's niece),
7, 11, 35, 83
Plymouth, Eng., 108, 110
Portland, Me., 153, 155, 157, 158
Portsmouth, N.H., 34, 52, 58, 72,
75, 108, 174, 175
"Dr Potter," 35, *93–4*
Potter, Thomas, 20, 25–6, 35, 93
Powell, Catherine Goldthwaite
Gardiner, *46–7*, 95, *96,
102–3*, 108, 190
description of, 35
Powell, William, 35
privateering, 38, 52
Providence, R.I., 73, 118

Quakers, 132
Quincy, Mass., 165

*Records of the Life of the Rev. John
Murray* (JM's autobiography),
8, 16, 18, 21–3, 25–6, 30–2,
194–5
Redding, Rev. Robert, 35, 153, *153*
Relly, Rev. James, 3, 4, 10, 20, 24–6,
30, 38, 41, 71
Rellyan Universalism, 15, 30, 34, 58,
162–3
see also Universalism, evolution

and development of
Rhode Island, 26–7, 35, 89
Robinson, Capt. Andrew, 37
Robinson, Judith (JSM's
grandmother), 37
Rossi, Alice, 18
Roxbury, Mass., 179
Russell, Joseph, 35, 87, *96, 101,*
108–10

Saint Eustacius, West Indies, 12, 88,
91, 94–5
Salem, Mass., 3, 12, 17, 28, 56, 73,
82–3, 116
Salisbury, Mass., 45
Sampson, Deborah, 39
Sargent family, 5, 9, 10, 17, 30, 55,
92–3, 177, 190
mansion of, 3, 26
Sargent, Anna Parsons (JSM's sister-
in-law; Mrs. Fitz William
Sargent), 123, *150, 157,* 153,
157, *157–8,* 158, *159, 170,
172,* 174, *175*
description of, 36
Sargent, Caroline Augusta
(JSM's niece), 14
Sargent, Catherine Osborne
(JSM's aunt; Mrs. Epes
Sargent), *91,* 132
description of, 36
Sargent, Charles, 146
Sargent, Charles Sprague, 36
Sargent, Daniel (JSM's uncle), 37
Sargent, Dorcas Babson (Mrs. Epes
Sargent), 36, 48, 145, *146,* 146,
154
Sargent, Dorcas, 147
Sargent, Epes (JSM's uncle), 10–11,
26–7, 36, 43, 48, 76, 80–1
Sargent, Epes, 37, 81, 83–4, *131–2,*
146, *148, 149–50, 151–3,*
153, *154, 162–3, 166,* 166

description of, 36
Sargent, Epes, 147
Sargent, Esther, 36, 161
Sargent, Fitz William (JSM's
   brother), 36, 59, 67, 93,
   115–16, 123, 153, *161, 170,
   179*, 181, 189
   description of, 36
Sargent, Henry, 37, 122, 158
Sargent, John James, 166
   description of, 37
Sargent, John Singer, 36
Sargent, Judith Saunders (JSM's
   mother), 4, 9, 26, 56, *78–9*,
   82, 89, 92–3, 95, 112, *112-13*,
   115–17, 121, *130–1*, 131,
   132–4, 135–6, 137, 143
   description of, 37
Sargent, Lucius Manlius, 17
Sargent, Lucy Saunders (JSM's aunt;
   Mrs. Paul Dudley Sargent),
   163
   description of, 37
Sargent, Mary McIntosh Williams
   (JSM's sister-in-law; Mrs.
   Winthrop Sargent), 38,
   169–70
   description of, 37
Sargent, Mary Turner (JSM's aunt;
   Mrs. Daniel Sargent; "Maria"),
   103–7, 108–9, *112*, 115, *116*,
   118–19, 125, *126, 129–30*,
   136, 137, 144–5, 145,
   159–60, 160, 167–8
   description of, 37, 50
Sargent, Paul Dudley (JSM's uncle),
   37
Sargent, Winthrop (JSM's father),
   7, 9, 50, 67, 78, 80–3, 85,
   87–8, *89–91*, 92, 98, 108, 112,
   112–13, 115–17, 129, *130–1*,
   132–4, 135–6, 137, 139, 156
   description of, 38

health of, 47, 50, 55
travels of, 47
as Universalist organizer, 3, 4,
   7, 10–12, 26, 38, 56
Sargent, Winthrop (JSM's brother),
   17, 37, *71–2, 92–3, 94–5*,
   107–8, 109, *114–15, 120–1*,
   131, 135, *138*, 146, *146, 153*,
   154–5, 169, 169–70, 170,
   171, 173, 174, 176–7, 178–9,
   179, 180, 180, *181*, 181, *182*,
   183, 184, 185, *186*, 187,
   188–9, 189, *189*, 189, 190,
   191, 194, *194*, 195, *195, 196*
   career of, 14, 37, 38, 50
   children of, 14–15, 17, 37–8,
      154–5
   description of, 38
   education of, 9
   health of, 56
   opposition to JSM's and JM's
      marriage of, 12, 38, 103,
      106–8, 114–15, 118, 120–1,
      127, 137
Sargent House Museum
   (Sargent-Murray-Gilman House),
   17, 31, 32
Saunders family, 9–10, 35, 37
Saunders, Judith, 8, 15
"Miss Saunders," 92–3
Saunders, Thomas (JSM's
   grandfather), 37
Scots/Scottish, 32
Sherburne, Henry, 14
Sewall, Mitchell, 59
shipping and trade, 11–12
shops and goods, 49, 72–3, 116,
   139, 167, 172, 178;
   furnishings, 135–6, 146
slaves, 39, 134
Spring, Dr. Marshall, 39
smallpox, 47, 50, 55
Smith, Bonnie Hurd, 18, 41

Spanish Consul, 167
"State Bank," 189
Stevens, John (JSM's husband),
    35, 39, 43, 46, 56, 94
    death of, 7, 12, 94–5
    financial difficulties of, 11–12, 35,
        62, 77, 78–89, 91
    marriage to JSM of, 7, 10, 12,
        103–4
Stevens, Judith Sargent
    see Murray, Judith Sargent
Stoughton, Mass., 90
Suffolk bank/funds, 186, 189
Sullivan, Maine, 37, 163
Sullivan, William, 39, *186*

Taunton, Mass., 90, 137
"Mrs Terrell," 39, *187*
"Mr Thompson," 39, 187
travel, by land, 49, 129, 163–5,
    179, 182–3
    see also Murray, Judith Sargent,
        travels of; and Murray, John,
        travels of
travel, by sea, 25, 28, 98–9, 108,
    124, 157–8
    see also Murray, John, travels of
The Traveller Returned (JSM's play),
    8, 13, 149–51
Thompson, Anna Williams,
    (JSM's niece), 8, 15, 37, 173,
    187, *188*
    description of, 39
Torys, 43–4
Trinity Church, Boston, 33
Truro, Eng., 35, 153
Tupper, Rebecca, 38
Turner, Dr. Phillip, 136
Tyler, John S., 149

Union College Press, 18
*Union, or, A Treatise of the
    Consanguinity and Affinity*

between Christ and His Church
    (Universalist book by James
    Relly), 10, 24, 30, 38
Unitarianism/Unitarians, 15, 29, 30,
    32, 162–3
Unitarian Universalist Association, 32
United States General Convention
    of Universalists, 21, 31
Universalism
    definition of, 24, 25, 41–3, 51,
        53, 133–4, 162–3, 183, 187
    evolution and history of, 15,
        20–1, 25, 28–32, 184, 190;
        conventions, 20–1, 129,
        134, 148
    see also Ballou, Rev. Hosea;
        Murray, John, preaching and
        ministry of; Relly, James; and
        Universalists in Gloucester,
        Boston
Universalists
    in Gloucester, 3–5, 7, 10, 16, 17,
        21, 29–31, 42, 56, 70, 75–7,
        100–2, 140, 190; expulsion
        from First Parish, 7, 10–11,
        20, 26–7, 102; Articles of
        Association, 7, 11, 20, 27, 54;
        goods seized, 11, 20, 27, 74,
        102; law suits, 11, 20, 27–8,
        35–6, 74–5, 98, 101–3,
        108–10; publications, 76;
        dedication of meetinghouse, 7,
        11, 20, 27, 38, 55–6, 102, 190;
    in Boston, 8, 10, 13–16, 21, 26,
        29–30, 33–5, 56, 137, 140,
        145, 148, 151, 155–7, 161–4,
        167, 171–2, 175–6, 178–9,
        180–2, 185–7, 189–90, 194,
        196–8; meetinghouses, 146,
        166, 196–7
Universalist catechism (JSM's), 7, 11,
    18, 57–9, 61, 70–1
Universalist Heritage Center, 32

The Universalist Quarterly, 17
University of Maine, 17

Vermont, 148

Wait, Mr., 82
Wales/Welsh, 24, 29
Walker, Elizabeth Stevens Elwell
    (JSM's sister-in-law), 62,
    77–8, 85–6, 88, 94
    description of, 39
Walker, Robert, 39
Wallach, Mr., 152
"Wallingsford," N.J., 35, 93
War of 1812, 16, 30
Washington (capital city), 16,
    30, 189
Washington, George, 7, 13–14,
    27–8, 34, 38, 114, 134, 166–7
    description of, 135, 186
Washington, Martha, 7, 13, 34,
    135–6, 168
Washington Monument Association,
    39, 186
Watertown, Mass., 39
weather conditions, 3, 25, 49, 53,
    73, 79, 99, 123, 126, 129, 133,
    139, 142, 162; storms, 157–8
Webber, Capt., 95
Wesley, John, 20, 22–3
West Indies, 7, 9, 12, 94
Wheat, Sarah, 39, 173
Whigs, 43–4
Whitefield, Rev. George, 20, 23–4
Winchester, N.H., 21, 32
Williams, Anna
    see Thompson, Anna Williams
Williams, David, 37
Williams, David Jr., 37
Williams, James, 37
Williams, Mary, 37
Wood, Sally, 14

Wright, Mr., 172
"Mrs Woodrow," 39, 143, *144*

York, Me., 35

Judith Sargent Murray